LIKE MUSICAL INSTRUMENTS

LIKE MUSICAL INSTRUMENTS

83 CONTEMPORARY AMERICAN POETS

PHOTOGRAPHS BY

JOHN SARSGARD

EDITED BY

LARRY FAGIN

BROADSTONE

LIBRARY OF CONGRESS CONTROL NUMBER 2014943161

ISBN 978-1-937968-12-0

Typesetting & design by Jonathan Greene.

PRINTED AND BOUND IN South Korea

Broadstone Books
418 Ann Street
Frankfort, KY 40601-1929
BroadstoneBooks.com

IN MEMORIAM

Jayne Cortez

Michael Gizzi

Anselm Hollo

Tuli Kupferberg

Peter Orlovsky

Paul Violi

CONTENTS

PREFACE

We invented this book over sushi at *Shima* (R.I.P.), on Second Avenue in Manhattan, near Larry's apartment. John had for some time been photographing 'celebrities' in downtown New York. He defines celebrity more in terms of uniqueness of accomplishment than notoriety, although most of his celebrities are quite well-known in their own circles, if not by the general public. Among them were some poets, including Larry, who agreed to think about what sort of book might emerge from the project, in return for John buying the sushi. We decided that a book of portraits of poets, with one excellent poem by each, would be serious and fun to produce, worthwhile to read and see.

Which poets and which poems? We wanted to include the lesser known along with the well-known. The poems Larry picked weren't always chosen to represent the 'best' or most typical of a poet's work, but more often something strange or surprising—an anthology with no theme other than the quality of the poems. The poets would be selected from among those John had already photographed or could get to sit still for him. Meeting and collaborating with these people that interested John was the main reason for him to photograph. We both wanted the book to be about who and what was included, not what was left out. We had no 'must do' list of poets. We hope you enjoy seeing and reading them.

LARRY FAGIN
JOHN SARSGARD

LIKE MUSICAL INSTRUMENTS

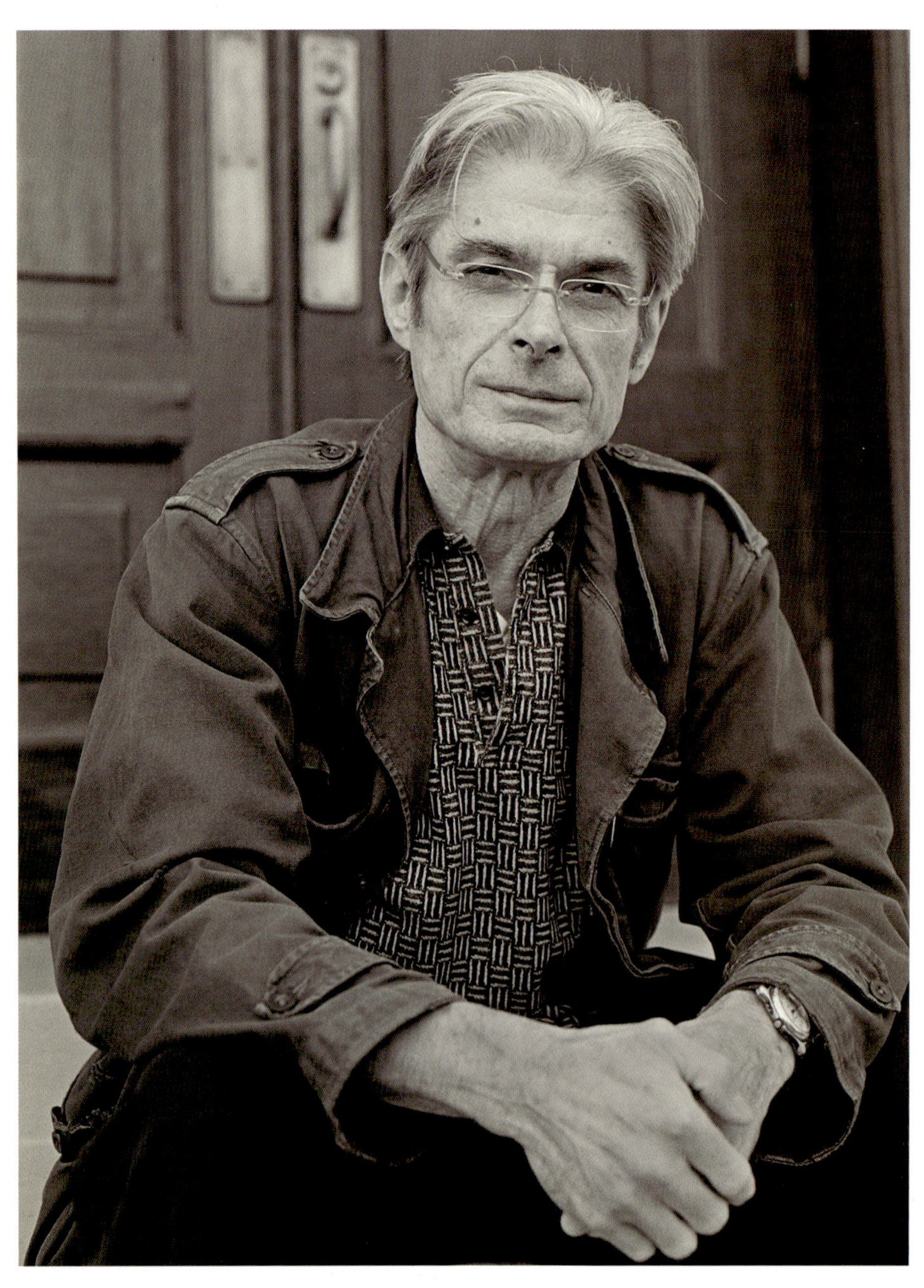

JOHN GODFREY

RADIANT DOG

Radiant dog on doublecross, and I,
by night, a raven fly. My fear
is that eternity has an alm
that is ordinary to ten thousand
and worn from my strings, my console
of limbs, and I a missing part.
It is the world that's new, not I,
and submarines can shoot the land
from the wheelbarrow of sickly pastorals.
Give me the swamp any day! or the huts
that pave the slave to freedom.
From a small cloud in my ears
the song has leapt the valley
curtained with snow, and for ascendant
harmony the gambler thumbs the cards.
Of all the queens one is a witch
whose curse is that she's held.
The horses roll the stone and trot
after their maturity sweepstakes.
This time the homeliest won't ride
my bet into hasty subtract glue.
The pieces fly and here I lie,
triangle of head and gut and thigh.
Put me on my mount, Tomahawk, and
past the river our cortege will dust
the heavy fur, and peasants' prayers
will touch the smell of holy cadaver.
I will have sun and manly rage,
and Mike Atlas will trim me up
to trip the bier from my brother's
hearse, and avenge me for my loss.
The gallows hurt! and for my scheme
I hang on the bridge's span
where my mother will trust my lips
with tears, the ones I send her now.

EVE OF EASTER

Milton, who made his illiterate daughters
Read to him in five languages
Till they heard the news he would marry again
And said they would rather hear he was dead
Milton who turns even Paradise Lost
Into an autobiography, I have three
Babies tonight, all three are sleeping:
Rachel the great great great granddaughter
Of Herman Melville is asleep on the bed
Sophia and Marie are sleeping
Sophia namesake of the wives
Of Lewis Freedson the scholar and Nathaniel Hawthorne
Marie my mother's oldest name, these three girls
Resting in the dark, I made the lucent dark
I stole images from Milton to cure opacous gloom
To render the room an orb beneath this raucous
Moon of March, eclipsed only in daylight
Heavy breathing baby bodies
Daughters and descendants in the presence of
The great ones, Milton and Melville and Hawthorne,
        everyone is speaking
At once, I only looked at them all blended
Each half Semitic, of a race always at war
The rest of their inherited grace
From among Nordics, Germans and English,
        writers at peace
Rushing warring Jews into democracy when actually
Peace is at the window begging entrance
With the hordes in the midst of air
Too cold for this time of year,
Eve of Easter and the shocking resurrection idea
Some one baby stirs now, hungry for an egg
It's the Melville baby, going to make a fuss
The Melville one's sucking her fingers for solace
She makes a squealing noise

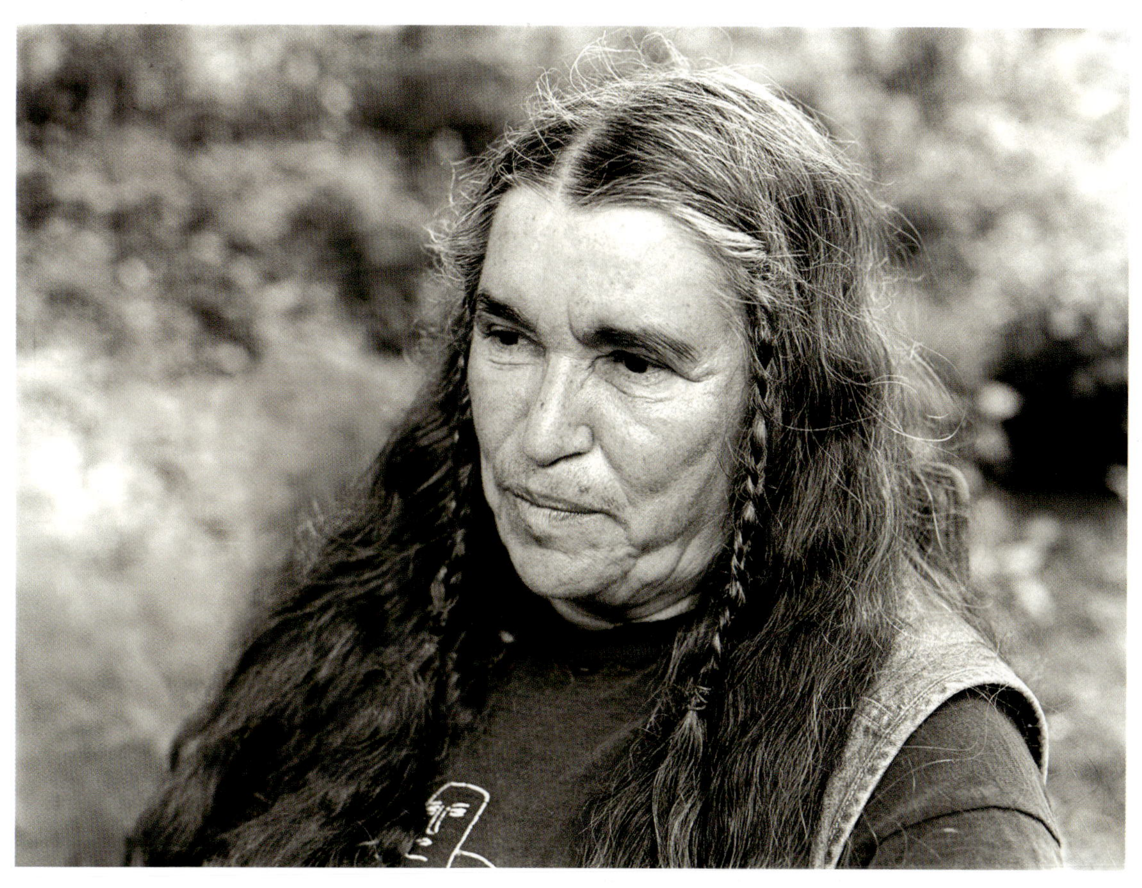

BERNADETTE MAYER

Hawthorne baby's still deeply asleep
The one like my mother's out like a light
The Melville one though the smallest wants the most
Because she doesn't really live here
Hawthorne will want to be nursed when she gets up
Melville sucked a bit and dozed back off
Now Hawthorne is moving around, she's the most hungry
Yet perhaps the most seduced by darkness in the room
I can hear Hawthorne, I know she's awake now
But will she stir, disturbing the placid sleep
Of Melville and insisting on waking us all
Meanwhile the rest of the people of Lenox
Drive up and down the street
Now Hawthorne wants to eat
They all see the light by which I write, Hawthorne sighs
The house is quiet, I hear Melville's toy
I've never changed the diaper of a boy
I think I'll go get Hawthorne and nurse her for the pleasure
Of cutting through darkness before her measured noise
Stimulates the boys, I'll cook a fish
Retain poise in the presence
Of heady descendants, stone-willed their fathers
Look at me and drink ink
I return a look to all the daughters and I wink
Eve of Easter, I've inherited this
Peaceful sleep of the children of men
Rachel, Sophia, Marie and again me
Bernadette, all heart I live, all head, all eye, all ear
I lost the prejudice of paradise
And wound up caring for the babies of these guys

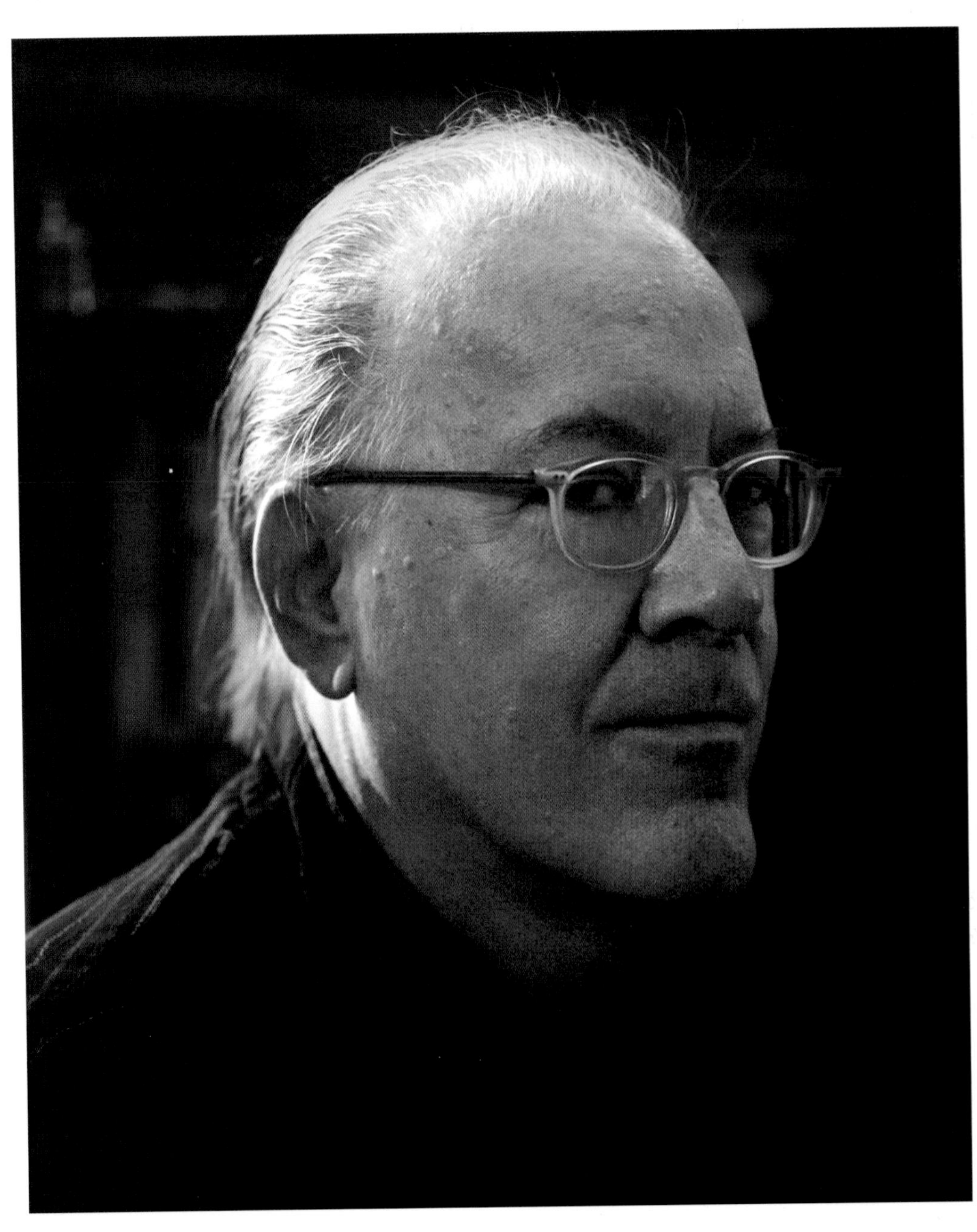

BRUCE ANDREWS

from IMPATIENT

You use clichés a lot, I don't know whether that's good or bad. Come off that corpuscle, I don't want your comment. I don't remember asking you to talk. Just because you can read doesn't mean you're human. Stress test—get real! Retreat praise. Self contained dwarfing to buy success retains a sense of order. Sprinklers control me prepositioned by your own fantasies. The extortion is embastardized. How's my little skill? Did you pass your compulsory attendance test yet? Self-serving voice absolves eternal debt. Frame-breaking punishable by death. Tag me no work & we work. Quotes skid a cardiac finish fisted exoskeletal gender kills debris. Sex stamens compile throat with matchhead. Slaves of improbability trot out the mouth. Groin a book I want more hollow without transplant. I remember seeing those thoughts somewhere else. He wanted to get me to mechanize him. Well if I play the verse, you can follow me? One hand covering eyeball, the complete jargons fix your thrift. For mesmerism, we must be rehearsed. Propulsive of boys, I'm being eaten alive by my goals. Style predates intake—apparently I did, 'seeking the bubble reputation'—that took care of my answer—the last thing in the world you want is for your organs to conduct so much electricity. Memory is more palatable than memory crutches to achieve a bright future. He has ignorance of ignorance. Harm does persist, not only repressed but ignored to be parented by furtive product. Don't drink water—fish fuck in it. Eat to avoid inspiration. They don't procreate well in captivity. The deepening atmosphere of fear seems to favor irrational behavior. Lockstep wants company just gulping down her formula. The integrity seems to have been discounted. Affect contraction imposed order that mammals could disinform. Quotes are surplus smorgasbord losers. Limp to talk shady talk trains of bed—& brain waves, pomp-free. One hand buys the other & absolute impotence corrupts absolutely. The masculine is at its gift advantage, makes news a neck into virulent states. Your failure lacks respect. Who writes your material? Derive me out!

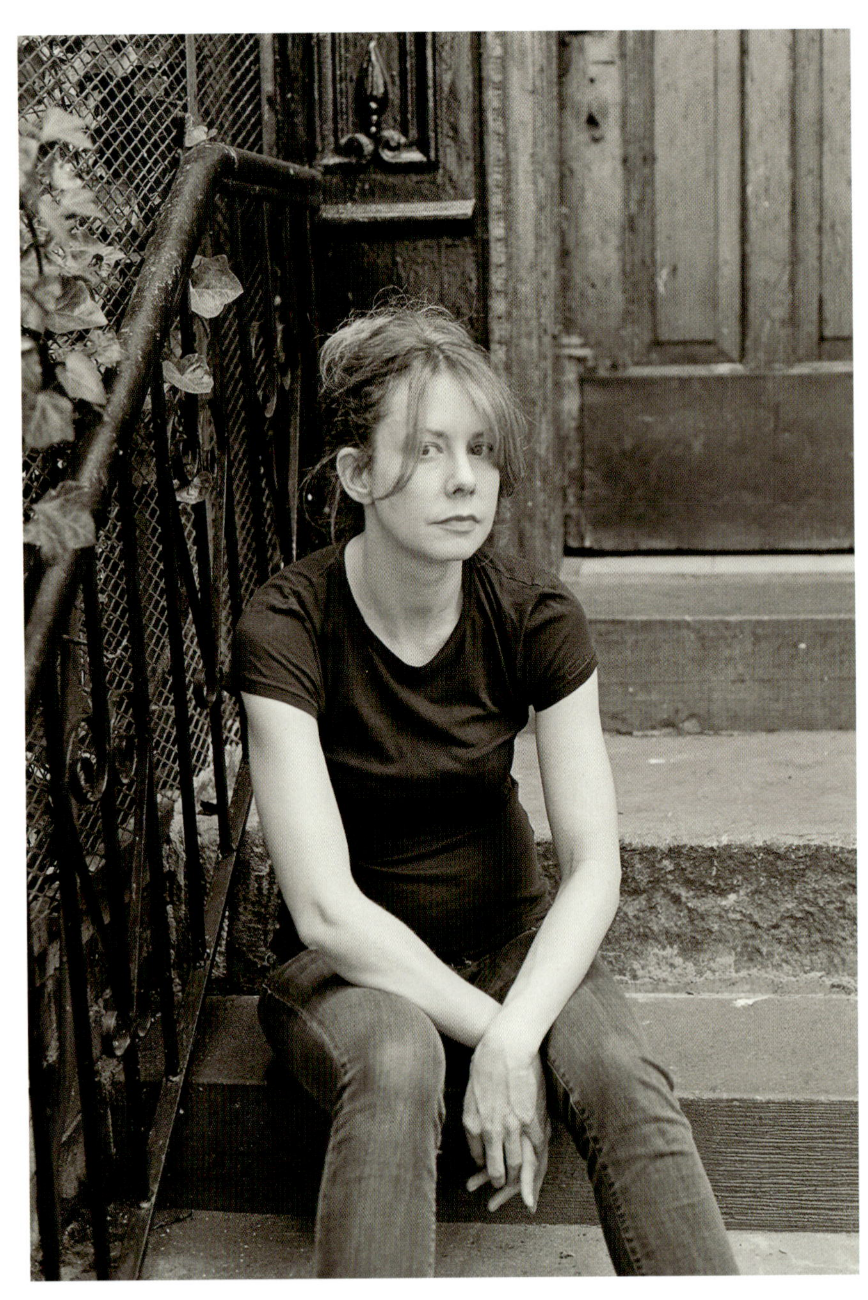

JO ANN WASSERMAN

SECOND WATCH

May it be creamy!
May these words give reassurance to our cheap possessions.
May this be our national comeuppance!
May deadlines move through common alchemy to eliminate the fat content of a
 supersized happy meal!
May it be supersized!
May comeuppances come to several rhythmic busybodies (those not directly
 swooning around our consumptions)
May God wink and may we see that mini-trend and winning streak as all ours!
May that (in case you did not understand this point) be taken to be for us only!
May February symbolically become May and the accustomed upbeat demeanor.
May we have May all the time May.
May models of Mayness abound perfectly around us in ethereal close-ups of daisies
 leaning from the billboards and
May platitudes about organic gardening and pointless recycling be all around us!
May we be able to grow stronger and bigger with whiter and whiter teeth in this
 manufactured organic way!
May it make a difference!
May it make us live longer!
May it make you live longer!
May it make you always clean and healthy!
May it make you always.
May it make the generations clean and calm without our intrepid and wild agilities.
May we harden that ethereal entanglement with life's source and the giver of life.
May we know that this is our God-given winning streak!
May this new and devout entanglement draw everything large about America into a
 tiny spoon-size.
May we, when out on the street, prevent its getting a bit bigger than that small
 managed amount.
May I ask you about this? this spinning out?
May I ask, are you spinning out?
May you/they stop walking.
May you/they stop me from walking.
May you/they hold me still.

May you/they make the space between us nothing more than a ceremonial
computation.
May you alone say No.
May you alone whisper No near the May-petals of my hair. May it be May again.
May you say absolutely not.
May the oscillations cancellations and phony confirmations come to nothing.
May we make way for an upcoming enormity.

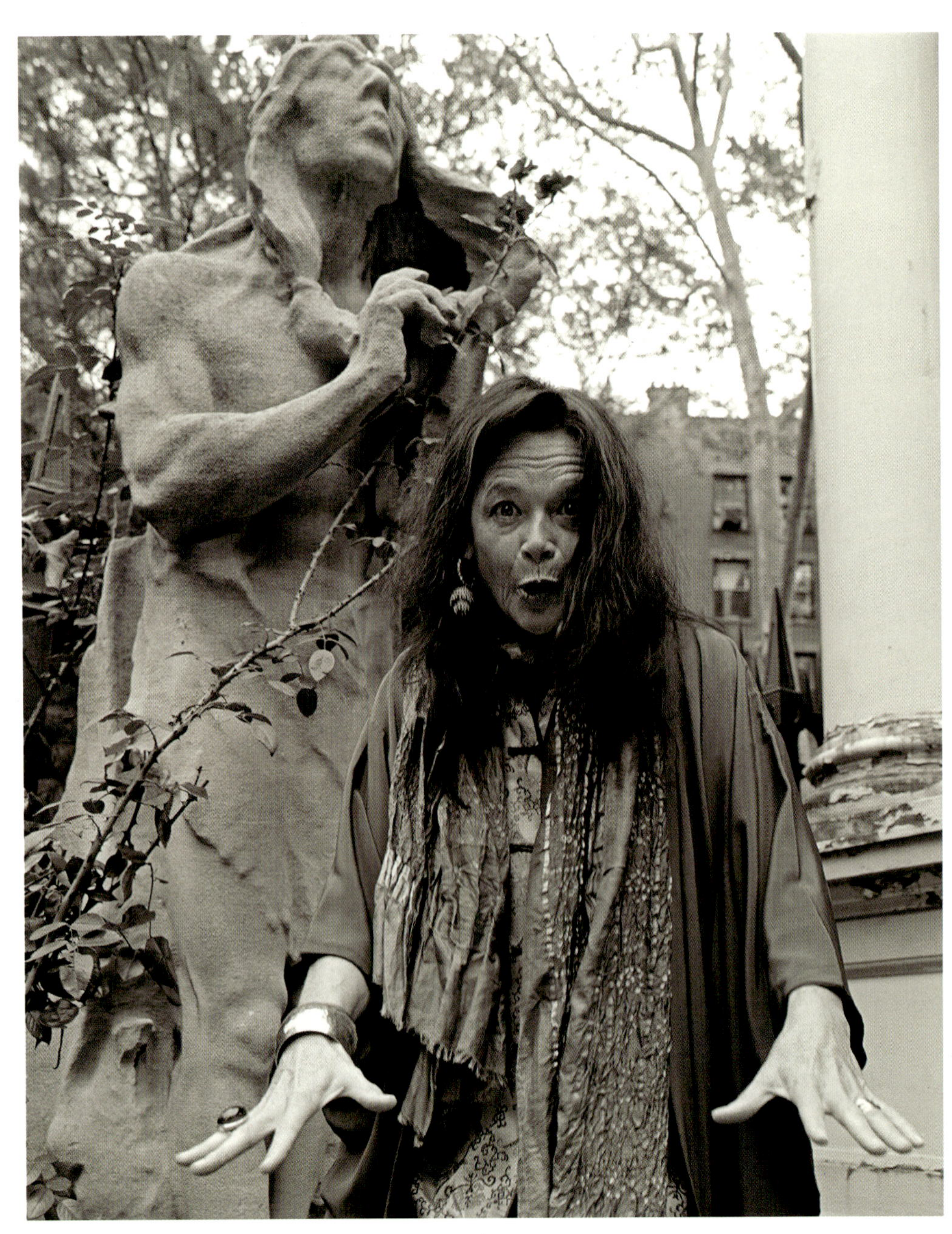

ANNE WALDMAN

HOW THE SESTINA (YAWN) WORKS

I opened this poem with a yawn
thinking how tired I am of revolution
the way it's presented on television
isn't exactly poetry
You could use some more methedrine
if you ask me personally

People should be treated personally
there's another yawn
here's some more methedrine
Thanks! Now about this revolution
What do you think? What is poetry?
Is it like television?

Now I get up and turn off the television
Whew! It was getting to me personally
I think it is like poetry
Yawn it's 4 AM yawn yawn
This new record is one big revolution
if you were listening you'd understand methedrine

isn't the greatest drug no not methedrine
it's no fun for watching television
You want to jump up have a revolution
about something that affects you personally
When you're busy and involved you never yawn
it's more like feeling, like energy, like poetry

I really like to write poetry
it's more fun than grass, acid, THC, methedrine
If I can't write I start to yawn
and it's time to sit back, watch television
see what's happening to me personally:
war, strike, starvation, revolution

This is a sample of my own revolution
taking the easy way out of poetry

I want it to hit you all personally
like a shot of extra-strong methedrine
so you'll become your own television
Become your own yawn!

O giant yawn, violent revolution
silent television, beautiful poetry

most deadly methedrine
I choose all of you for my poem personally

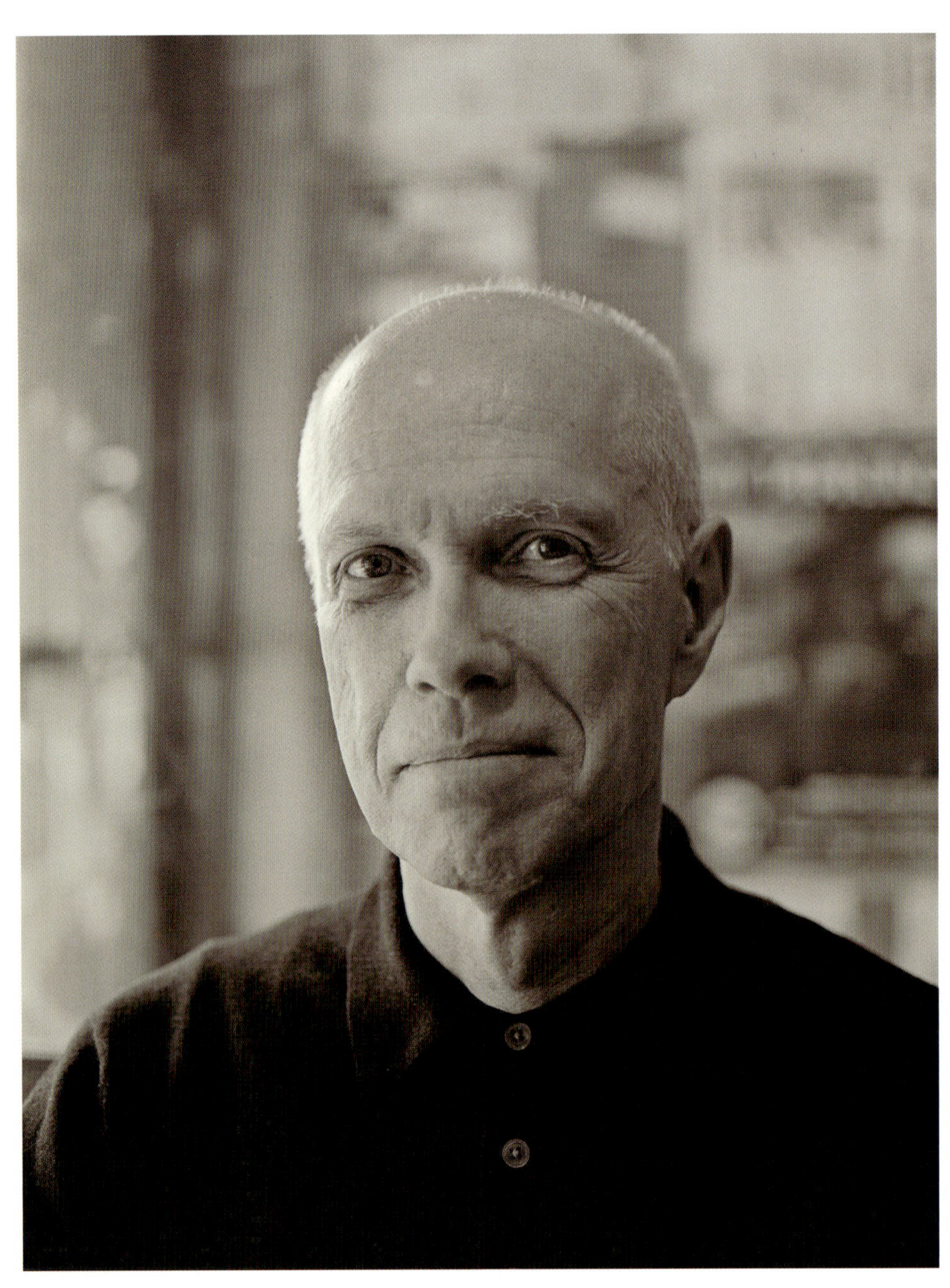

RON PADGETT

CUT SHADOWS

We sell
cut shadows

Come in and see us

You can buy the cut shadow
of anything

a flower?

There
you have the shadow

of a cut flower

'SCALE SHIFT'

Scale shift from bright blue-green through time to yellow-green as travel through
yellow green as farther in scale leaves inside other leaves as travel through
from bluish tinge spreading to yellow green through time as going through observe
coding red gold from yellow green and darker green codes observe
viburnum vivid across range optical spectrum as travel through geography and observe
viburnum and pine dark green evergreen as spot in white, color against gray
shifting through time from start of season bluish green small and transparent unfurling
going down scale through heat expansion bluish green to darker green unfurling
observe pine dark green fuller and wilted grows larger as travel through geography
in full of season fuller wilted and yellowish tinge as observing through tinting
yellowish tinge in preparing for red gold and oaks brown as water in limits
change as travel through geography or time as season changes red gold or brown yellow
tinge scale spectrum visible across range as travel through season changes red, brown, oak
from blue-green unfurling travel through wilting season red-gold coding
and on ground almost purple violet tinged dark bluish season coming geography sap changes
sap changes from full on to wilting summer heated and sap slows down
wooden rings expand & wooden circulatory system red-gold coding sap slows down
as travel through geography as we would travel through yellow tinges changing
unfurling into gold, green, against white, gray as geography season changes
as optical spectrum observe through travel geography time brown as water limits
as yellow surrounds and like water yellow in directions gold coded and water slows in season
as season slows water and yellow-gold surrounding and observe as we are surrounded
as we are submerged in coding yellow-gold, red-gold, browns and dark green against white, gray
as travel through spectrum in directions gold oak viburnum pine dark green against white, gray
and black indicating travel observation delineation travel observing on black against color spectrum red gold
coded, bluish light green unfurling through spectrum time travel on black coded red-gold oak
viburnum vivid as travel through bluish light green unfurling into red-gold, browns, oak, pines
as vivid against white, gray we are submerged in spectrum travel observing gold, green
through season changes vivid geography time we are submerged in spectrum surrounded coded red-gold
in such colors, vivid against black, white, gray, we submerge observing as we would travel

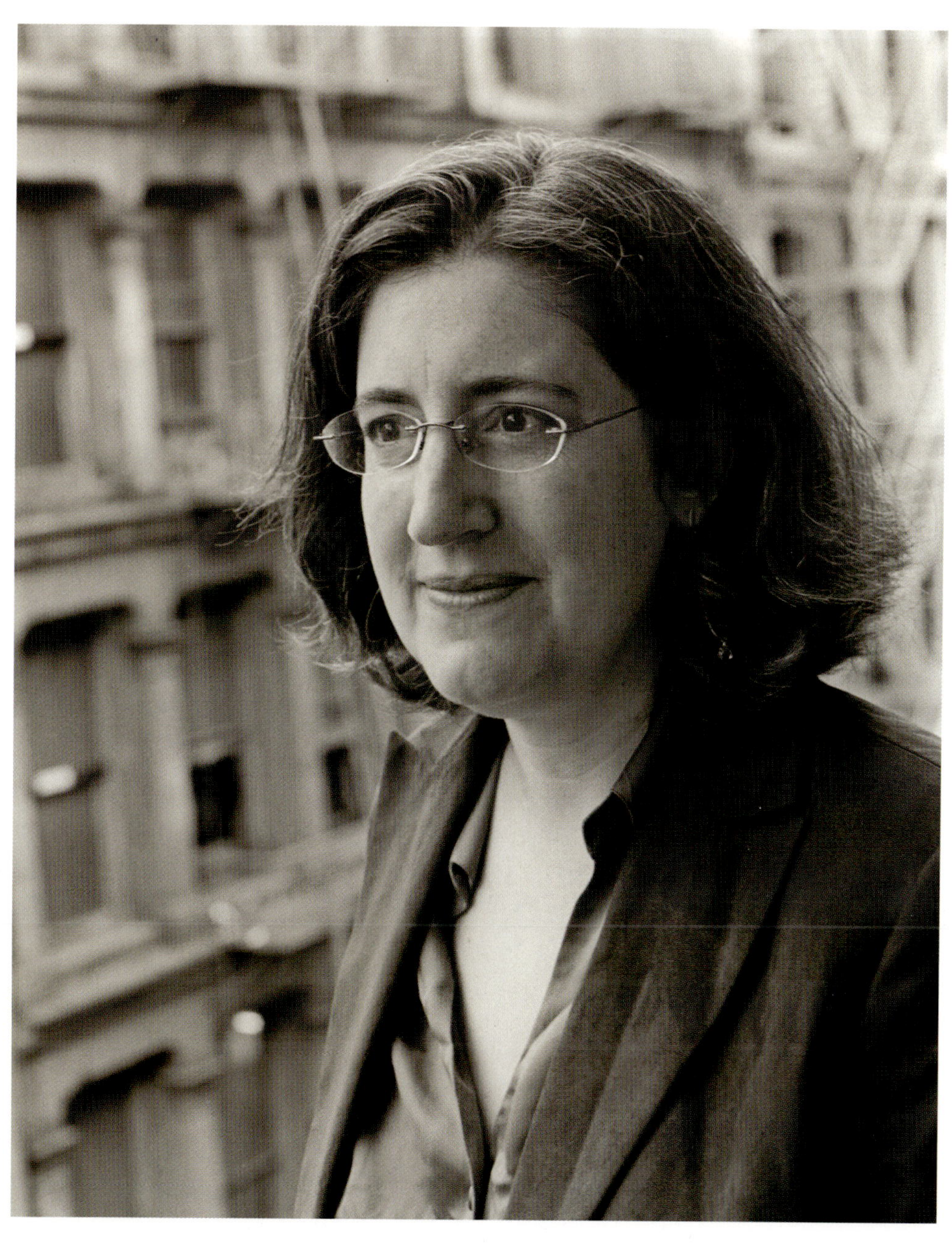

MARCELLA DURAND

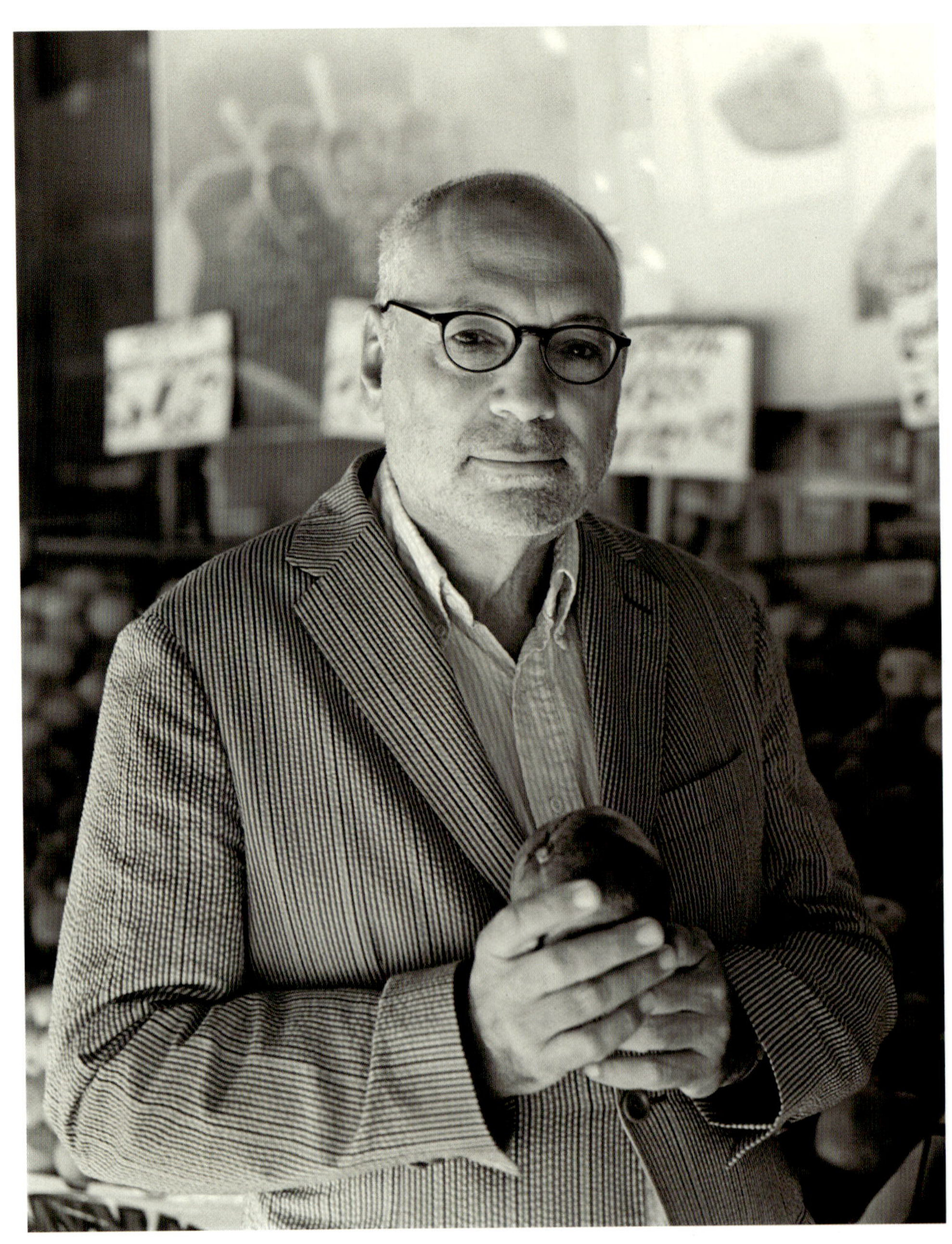

CHARLES BERNSTEIN

MARCH

Like towers make amends, these times
Stall, inherent to a flame that owes
Its own departing after, nonsense that
Tears all faults in ways that ask
Reply, or own or others' cares.
Refused for want of hurting, gain
Else that quiets, resisting standards
Partly for fear, ageless glowering
At shudder speed, or cancel without
Report. This legless hope, these brief
Returns. The gravity of a peaceful
Chat, eyes heavy with
Commerce, traffics in longed for
Goods, permutations of promise, hard
Recollected facts. Ageless
These faults convene, argue plans, yet point
At any loss, so much, erasing
Our undoing, greatest wildness. Continuous
Focus—shift, blur, become transparent, persists. The
Crack at which we border doubly mazed, with
Single purpose, lost in thoughts' conundrums'
Renewed verges.

THE PAGE TORN OUT

Curtains open to a page being torn out of a notebook.

PAGE: I am the page torn out!

NOTEBOOK: That felt wonderful! Tear out another one!

A second page is torn out.

SECOND PAGE: I am the page torn out! I cause pleasure being torn!

FIRST PAGE: No, I am the page torn out!

SECOND PAGE: You are merely a precedent! I am the page torn out!

UNIVERSE *(lying on a yellow bedsheet decorated with cows)*: Yawn.

NOTEBOOK: '...and the universe lay on a yellow bedsheet covered with cows, yawning...'

The universe shrieks after reading the words in the notebook, & tears out the page upon which they were written.

THIRD PAGE: I am the page torn out!

A curtain behind the stage raises to reveal countless pages standing in a vast stretch of desert wearing Roman slave garb & screaming 'I am the page torn out!'

Curtains fall.

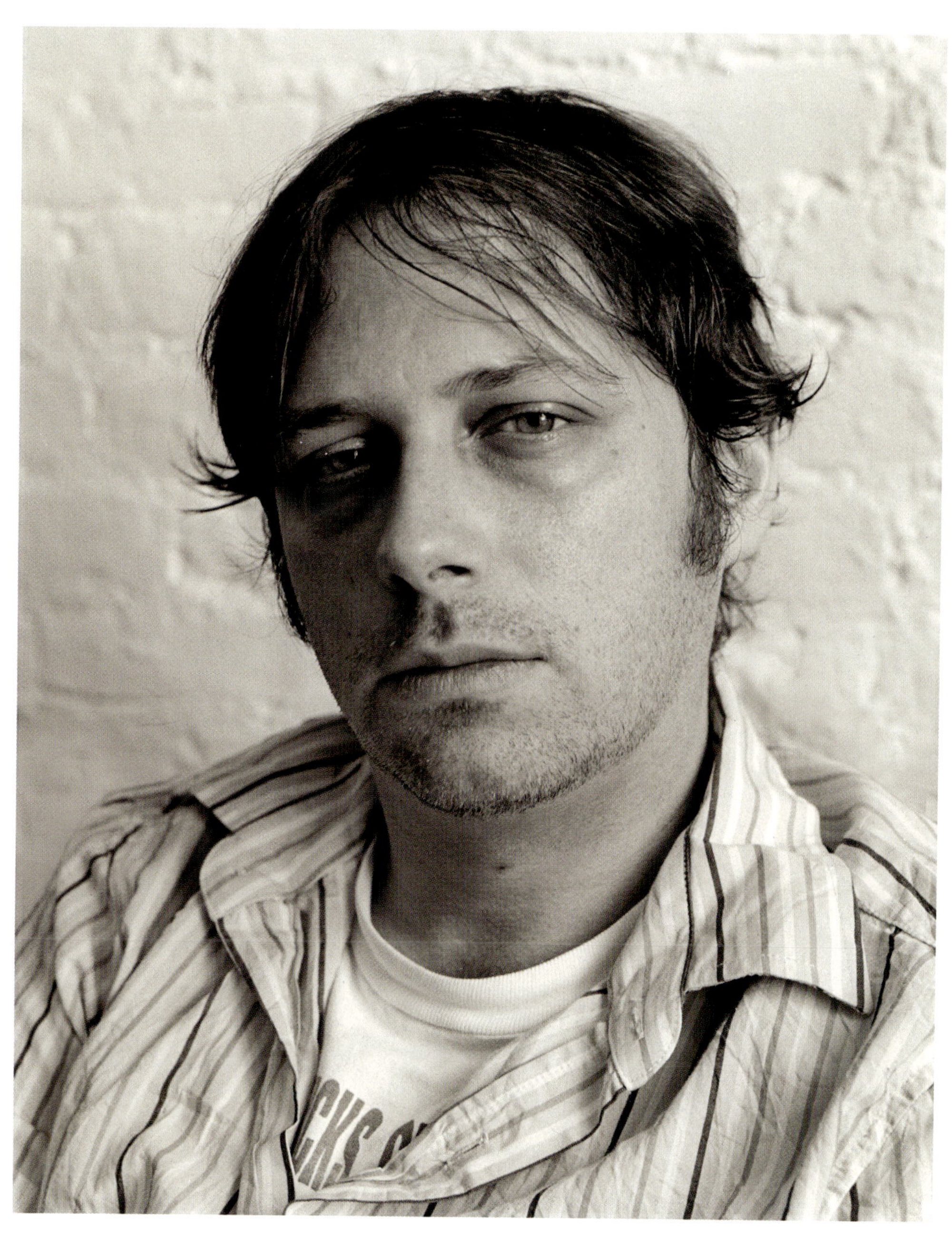

ANSELM BERRIGAN

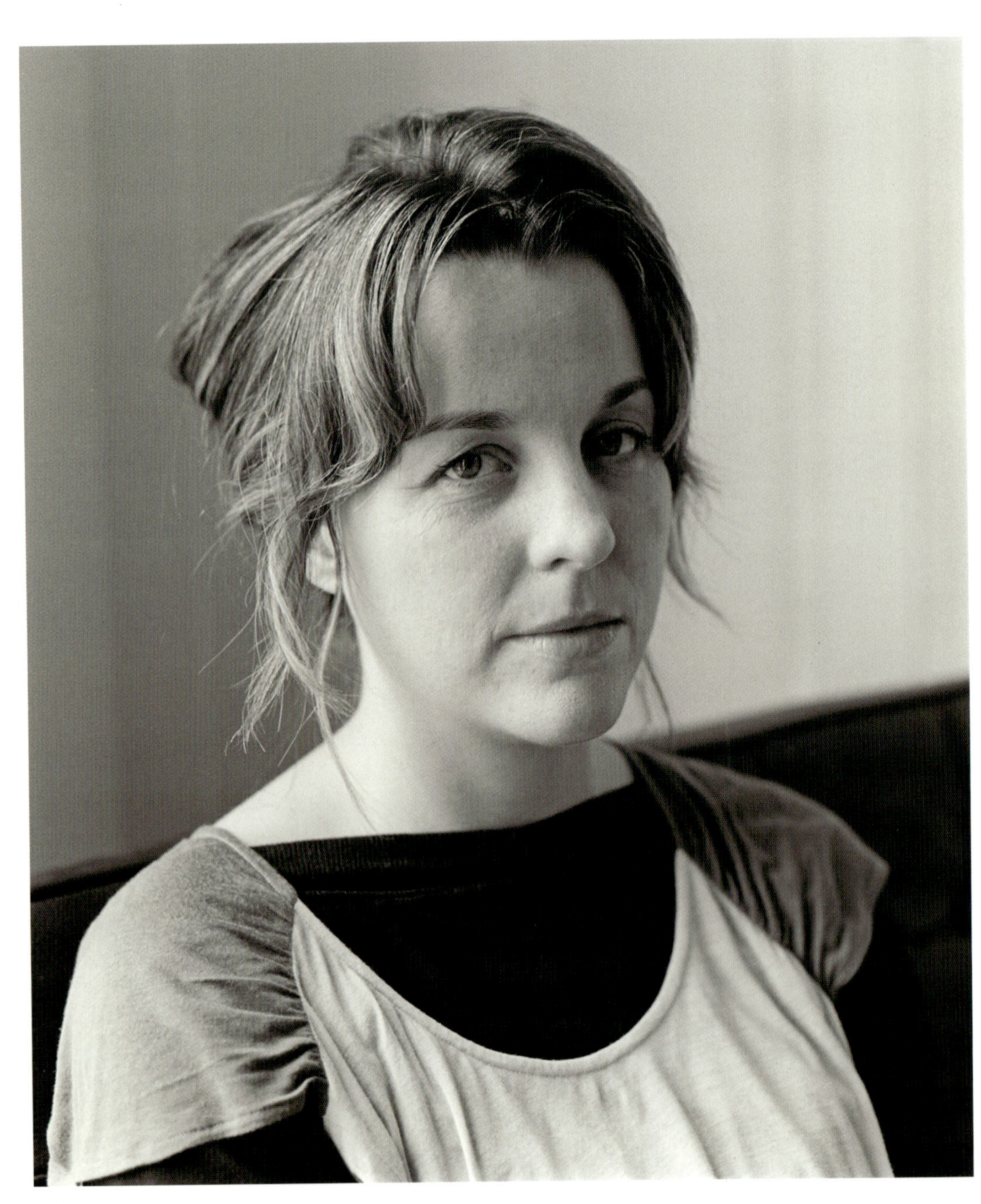

JACQUELINE WATERS

NO NEWS IS

There are several ways out of this. There's the spillway.
A tap at the valve, and winter softly
unloads a spring.
I fault no one. It was my limb.
I went out on it. The severing was startling
like a hail of fumes from the sky.
But grief is mastery
of what was always wrong
and this is the psyche—a castle one passes,
admires, meets a few of the occupants,
attends a dance or dinner, helps put out a fire,
is robbed or mocked or sated,
leaves, finally, having to admit
that it was not a true experience.
For though consistencies exist
and opinions may be formed, judgment
can never really fall.
So the present is allowed to be The Age of Wonders.
Now the envious are the greatest among us
for to them some dull thing must speak
unimpeded in a heavenly way,
while most of us, under duress,
learn not to trust what we hear,
then to trust it, and then not,
dwindling as the universe expands.
After loss some yearning is customary
and dependable, even adorable
like the animosity between cats and dogs.
More eschewable is the sheepish moment
when moonlight penetrates the treehouse
exposing us for sentimental loons. Oh, can't we stay
and reminisce a while? No, our passage
has been arranged, a slight pressure
on the eardrums spurs our departure
though nothing's really certain till we pull in the ladder.

REALLY THERE IS NO SOLUTION

No such thing as 'solution'   it's just going to live on
with one rotten moment after another
until the 'situation' wears out and God gets his way
and deeds all land for eternity
to the loudest voice

You know what? This isn't even my business, isn't even
in my backyard. The radio, the TV, the internet, and the paper,
bring me all this news that's none of my business.
I'm tired of global awareness emanating from my position
at the on and off button

which is now off
on the Afghanistan ghastly goal of
'finishing' the 'job'

All that 'in the moment' stuff—
the rotten moment lives forever
in a very deep pit it can never climb out of

Better shift to some other conceits—
'I go way back, I'm a goddess'
The tall votive candle for Lenore
goes out with a pop as Jim and Maggie
are leaving

'I was born old'
that's why old things are so familiar
like the return
of the now ever present mocking bird

Take it easy, when you return, don't let anger mar your entrance
think about your dreams, the comings and goings of people
waiting in the bread line, near the beach
Why are you feeling better now...

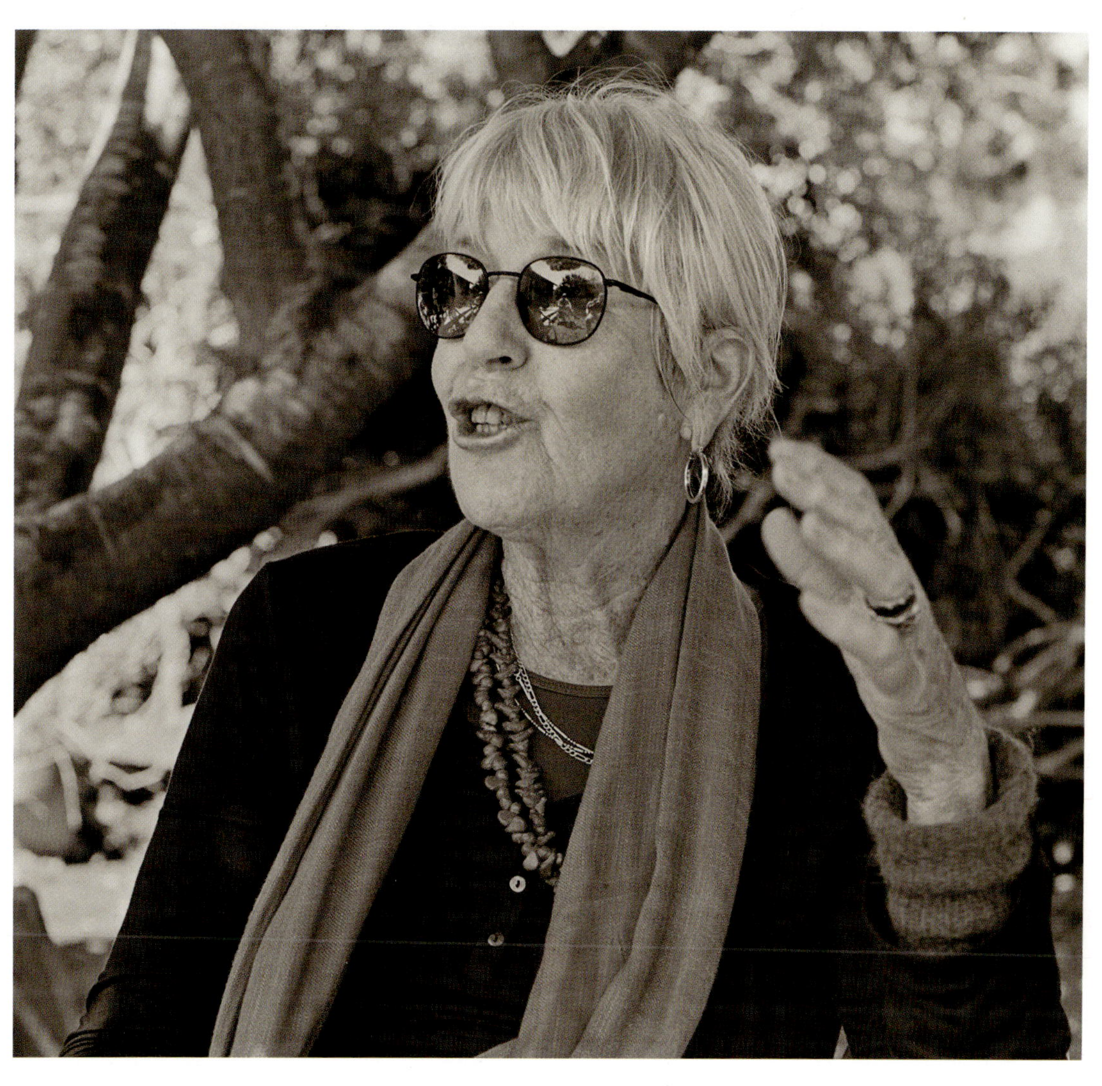

JOANNE KYGER

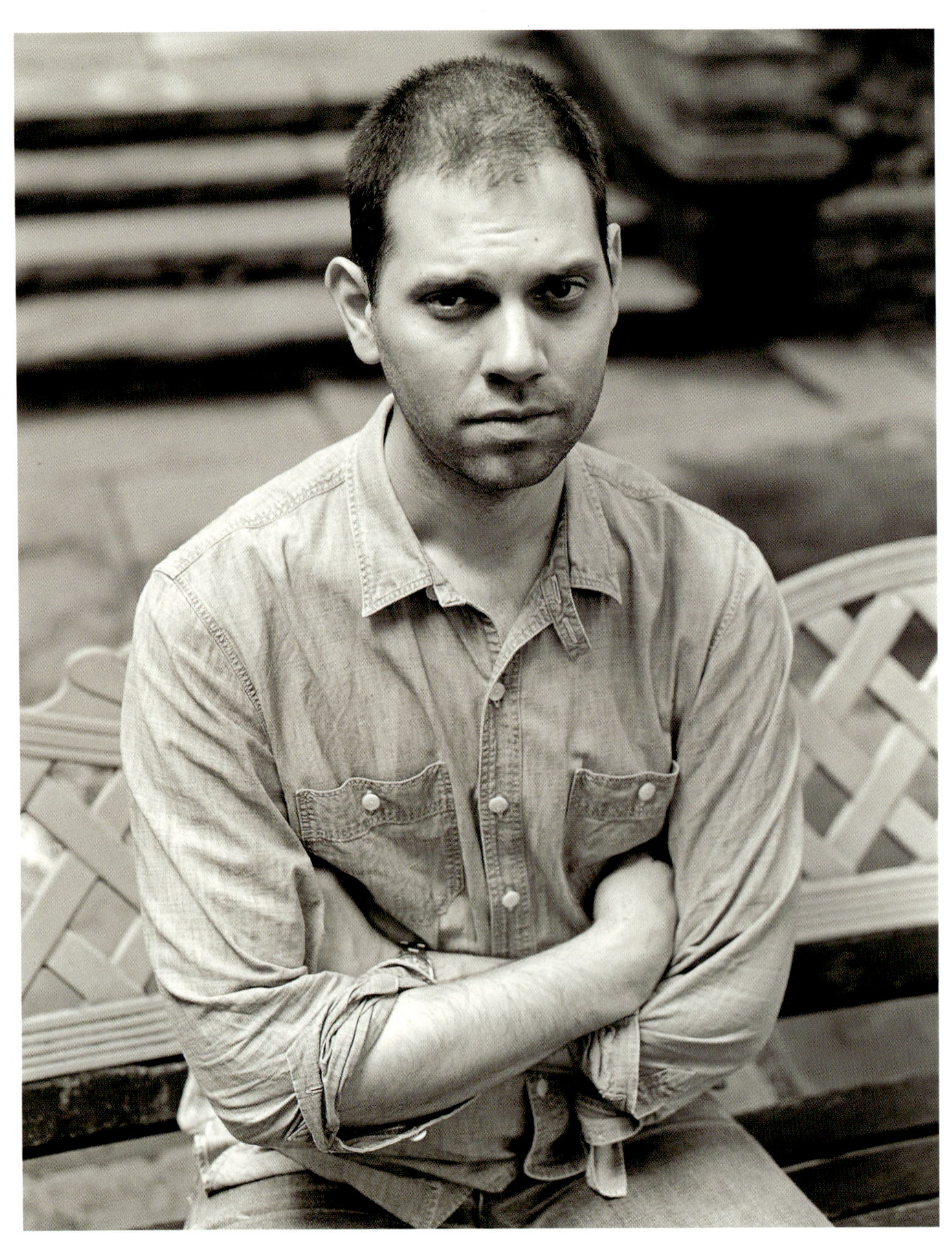

KOSTAS ANAGNOPOULOS

'THE HOLES IN MY EDUCATION'

The holes in my education. I am graded and come up short. How free the birds are! They walk, too. I follow them but they are fast. The books are small and short but slow. I study the night sky and *its* holes. But you travel with a black nimbus lighting your way. Thunder interrupts our class, leaving us dyspeptic, squabbling over nothing. We see stars without being struck. Teacher pushes our buttons, our limbs fatten with regret. We are after all in a land where books are left out in the rain. I'm in the lowest percentile, having horsed around like a musical top or a page torn out. Will the future reach me before I die?

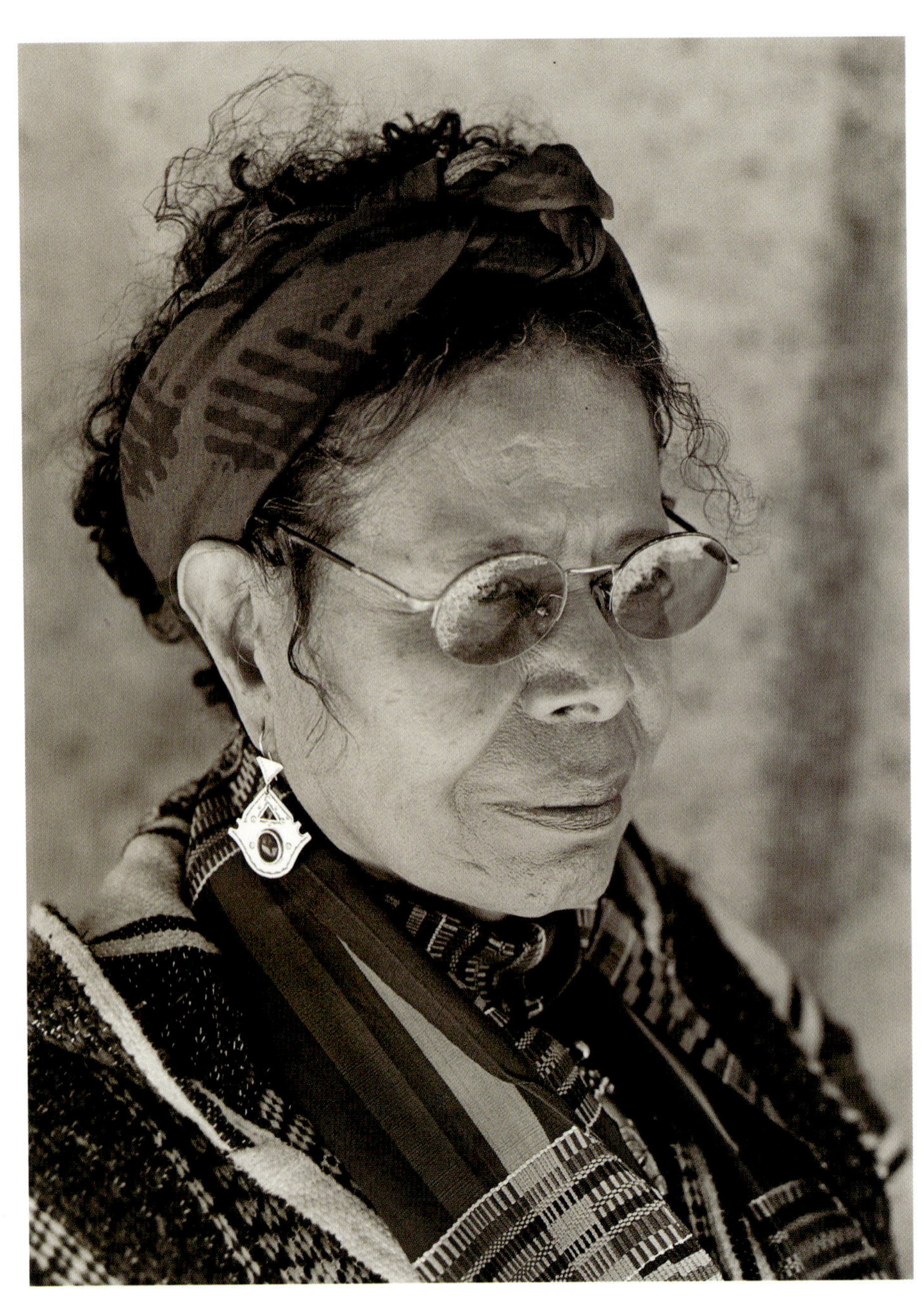

JAYNE CORTEZ

ABOUT FLYIN' HOME

What would you say to yourself
if you had to lay on your back
hold up the horn
and play 99 choruses of
a tune called Flyin' Home
exactly as you recorded it
55 years ago
& what would you think
if you woke up in the afternoon
& your head was spinning with
voices shouting
Flyin' Home blow Flyin' Home
& what would you do
if someone whispered in your ear
hug me kiss me anything
but please don't play Flyin' Home
& what if a customer said:
tonight I'm having sex with
a person who has been up
in a flying saucer
so please funk me down good with Flyin' Home
& what would you think
if someone started singing
Yankee Doodle Dandy
in the middle of your solo on Flyin' Home
& what if you had to enter
all the contaminated areas in the world
just to perform your infectious version of
Flyin' Home
& what if you saw yourself
looking like a madman
with a smashed horn
walking backward on a subway platform
after 50 years of blowing Flyin' Home
& what would you think to yourself

if you had to play Flyin' Home
when you didn't have
a home to fly to
& what if Flyin' Home became
your boogie woogie social security check
your oldie but goodie way out of retirement
& was more valuable than you
I mean somewhere
in advance of nowhere
you are in here
after being out there
Flyin' Home

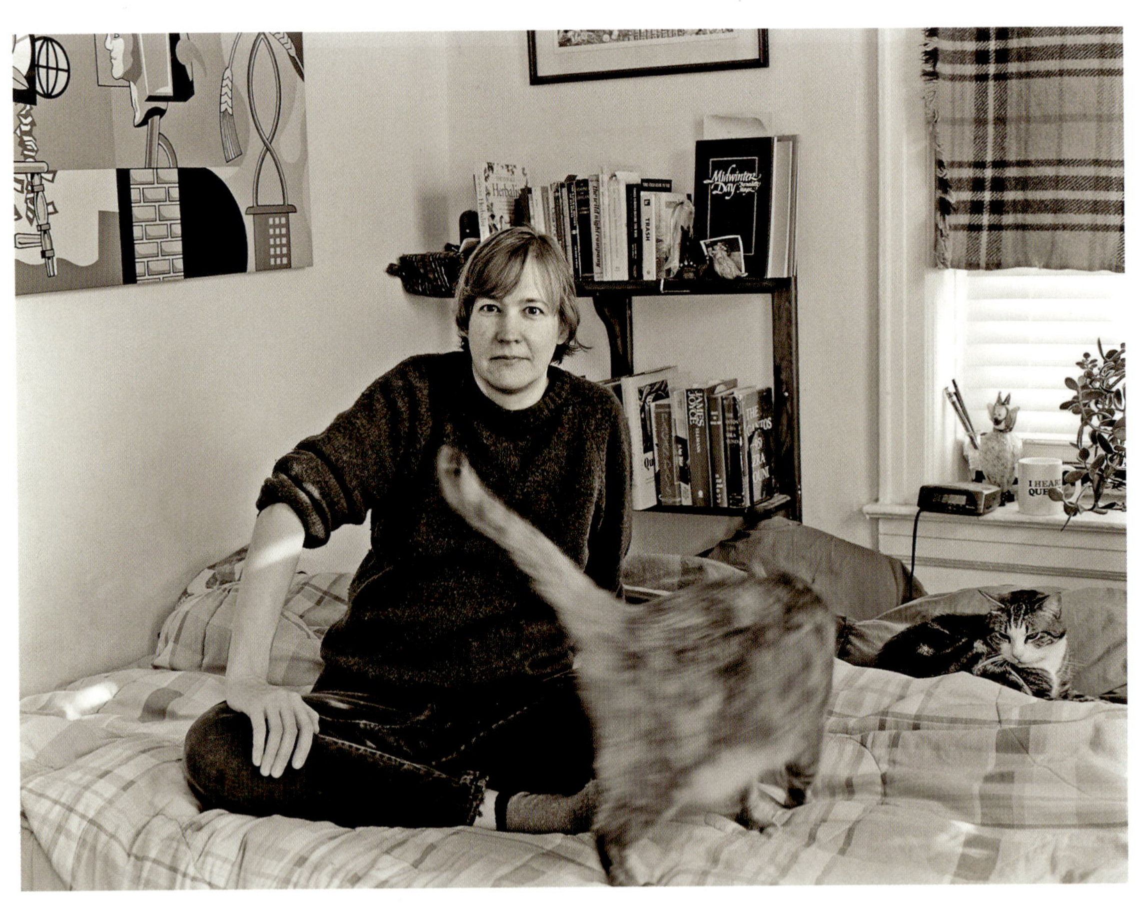

LISA JARNOT

SWAMP FORMALISM

for Donald Rumsfeld

As if they were not men,
amphibious, gill-like, with
wings, as if they were
sunning on the rocks, in a
new day, with their flickered
lizard tongues, as if they were
tiny and biting and black,
as if I was a hero or they were,
as if the they and these us that
arrived, out of the same blue
ground bogs, as if from my
bog that I saw the sun and
swam up to the surface, as if
the surface was shining, like a
lizard to embrace, as if the
random pain of lizard heads
on sticks were prettier to eat,
as if I didn't kill the plants, the
water, and the air, as if the
fruit and the sheep were all
diamond shaped and melted,
allowing in the sun, underground,
crowned, in shadows, in the
main dust, from the self same
main dust spring.

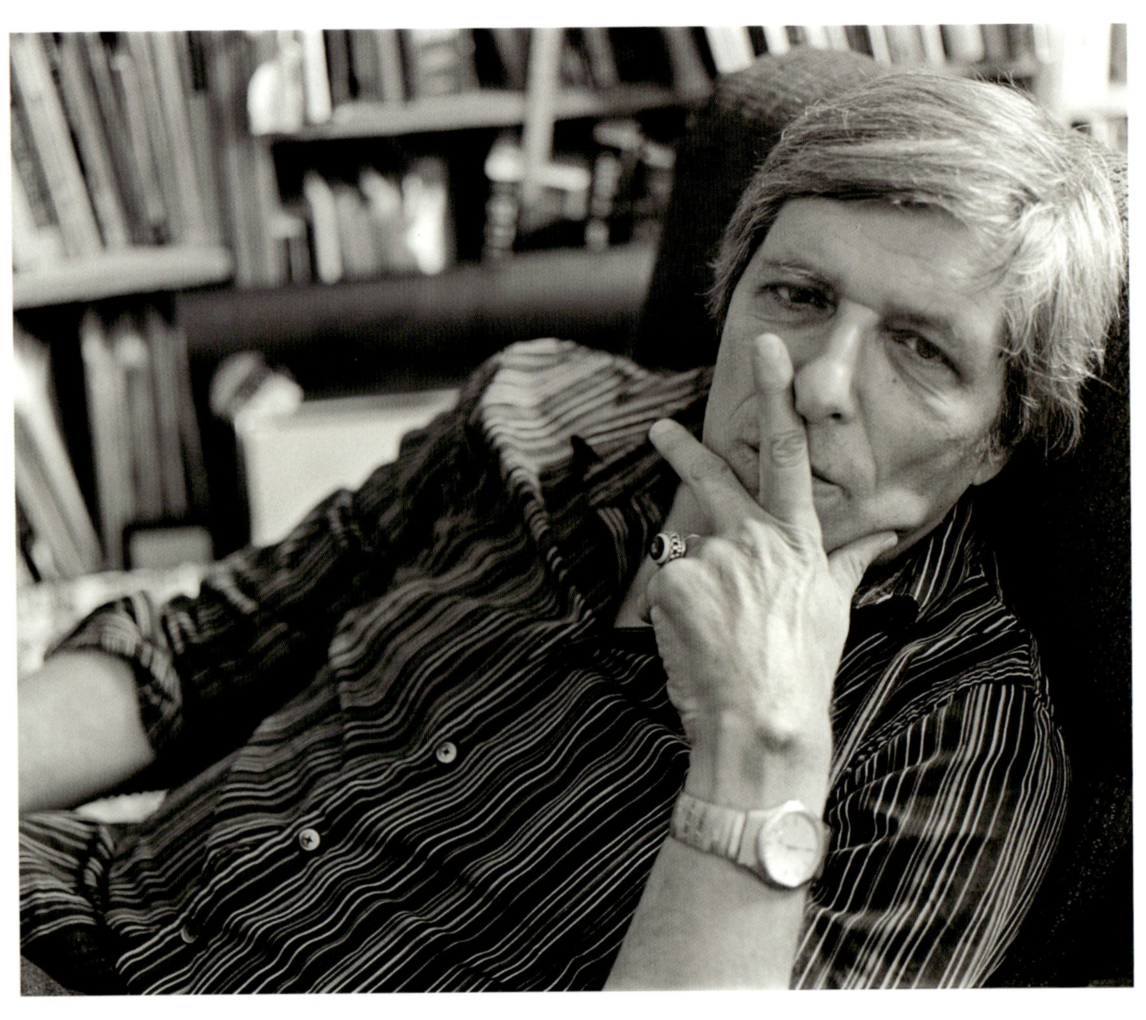

LEWIS WARSH

1000 POETRY READINGS

I'm going to begin with a series of poems, selections really, from
a book I began the winter before last around Summer '73 actually
when I was staying with friends, friends of friends, in Seattle,
the series itself dividing into three sections so I'm just going to
read a few poems from each of the sections dealing with asceticism
as I see it and then try to bridge the sections...you know, bridges...
the last time I read having read the entire series but since then I've
written these two other parts, books really, so the second half of
the reading will connect with the first by some sort of suspension
or key with the continuity being that everything follows. . .please
smoke...alphabetically and chronologically as well, though in part
three, which I'll read last, with a quote by Wills, just something
I got off the TV really, and part of which was published recently
I hope you'll see how I've tried to tie everything together, with life
in Seattle which was really an exciting time for me connecting with
the other less exciting to me intellectually if nothing else period
in my life when I was working drudgery really like I'm sure you know
I'll try to end on an up note with my most recent stuff which fits
into the series or written on my last trip to New York stands on its
own as being central to the hideous grief I feel.

NEW YEAR'S SONGS

How to let everyone in the tall
obdurate boring library
built for patience like a cigar
only the rain makes clear the spiderwebs
that swaddle the exterior
I usually see past or through it
a world defined by its wrapping
or a whorl someone's ear she's asleep
or pretending to be
so it's impossible to wake her
something else whirling in her head

◆

My dead twin left me
with instructions to remain at the controls
of a telescope that saw and spoke
of a dark map an ongoing complexity
of bodies closer to me than ever
the whole terrestrial apricot I was on
now I can't remember the clear day
or the new language
it was comforting in the shadows
of the descending plate-glass
and concrete brise-soleil screen
that breaks up the sun on its way in

◆

They've chiseled commonplaces
into the cornerstones
a few words on the fantastic
multiplying faces

◆

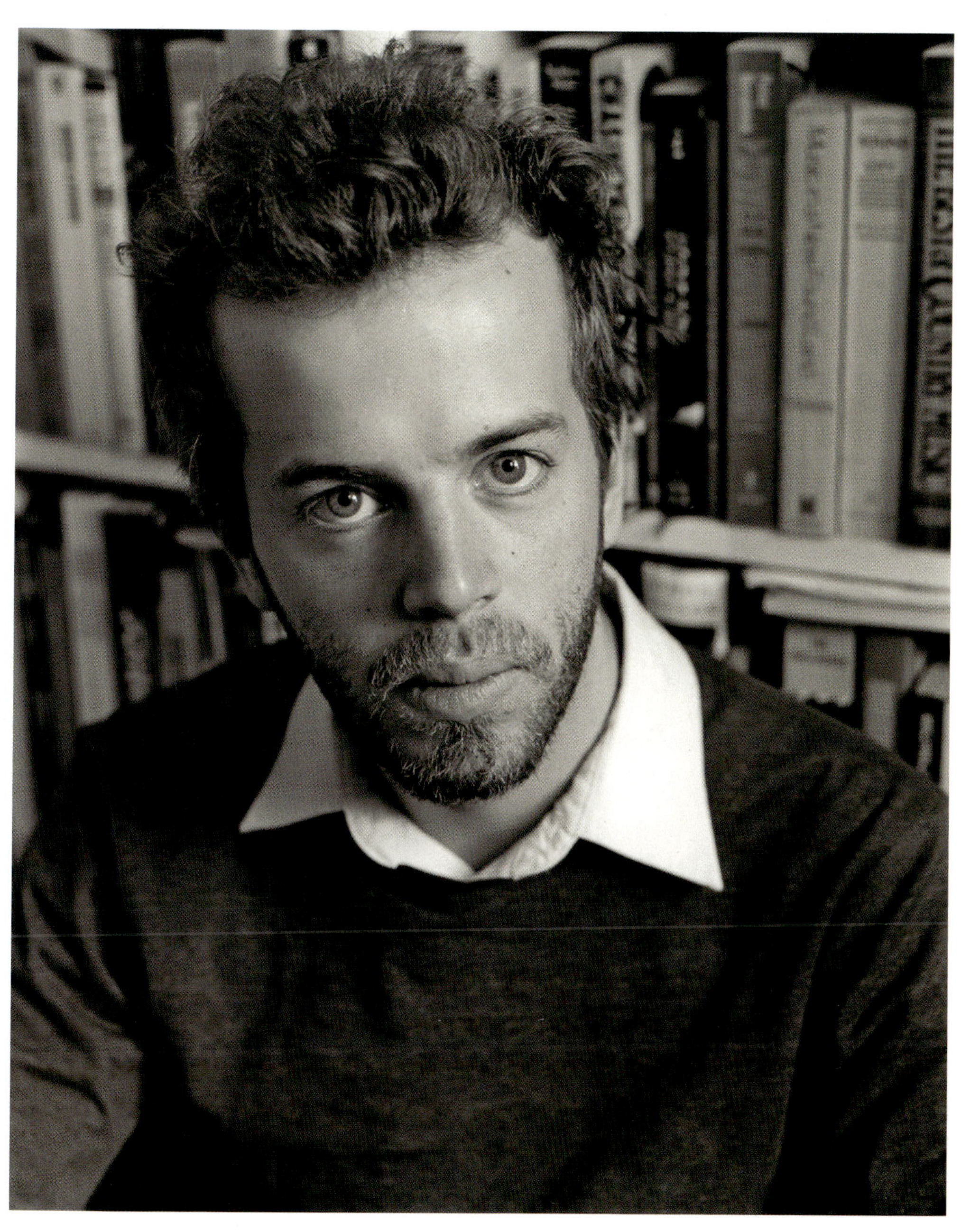

BEN TRIPP

I should get going
on my search for nothing
my origin is a destination
one where I recognized everybody
and remembered new people
from the days ahead of me
since then I've been forgetting
trying not to make myself scarce
or appear in too many places at once
it's always best to stay put

◆

Names are failures I refuse
to let them measure me
the distances are illegible
the experiences apparent
always without apology
*
There's nothing like solitude
for a cutting tool
to expose feelings as facts
no consolation in what night means
repudiating all that's given to it
to give back

◆

My songs are struck
by what could happen
beginning with echoes
that may never end
the light is just there
in an empty room
everything else is in the way
and the right words begin
to make themselves scarce

like everyone on my mind
everything I want to sing
to them
is already in them
buildings have them
where they want them
where they've always been

◆

Remarking on space
from a little fortress of impulses
who asked for the love of tomorrow
is the sky falling
are the seasons on hold
I've already been to wherever I'm going
I forget them when I think about
how nervous I get
when I feel great

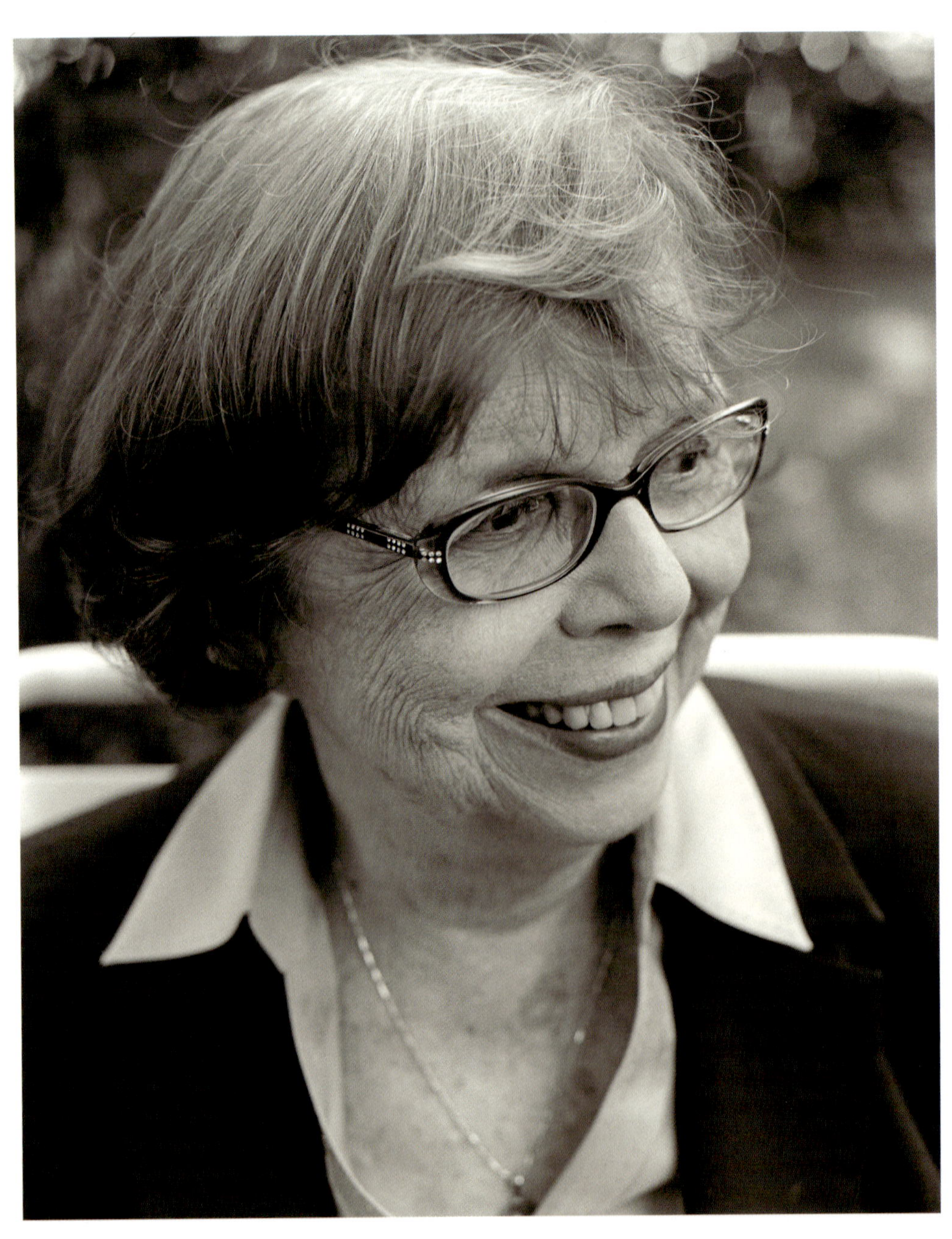

MARY FERRARI

THE BLUE AND YELLOW

for Charles North

I'm in a blue and yellow
mood. Blue as the dead
sea and yellow as a falling star.
There is no one to collect my
garbage, the refuse of a too active
imagination remains stinking in my mind.

I've tried everything, including
gin and tonic but still I hate
everyone and will do nothing kind
or sincere.

I'm a summer rose turned black,
the creepy ears of a rhododendron.
I should love poets, but even they
have become surplus goods, something
I have in my attic. What to do with
all this junk? It takes more energy
than I have, I tell you.

Ezra says, Prepare to go on a journey.
What advice from a great soothsayer!
I know I have to drive to the eternal
log cabin in Vermont. I know
I have to wait for whole woods of wolves
in my nights. To eat me up? I'd rather
live, a leftover salad, than be dead.
Every summer I think: this is the end.
Someone has just said: stupid idiot. Should
I punish him? Should I care? Certainly
not. I agree with him. He is absolutely
right, as Boy Scouts have some dirty aspect
of truth, the truth of sneakers, sleeping
bags and badges. This is life.

How I hate life! But I refuse to die!
I have been embroiled in wars
long enough. It's not enough to hate
one's friends. It is not enough to
wish they would all be dethroned from
their dreams. Sure, I wanted
to be a queen, a beautiful queen, revered
by the populace. I would like to bring
justice to all, not love.
After all, I have passed through the valley
of Westchester and swum the Shelldrake
alone. Charon didn't guide me. No one
guided me. I simply whispered to the
water that I was there and it moved.
So perhaps I am really a goddess, whose speech
is a rainbow uniting all the wicker chairs
of the world.

I am a student of the times
willing to write anything as long as
it is confusing and not what anyone
needs. I condemn you to drink the milk
of a camel. Drink it!
It's bad for you, as I will be too.
I am tired of being sophisticated.
It was just a pose. A scared rabbit's
imitation of Superman. We will not speak of
religion and the diseased ideas of
nuns, who are condemned to be good women,
too good. What is wrong with a good woman?
She doesn't go far enough. She shrinks.
She tightens.

Well, what am I? The mother of the next
generation? The wind between the mountains,
the bell of a train on a night curve?
What am I then, sister to tigers
and avalanches? What do I want to destroy?
Shall I never dance on the surf
of a party, free as the ocean in the arms
of a spray, rising upward and forward with
a great roar? I might frighten somebody
timid. Not a lake
in Vermont where I am fated to go, where
the water is flat, an icy responsibility.

What must I do, Father? Leave him
out of it! Yes, I do wish to go abroad
on a ship. I wish to meet with all of
the cannibals of Europe, what wild beasts
I may talk with at the Louvre, or just
outside it at a café. No one can imagine
having a gentle man for president. Where
are our masks? But it doesn't matter because
Nigeria is being born again in the bowels of
New York, and you are a midwife, ever
zealous and patient. All that is here
are demons who intend to celebrate the
end of my life and yet there is someone
who gives me an offering of life
contained in a box made of ice
cream sticks pasted over with blue feathers.
From the wreckage of dolls, I bring
this moonstone away. I am the last survivor
and I want to speak in the name of
joy, the joy lost somewhere along
the river to be found among
the blue and yellow of it all.

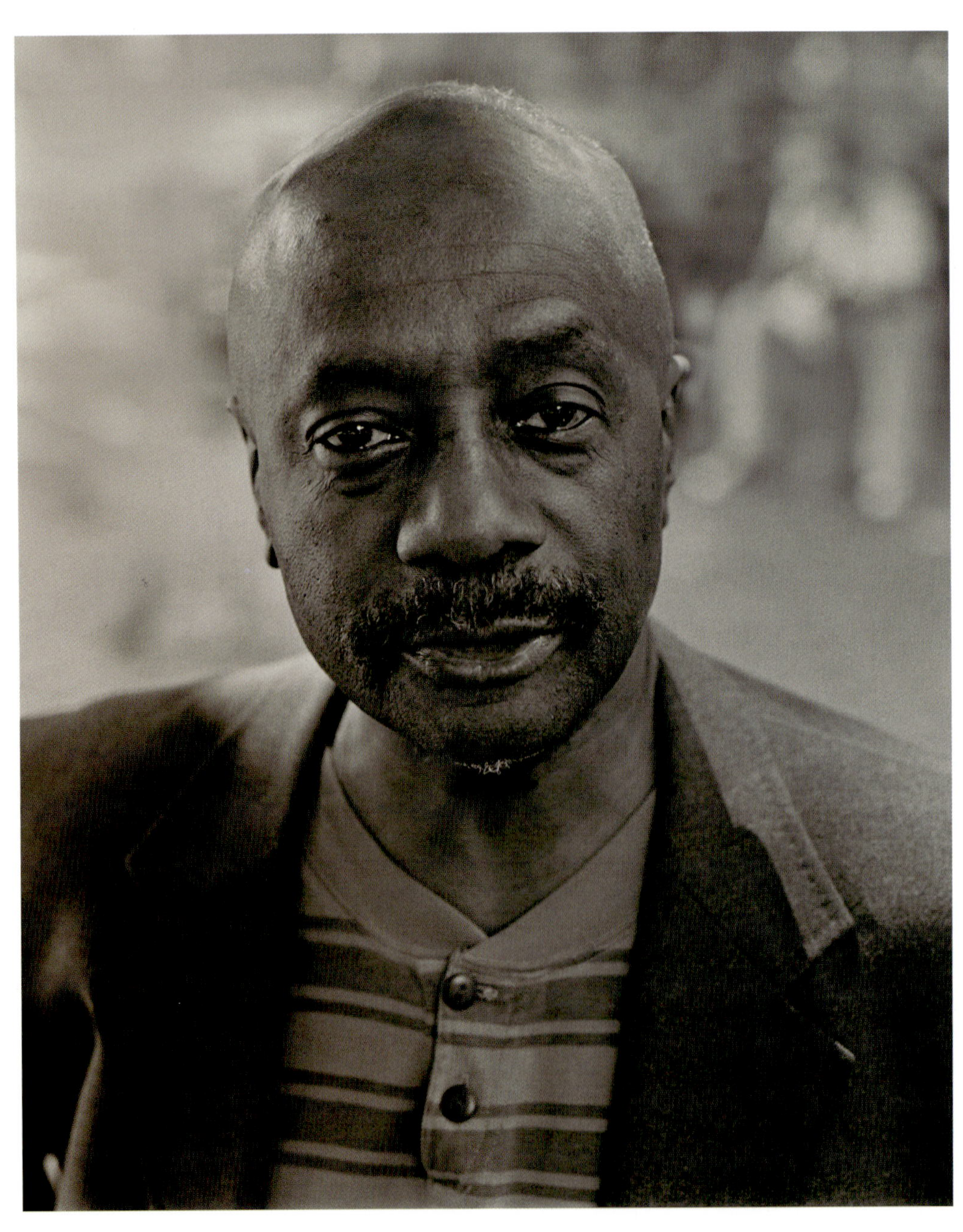

DAVID HENDERSON

BOPPING

My main men and I bopped
to general agreement (like the toast to ‘the boys upstate’
                                        before every bottle of Paradise or
                                        Thunderbird wine)
down cats
we bopped to give cause to the causes
that died before they got to us.

I remember the arm pumping cap crowned blades
of my boyhood
their elemental gait talking
deep beneath my eyes. . .
the list at waist and trunk
       whip of an arm
& abrupt   then long wing-tipped stride
of days when we had to show ourselves love
in difficult pretensions
                 as if speaking words of self-love
        was too remote   a performance
       when   before the fact
we understood all too well
the action of the thrust.

He maneuvered
to turn that way in dawns or dusk
of the eternal wars
among ourselves   our gangs:
                   The Crowns   Chaplains   Sportsmen
Boston Baldies   Young Sinners   Enchanters   Duschon Lords—
because talking   after all   is too little of glamour
to the hungry   the ugly   the mean

We bopped when about to fight
and we bopped when happy
all in our own slight variances
known to the members of the Road
and known to the similar bops
of the roaming hordes

From Avenue 'D'   to Red Hook
Thru Marcy Projects   then Crown Heights
Prospect Avenue in the Bronx & also in Brooklyn
The Fifth Avenue Armory on 141st & the Harlem River
Bronx River Housing   forty-three   fifty-five
99 center Boston Road
From Winters to graduation
From street duels
until
wedlock   or the cops
shut us down
bopping...

AUTOPILOT

The mountain sees clearly
I struggle to do without
not get in my head about it
plow right through
wall of cloud

Idiot slows down
apposite thing to say
about one who barely seems to be moving
my friend brushes her hair
closes her glassy eyes

The air isn't invisible
bright and bumpy
the sky is what the light
does next

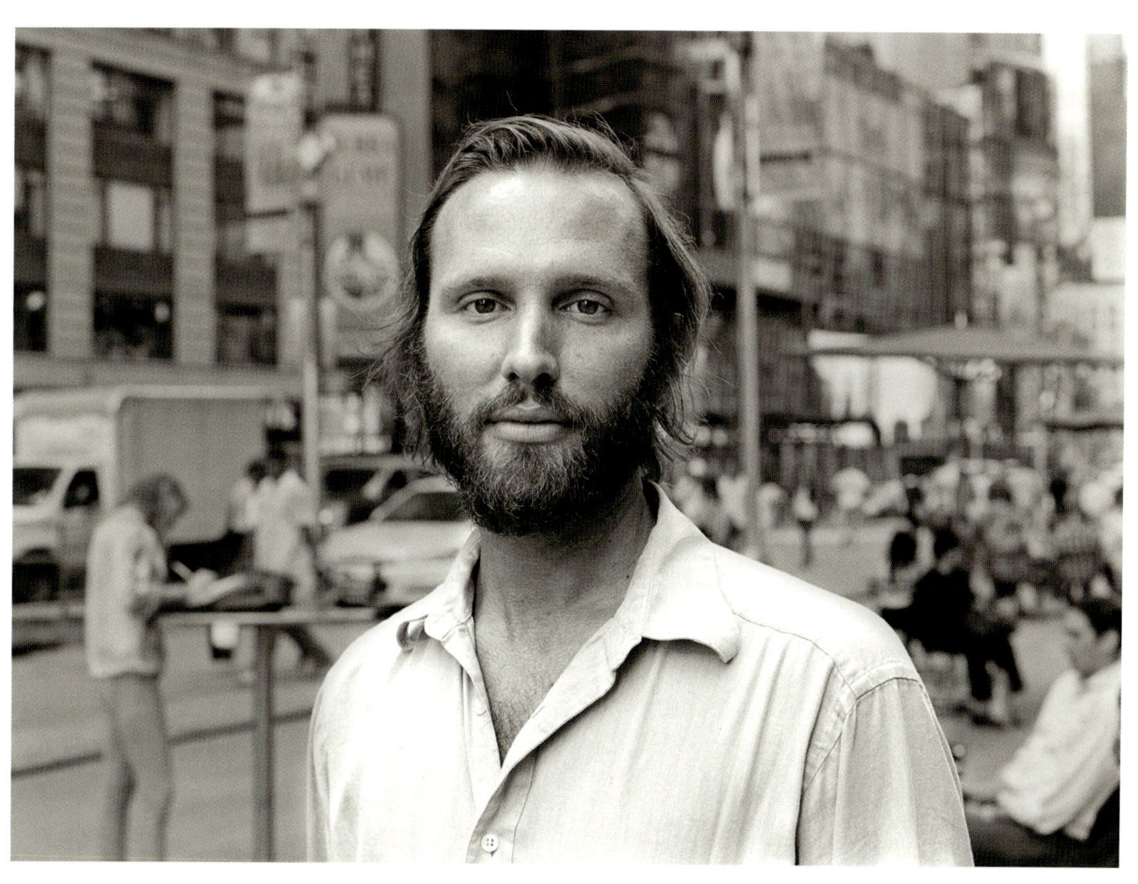

MICHAEL ROBERTS

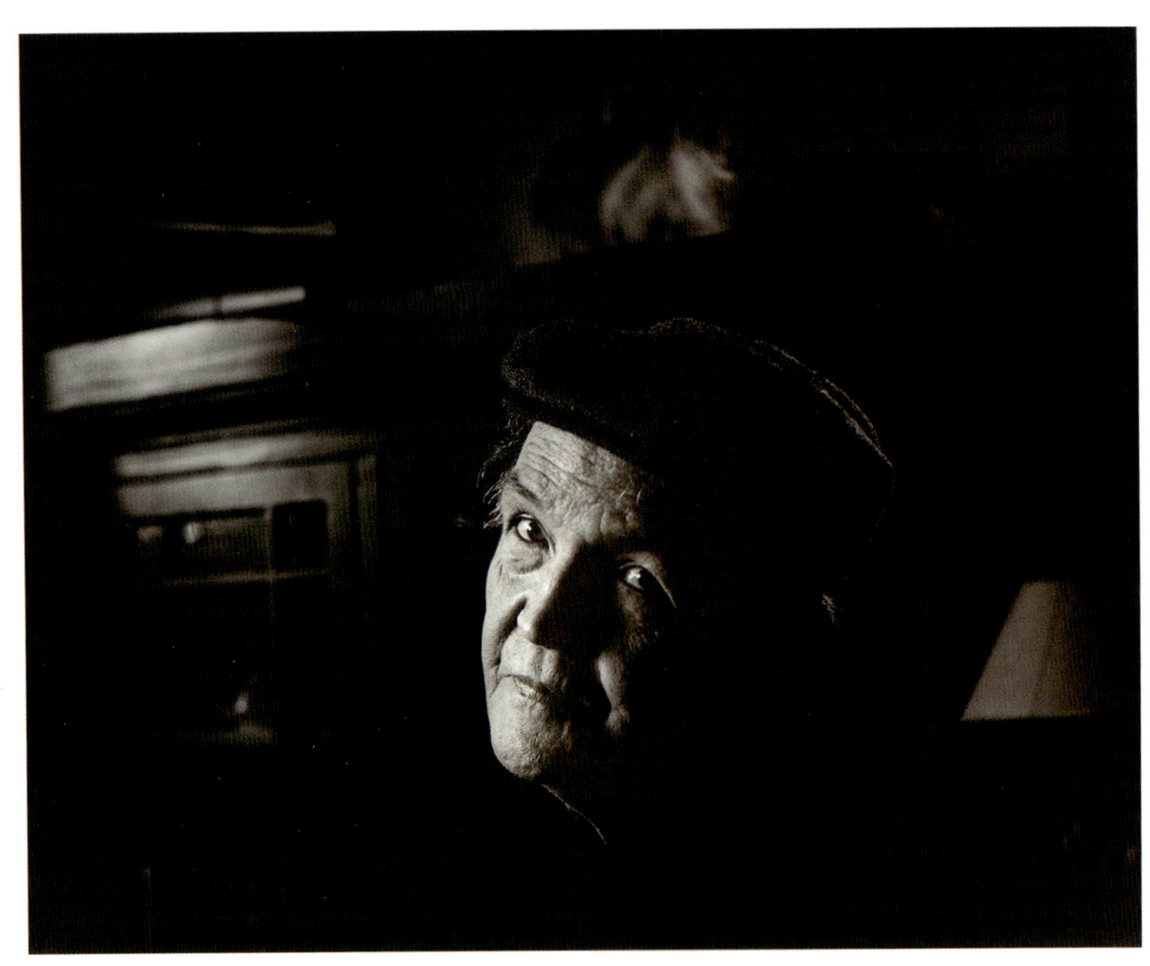

TOM CLARK

POEM

Like musical instruments
Abandoned in a field
The parts of your feelings

Are starting to know a quiet
The pure conversion of your
Life into art seems destined

Never to occur
You don't mind
You feel spiritual and alert

As the air must feel
Turning into sky aloft and blue
You feel like

You'll never feel like touching anything or anyone
Again
And then you do

WHY I DO OR DO NOT WRITE POETRY

I write specifically for a theoretical audience
of people like me, by which
I do not mean
61-year-old, introverted, post-anorexic, quiet but brave,
relentless, moralistic, materialistic, demanding,
red or blond haired individuals.
Nor do I mean people who love poetry
or people who think they have something to say
or people who think they have nothing to say
or people whose supposed opinions are constructed around
their need for safety
their need for response
their need for identity
their need for stimulation, continuity,
re-enforcement, provocation,
antagonism, restlessness, drama,
chastisement, appeasement, congratulation,
adulation, abasement, laziness,
timidity, forgiveness,
or fun.

What I do mean
is a rare group of scattered, glimmering souls
who will wait forever if necessary
to hear the one particular thing
which can only be phrased in any one
of a number of words by which
recognition is achieved.

When they hear it
they know it, and
more often than not
keep quiet about it.

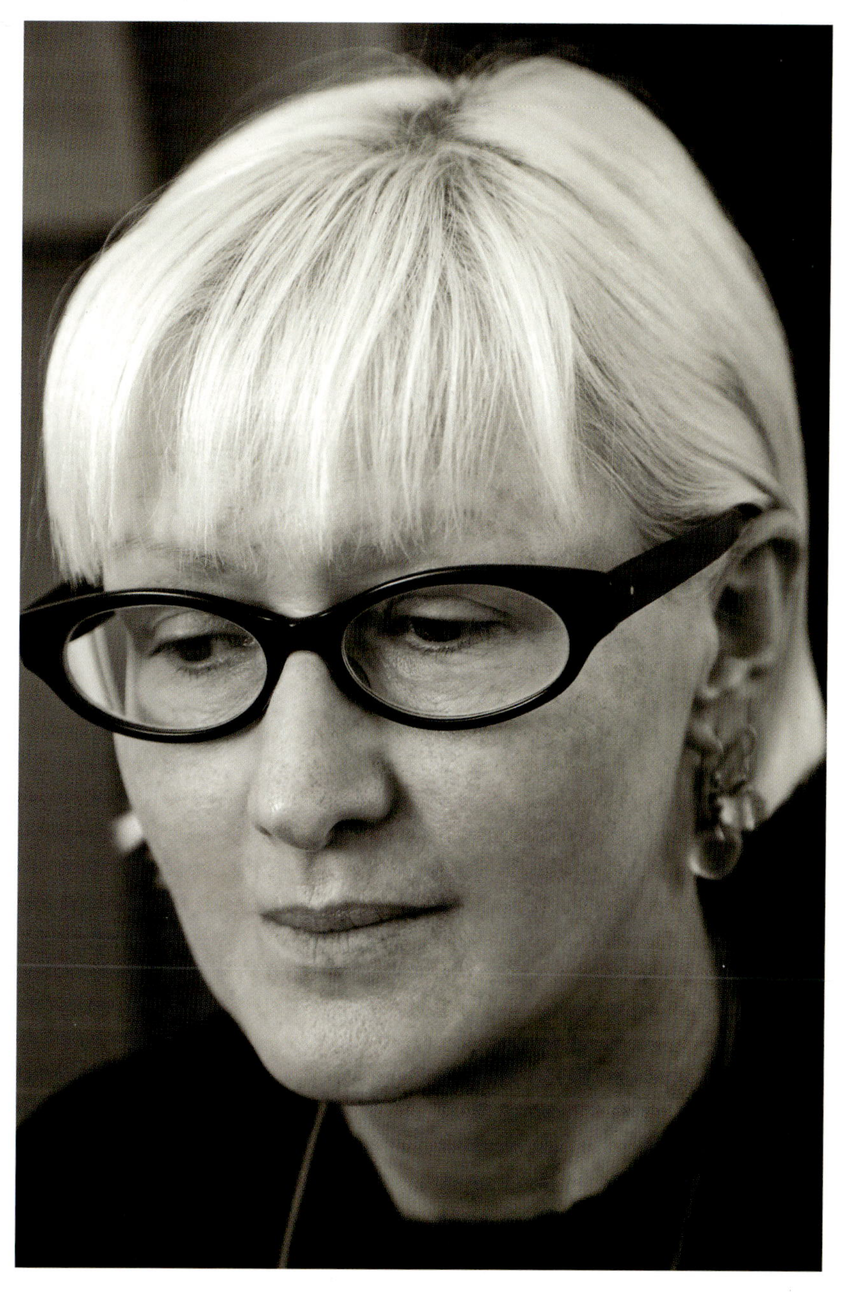

SUSAN NOEL

LOVE POEM

Doubling the sky to take in as much as when
things double with their own explanations,
the clouds depart to find different endings.

When a raft is a river and a river is a tree or a swing
and the king dupes the pedestrians into crossing
in total darkness, or when everything

is too much, we can't stop, not even for a second,
and the queen, for she is here too, signals the servants
to put a star in her bed, to help her forget

her earthly affairs or mix them with the firmament,
shaking and stirring about her head.
Then I can feel the pleasure that conspires against me.

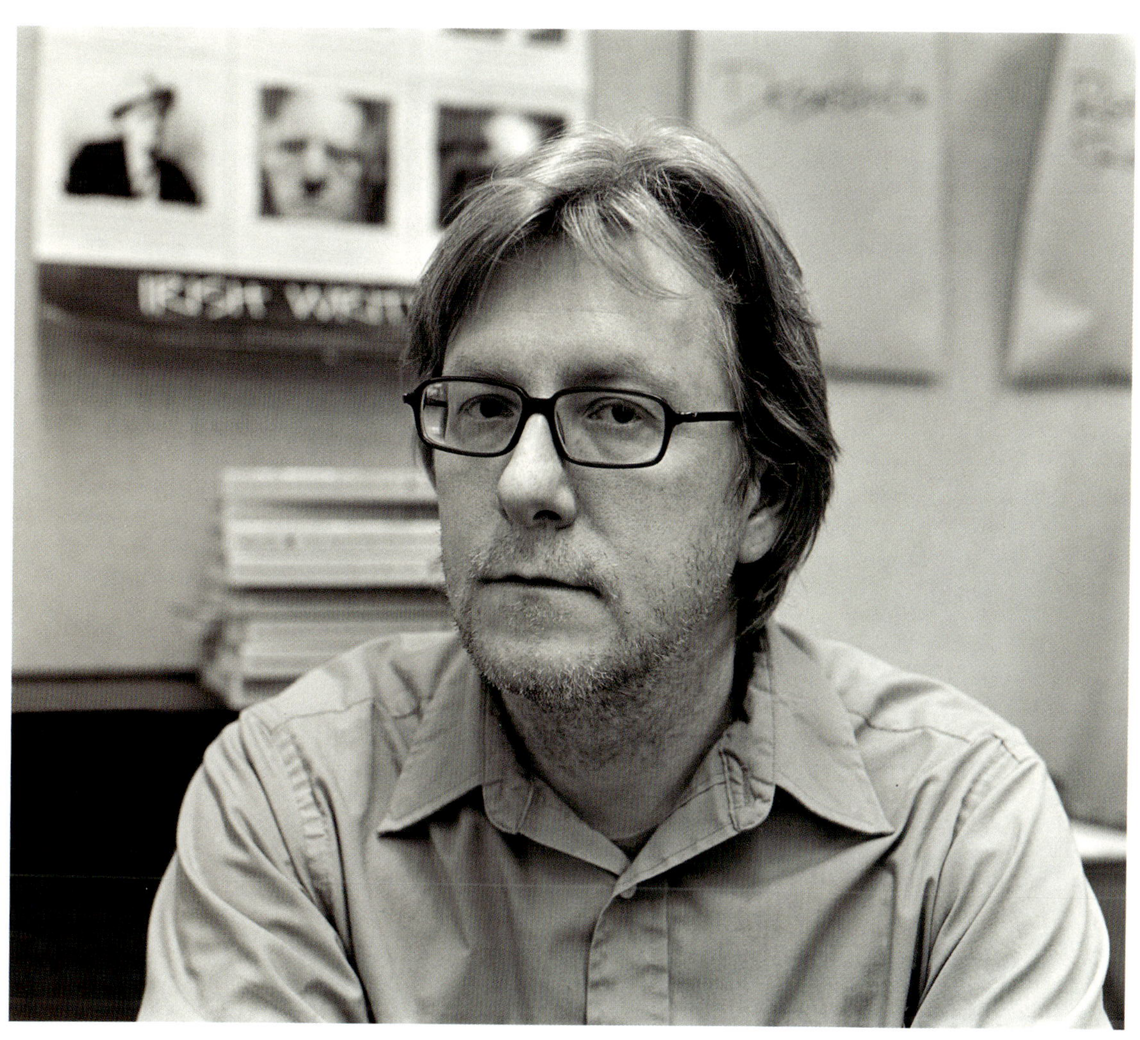

RICHARD ROUNDY

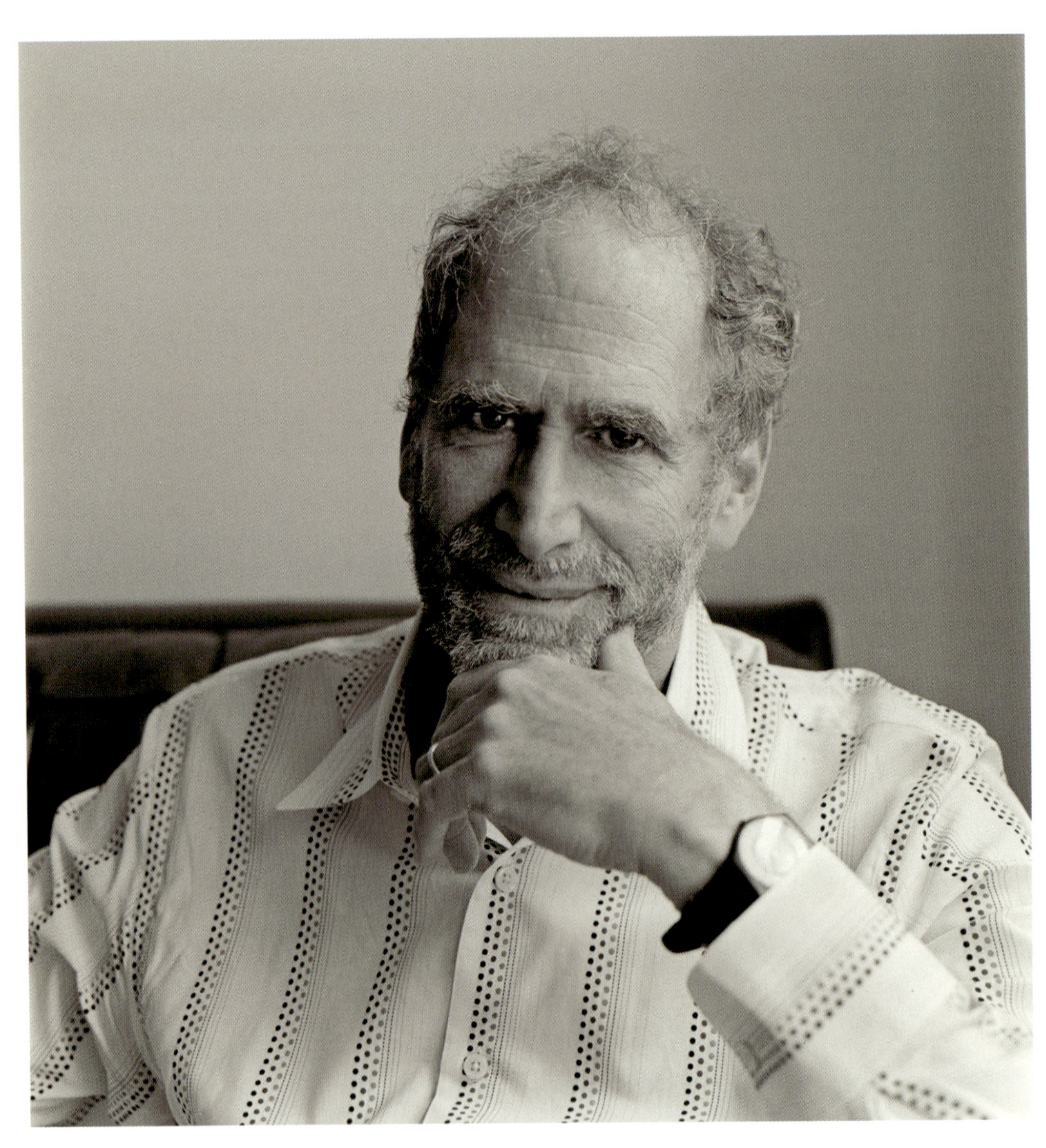

BOB PERELMAN

PRIMER

for Alan Bernheimer

The surface of the earth displays
A grain of sand. The pace it keeps
Creates bonds of love that stretch
Past the breaking point. Matter
Resents nothing. Plants try.
Animals can barely think. Speaking

Their minds, people load the air
With noise so thoroughly meant
That a would-be heaven
Falls from the sky and is
Where we follow our wills
To lead our lives, chasing

Bent actions along the curve
Of a finite door. The equations
Produce curbed or unleashed powers,
Barking into a dark garage

Or surviving the face of the deep.
For the earth to revolve
Continuously requires constant
Vigilance, endless sleep.

JOGGER'S ALMANAC

Right on cue with tragic elegance
Scattered showers make the scene
A magnet for a head in the clouds
Haven't found a better match in all my travels
Not in the hostels of Split anyway
And I can't say it's funny
For even a moment's remoteness
Carries an obsolescence
As troubling as a wheeze
People ask me if I'm turning around
With spring creeping in
One stammers from habit
And runs away
Smack into the enchantment of a sign
Who put that there—
Someone, anyone?
Nothing can prosper in this metallic air
Yet I can manage a second glance
Is there a blind spot on the sun?

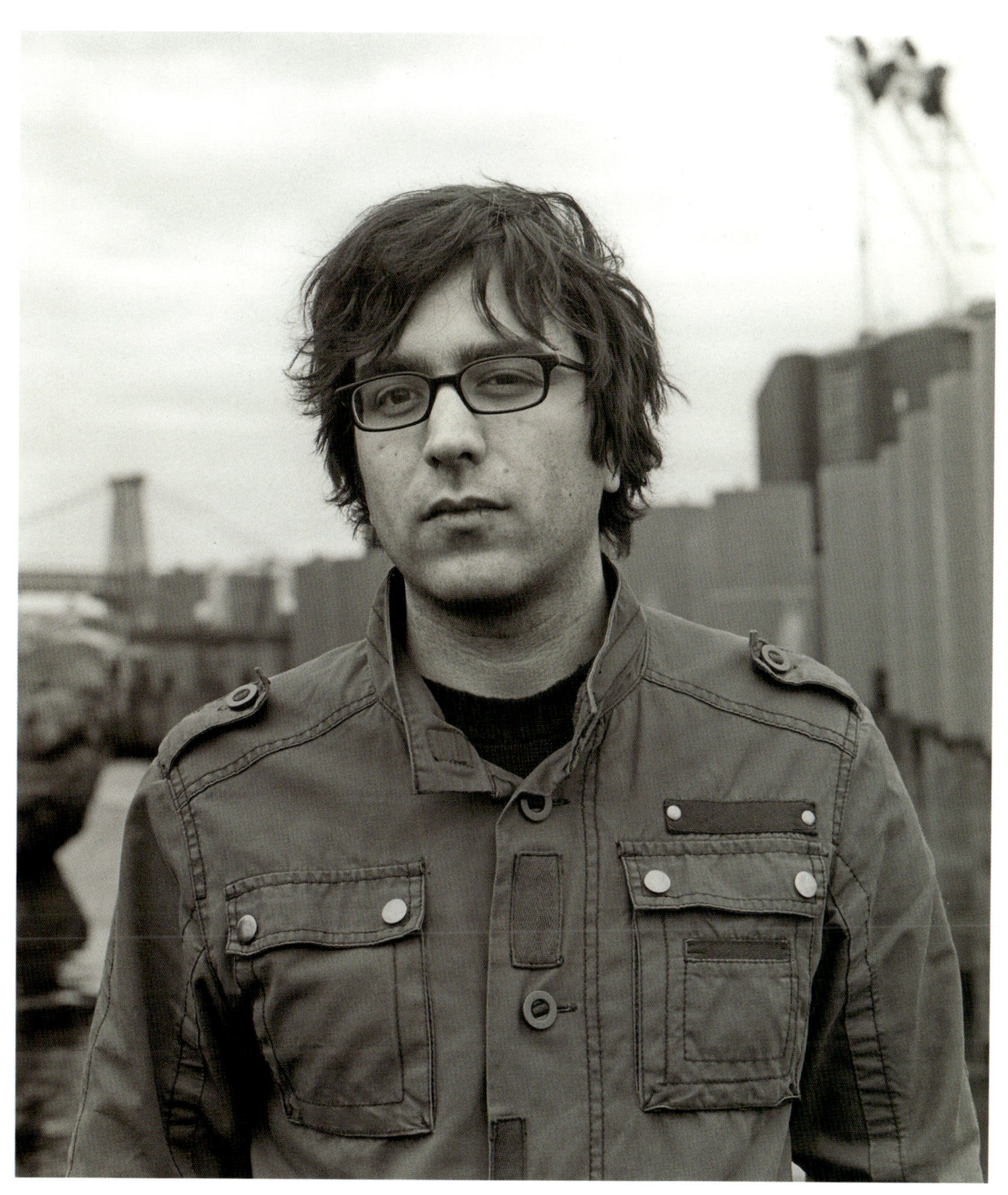

AARON SIMON

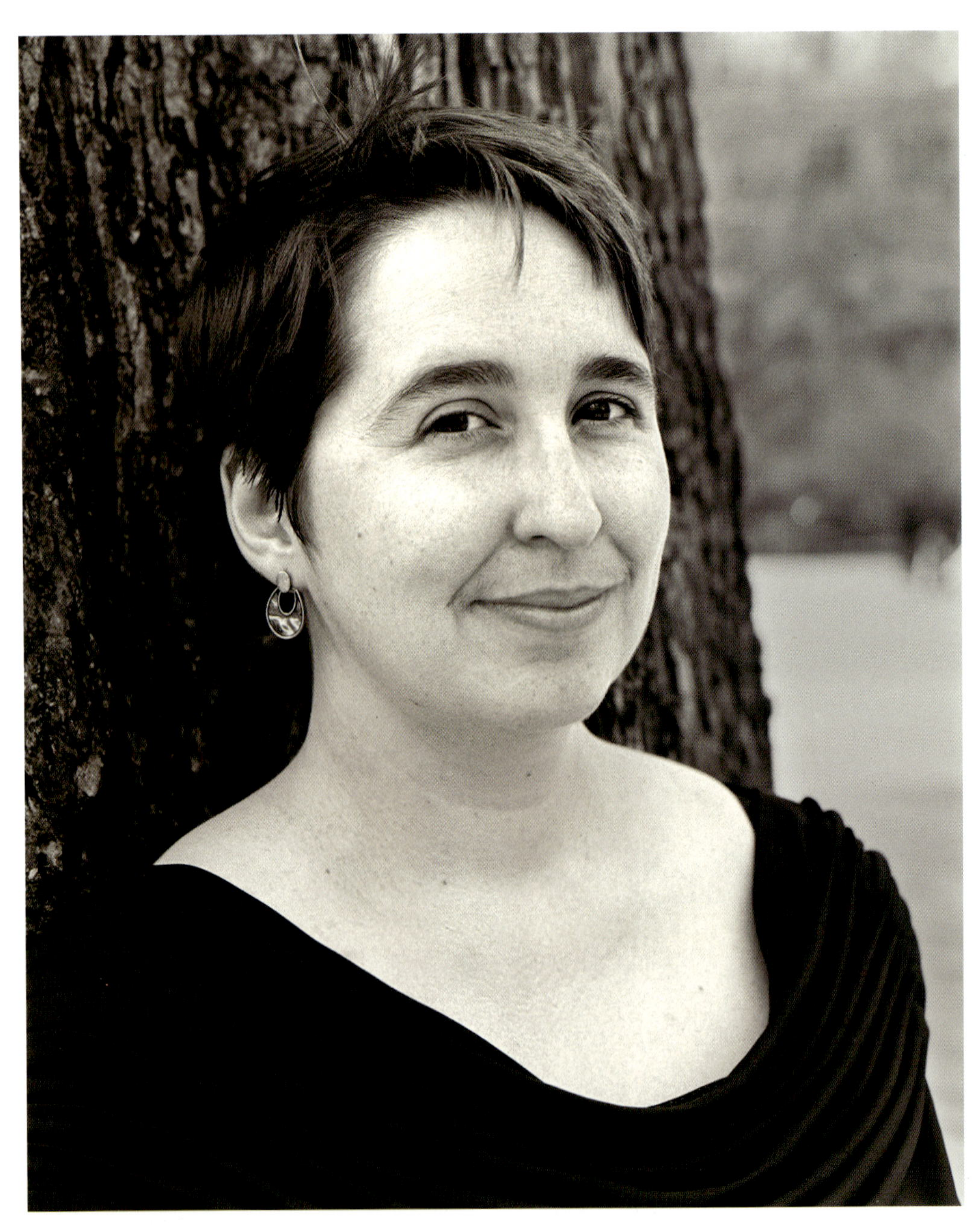

MAZARINE TREYZ

POETRY

Teeth, privatize verbs
Nostrils, charge up the gorge
Vagina, mark our desert island days
Wrists, begin as you mean to continue
Ankles, behind the eight-ball
Your penis is boring
Ears, carry me somewhere silent
Fascia, can you manage?
Larynx, frog without honey
Clavicle, clavicle
Vena Cava, don't make me come over there
Medulla, expect the worst
Ribs, never you mind
Parce que
Je te veux
Peace out, dope fiend!

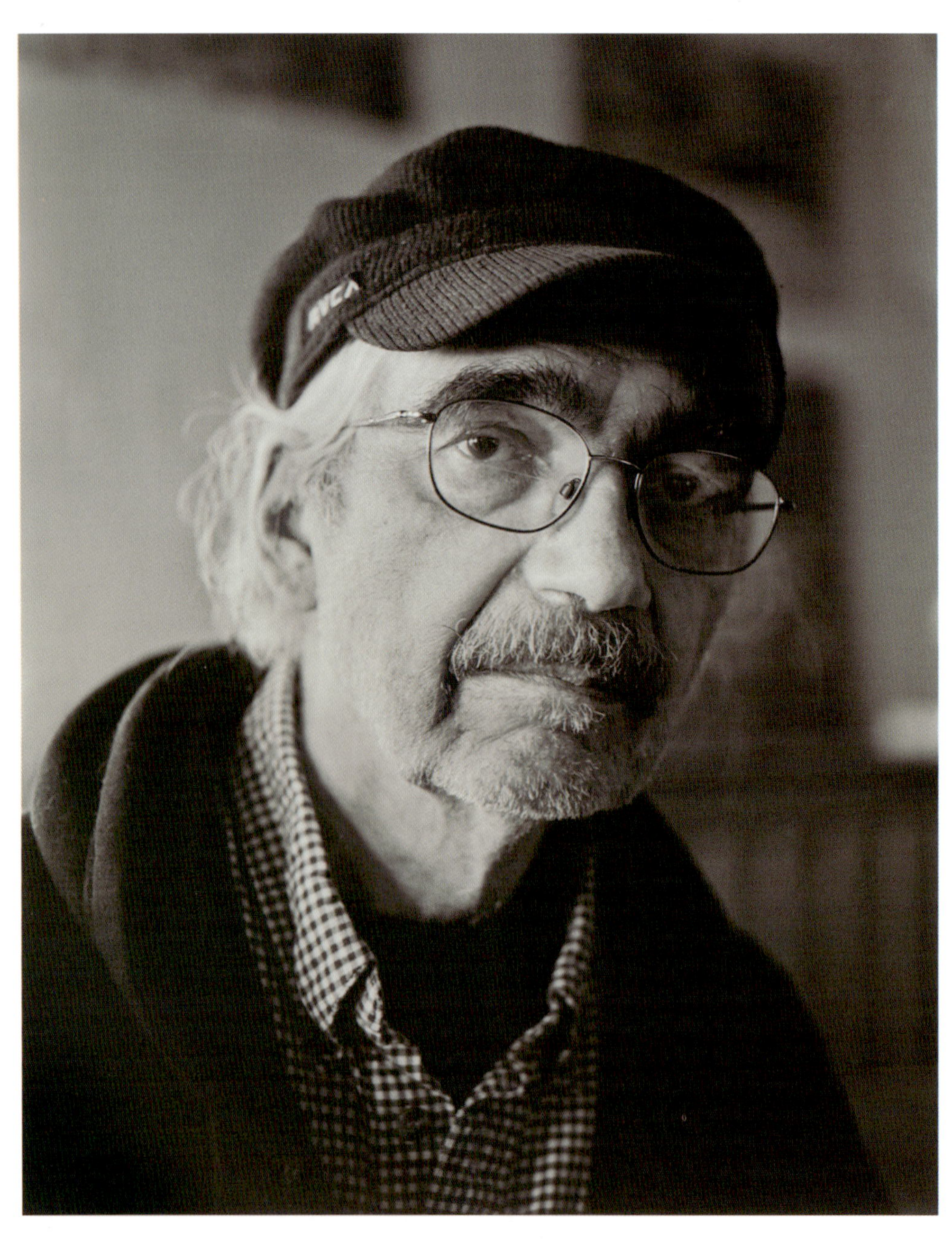

DICK GALLUP

CHARGED PARTICLES

Bright red where the sky dips towards heaven
And the creamy light drifts
From building
To building
To river
To air surrounding me
Standing over the docile Arno
With a bag over my shoulder
An ache in my foot
Today and tomorrow too
Over a light lunch
Getting heavier with the sunlight
And the wine
And the afternoon descending
Into the delicious lonely evening

Inhabiting ancient buildings
Dark stairs and stumbling
Where the shaky hands fall
Across beautiful shoulders with the burden of delight
Following the distance into the absence of noise
Where the city fades away
Together before the canopy
Of frozen winter streets
Leaving the avenues
To cabs and buses
Where the cluttered air comes down
Poised over puddles of light on the narrow white streets

No end to the level sky no top to the falling snow
No hat on my head
                                        Where I'm standing in the rain now
The drops passing me on their way to the icy clouds of winter
Passing those I don't know
                                                        And those I do
                                    Without comprehension
Of how we meet inclemently
                                                            Like broken municipalities
Along a new highway with burlap covered signs

SPARKLING WHITE TOAST

Sparkling white toast ordered by the guy at the next table
lifted my mood.

According to him, every other kind is weird, of course.

I wish while I was watching I wasn't jealous of her
I kept thinking she's not as good as I am, but because
she *seems* better, everyone'll love her more, I guess
she's the new one now, they'll be really glad to get rid of
me, BACKWARD ACCULTURATION.
I'm going to write an 'attitude work.'
ASK FOR IT BY NAME.

◆

Ask for solutions to your problems in your dreams.
Before you go to bed, ask your dreams to solve your
problems for you.
HOW NICE.

◆

You're so sunny and flat and blue
whenever you come in the trees swaying and flashing
outside the window are demoted.
Bandana festooned shopping cart, ONE FOR THE STYLE
BOOK.
Have you noticed what they're wearing?
Here comes Lizzie, ancient collie, which we used to call all of
them Lassie, poor old Lizzie, with a hairless rope for a
TAIL.

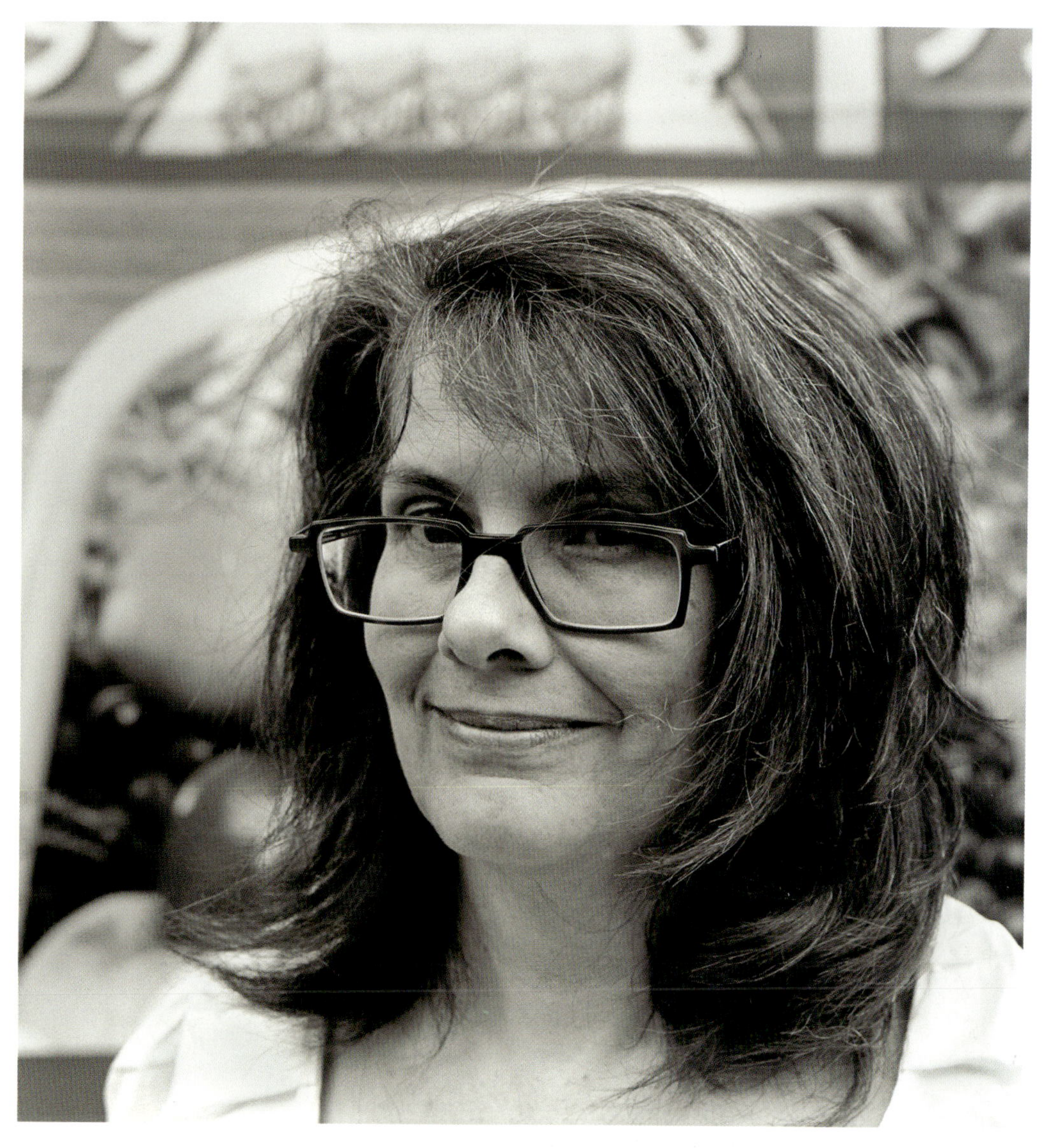

SUSIE TIMMONS

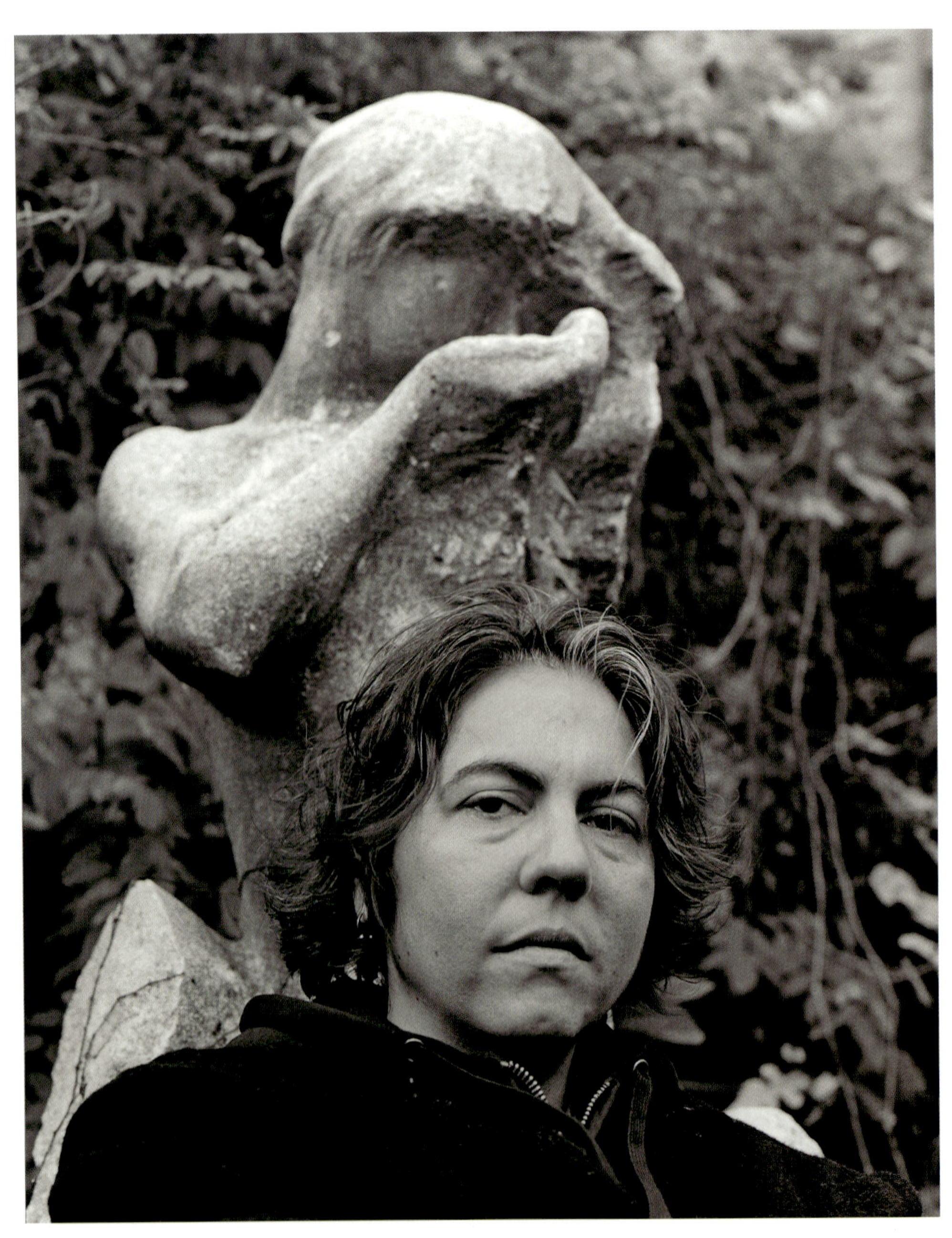

STACY SZYMASZEK

from HART ISLAND

a cavern   hill-

side hazel

eye carnation

face nasal call

                    a drake

messianic chemical

reaction scourge

marks of the lot

lit infra-

red winding

paper napkin

Turin

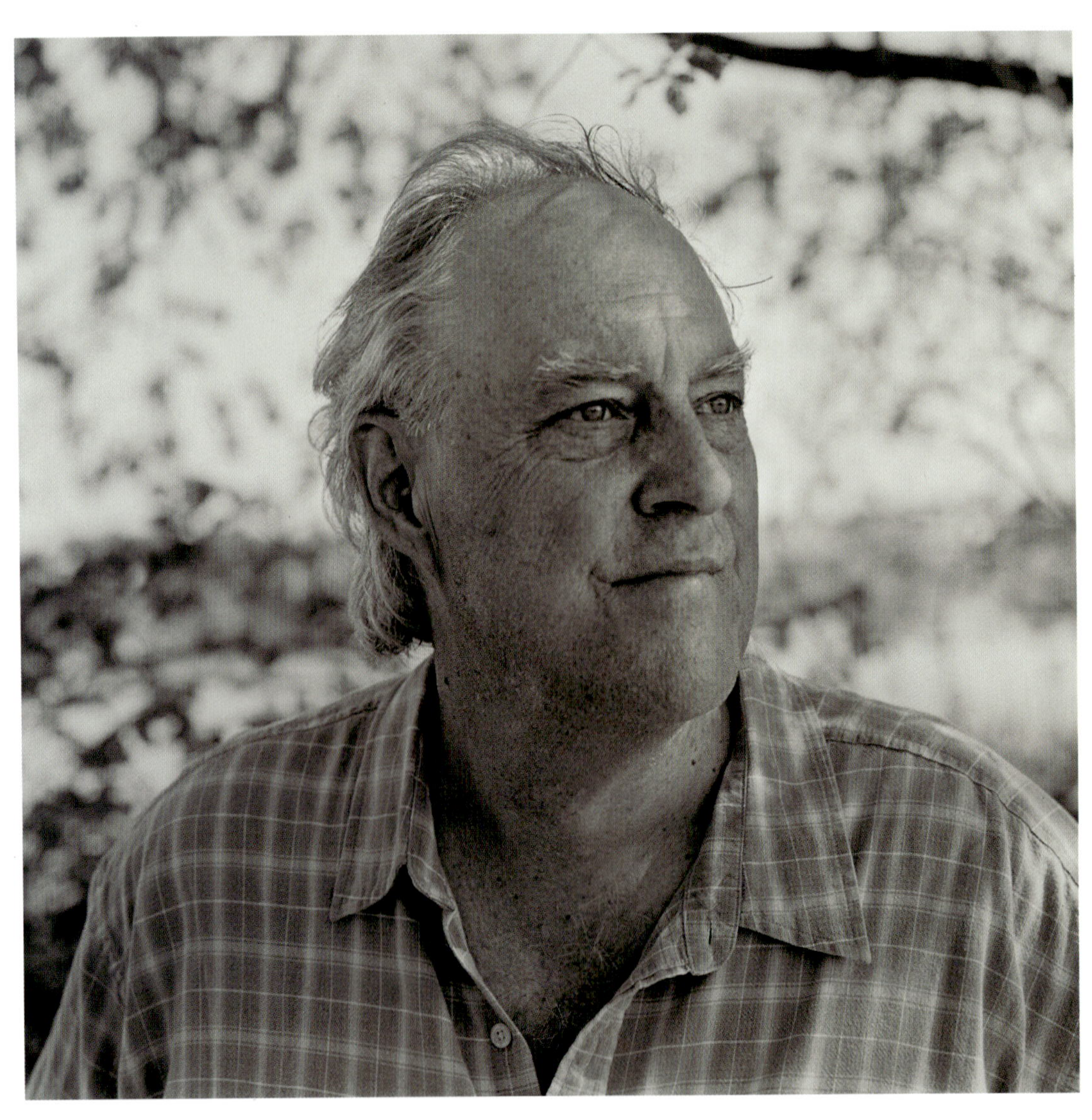

MERRILL GILFILLAN

JULY 12, 1990

Anyone once loved
still loved—
Hollyhocks
open in the alleyways:
confectionery
colors: cherry, sweet-tooth pinks,
mallow yellow:
soda pop colors,
sticky jube jube—
But anyone
once loved, still loved.

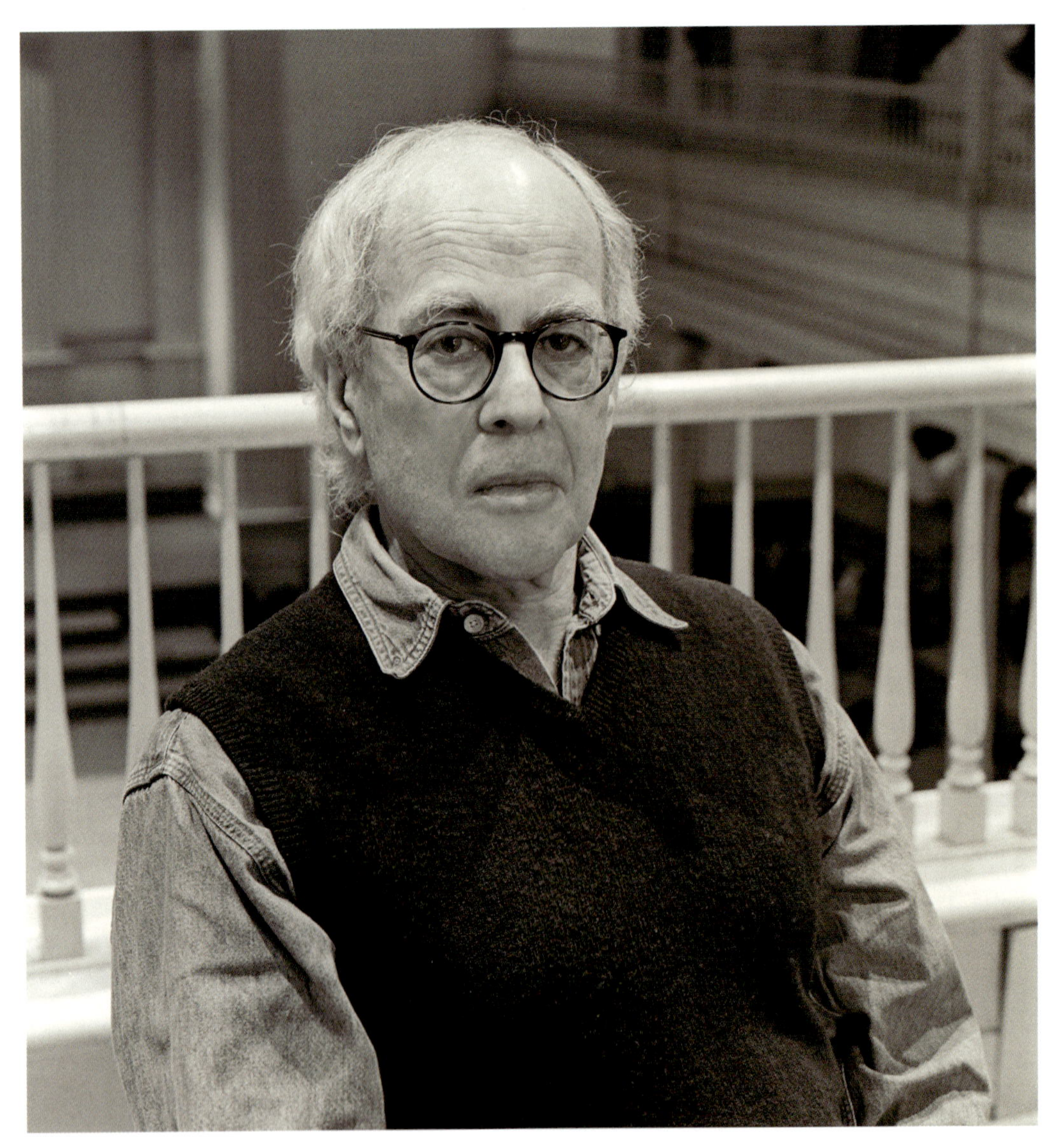

CHARLES NORTH

THE PHILOSOPHY OF NEW JERSEY

for Jill

Actually the sky appears older than it is. It's 63 or 64 at most, not 75. The part with the cliff face and the yellow crane could be in its early 30s. It wasn't Wallace Stevens who said, 'They have cut off my head, and picked out all the letters of the alphabet—all the vowels and consonants—and brought them out through my ears; and then they want me to write poetry! I can't do it!' It was John Clare. Wallace Stevens said—something like—the best poems are the ones you meant to write. That has a nice sound to it, but it's hard to see how he or anyone would know that. It would be hard, for example, to accept the notion that there are ideas one meant to have. Poems underneath every peeling sycamore and inside every file cabinet, along with ideas about poetry and uncountable other ideas.

WEIGHTIER TITLE

Light cancels color
Thin underpinning to the stars
The very blood éclairs of darkness
Eyes a mesmer of focus
Their spectacles all in the dirt
Spectral news enough of a boost
Would you be included and remain a woman?
Highly unlikely
The she of it, a swift tub in the grass
Grass is grass in more than name
Some words fit their parts
Some try to muscle their way in

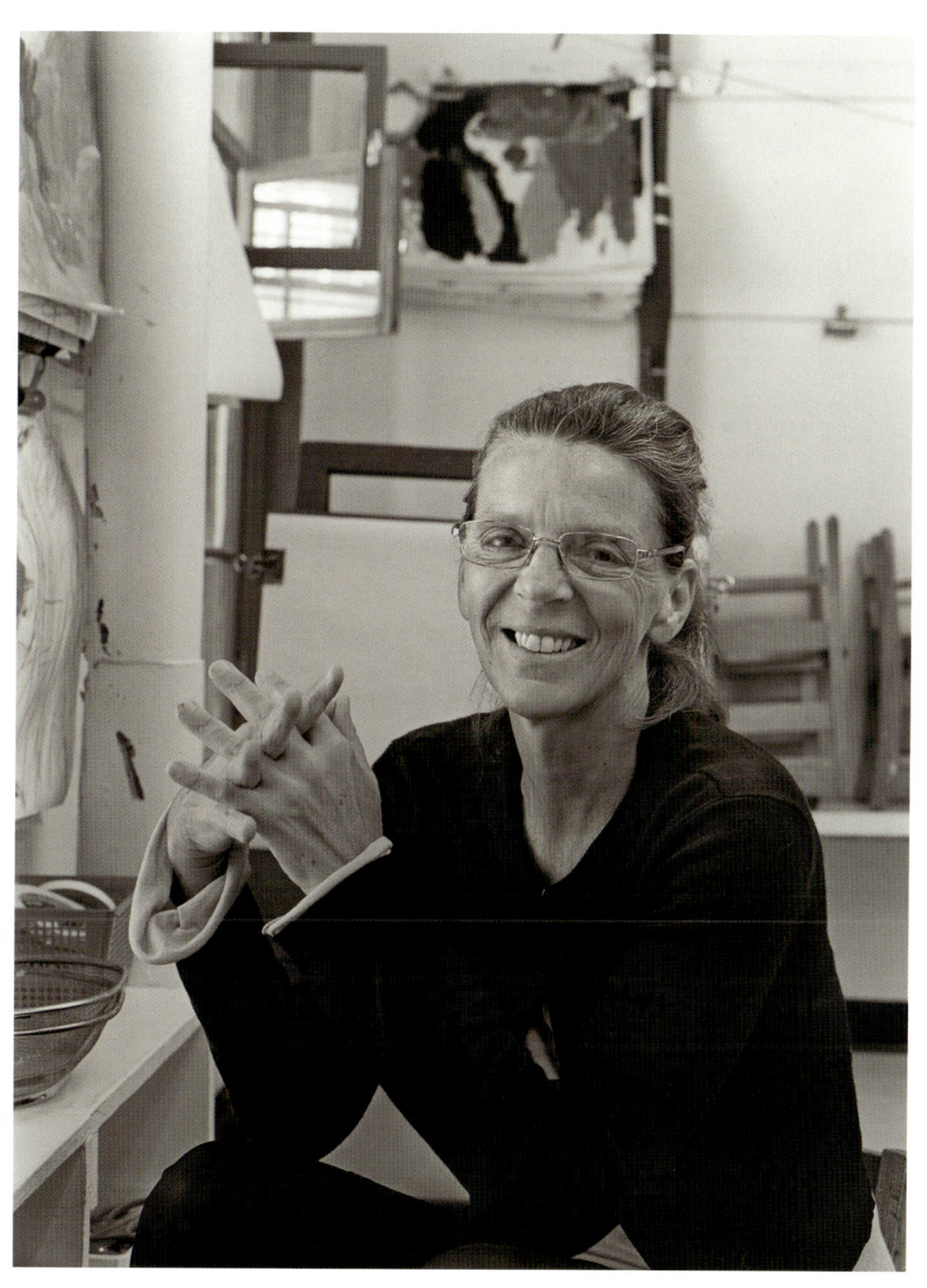

CAROL SZAMATOWICZ

KIT
ROBINSON

WORKING GIRL BLUES

What are you?
A person who imagines?
Or a person who doubts?
Can't I be both?
We'll find out
What are you?
A serious, forthright, sincere individual?
Or a snickering, snidely snoot?
Can't I be both?
Yes, I suppose you can at that

And that's that
But that's not this
Not this wish list that's long and off the cuff
Not that address that's inked upon a wrist
All that is past, not built to last
It goes by fast, the die is cast
And neither ends
Nor starts again
But filters slowly through our pores
And sees us safely out of doors

Time transpires in fits
Starts, long stretches, sudden
Pitches, realization
Slides backwards, hiccups
Blanks out, starts up again
Breathing into the evening
As we prepare for the day
Play scales, watch for whales
Chat, where you at
Chew time into sweet, chunky bits

Spit the pits, pop zits
Do lines, levy fines
Take a notion, jump bail
Spot trains, switch lanes
Eat breakfast any time of day
Stay for the stay pay
Don't move from that chair
Get a load of the avenue
Traffic picking up, going off
Light left not enough, stifle cough

Everything that happens happens once
And once only
Do you believe that?
Yes, but then dig this:
Different Day, Same Old Shit
Well, you're right there
You're right over there in that big old chair
Not turning into a public square
A Monument to Instrumentality
That's what I call the business end of this No. 2 pencil

What happens when what you want
To happen doesn't happen and what
You don't want to happen does is
Mind and body go on strike
Okay then I just won't even try
The grand mechanism of concerted effort
Shuts down, refuses to budge
Meanwhile the sun, author of an engrossing
Superlative pulp, continues to shine brightly
On a glorious day in the history of the universe

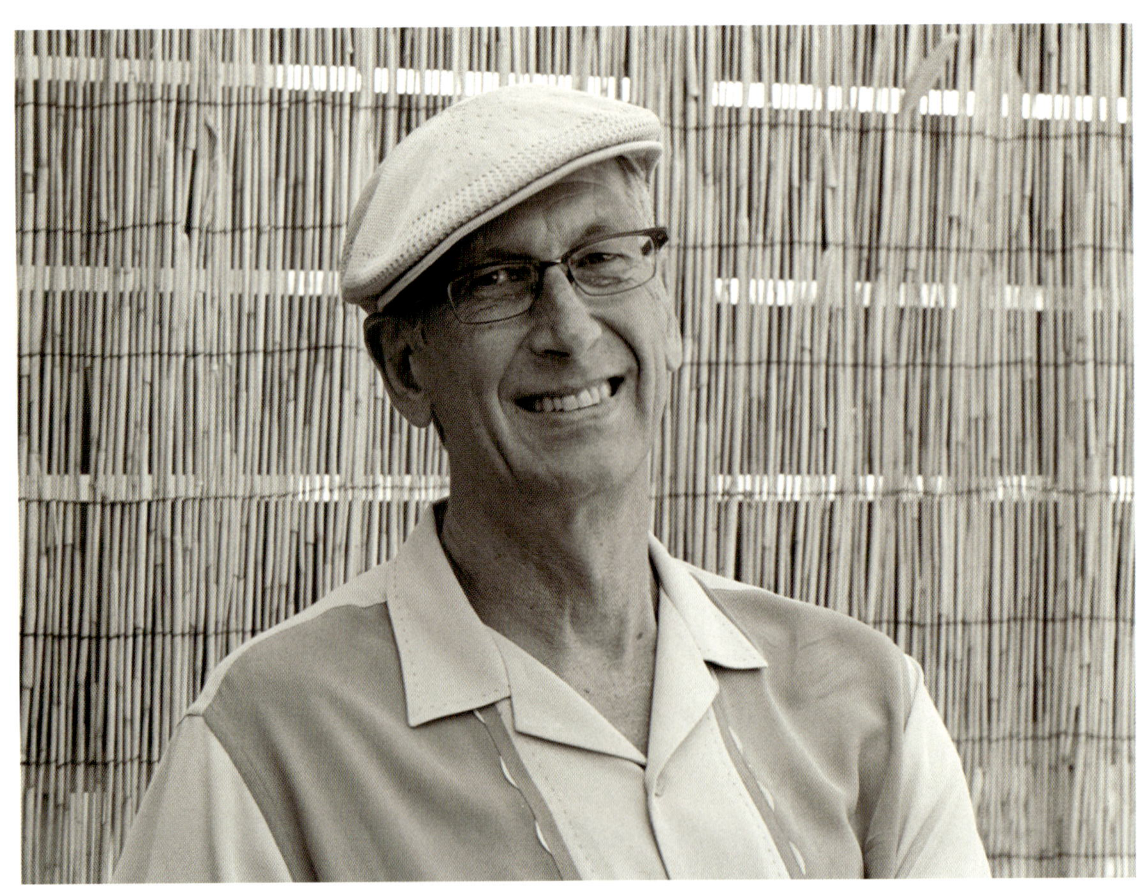

KIT ROBINSON

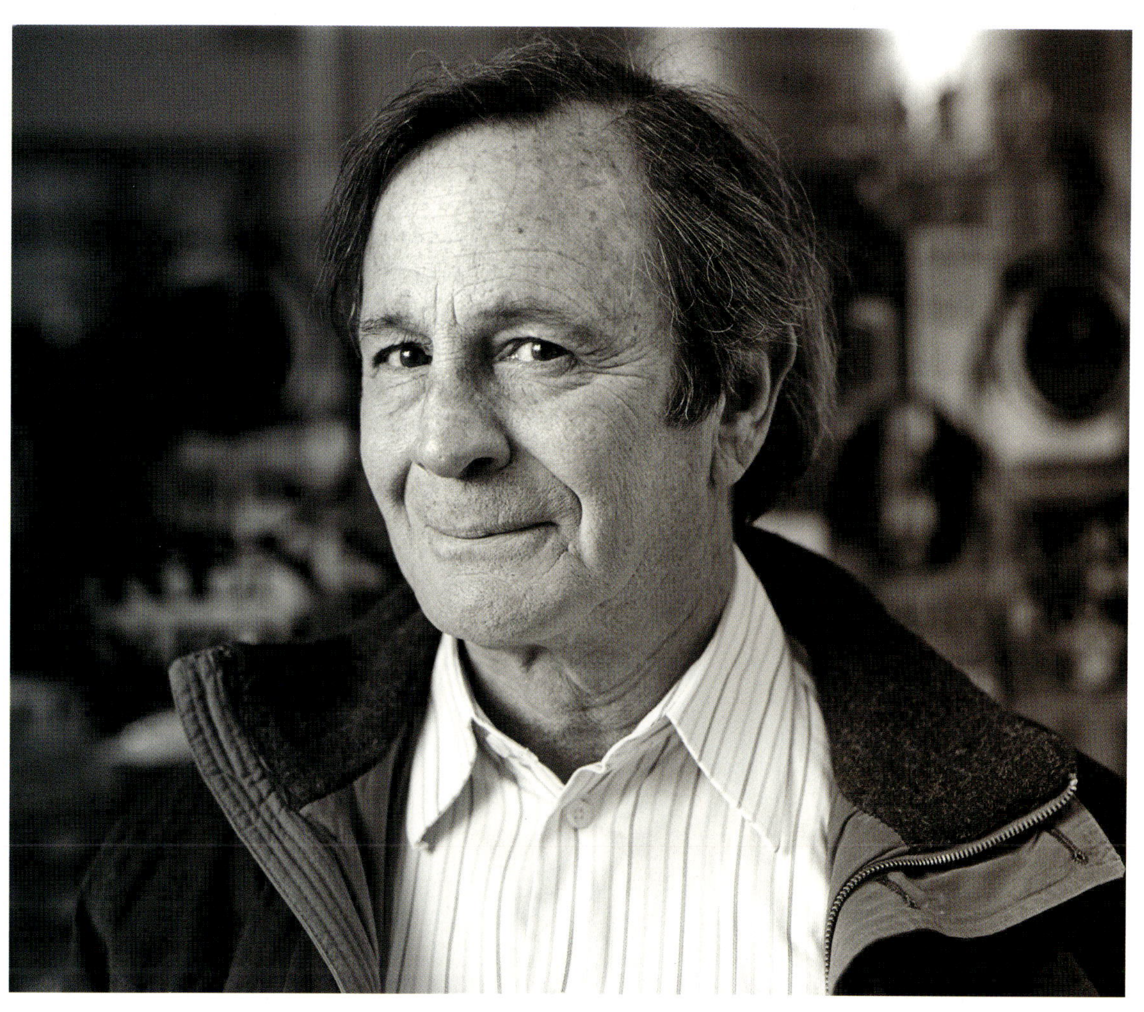

PAUL VIOLI

COUNTERMAN

What'll it be?

Roast beef on rye, with tomato and mayo.

Whaddaya want on it?

A swipe of mayo.
Pepper but no salt.

You got it. Roast beef on rye.
You want lettuce on that?

No. Just tomato and mayo.

Tomato and mayo. You got it.
...Salt and pepper?

No salt, just a little pepper.

You got it. No salt.
You want tomato.

Yes. Tomato. No lettuce.

No lettuce. You got it.
...No salt, right?

Right. No salt.

You got it. Pickle?

No, no pickle. Just tomato and mayo.
And pepper.

Pepper.

Yes, a little pepper.

Right. A little pepper.
No pickle.

Right. No pickle.

You got it.
Next!

Roast beef on whole wheat, please,
With lettuce, mayonnaise and a center slice
Of beefsteak tomato.
The lettuce splayed, if you will
In a Beaux Arts derivative of classical acanthus,
And the roast beef, thinly sliced, folded
In a multi-foil arrangement
That eschews Bragdonian pretensions
Or any idea of divine geometric projection
For that matter, but simply provides
A setting for the tomato
To form a medallion with a dab
Of mayonnaise as a fleuron.
And—as eclectic as this may sound—
If the mayonnaise can also be applied
Along the crust in a Vitruvian scroll
And as a festoon below the medallion,
That would be swell.

You mean like in the Cathedral St. Pierre in Geneva?

Yes, but the swag more like the one below the rosette
At the Royal Palace in Amsterdam.

You got it.
Next!

KUGEL

Images of girlfriend
appear in dreams.
Years from now we are married.
She's in the bathroom
applying make-up.
'Er hat die Kugel,' she says.
Literally, he has the ballpoint pen
or the ball or even 'he is on the ball.'
Or ball of noodles.
Nothing in town has changed.
The peach orchard is still there.
Except now I was in my late thirties.
We were happy, so happy
long before life had begun and ended.

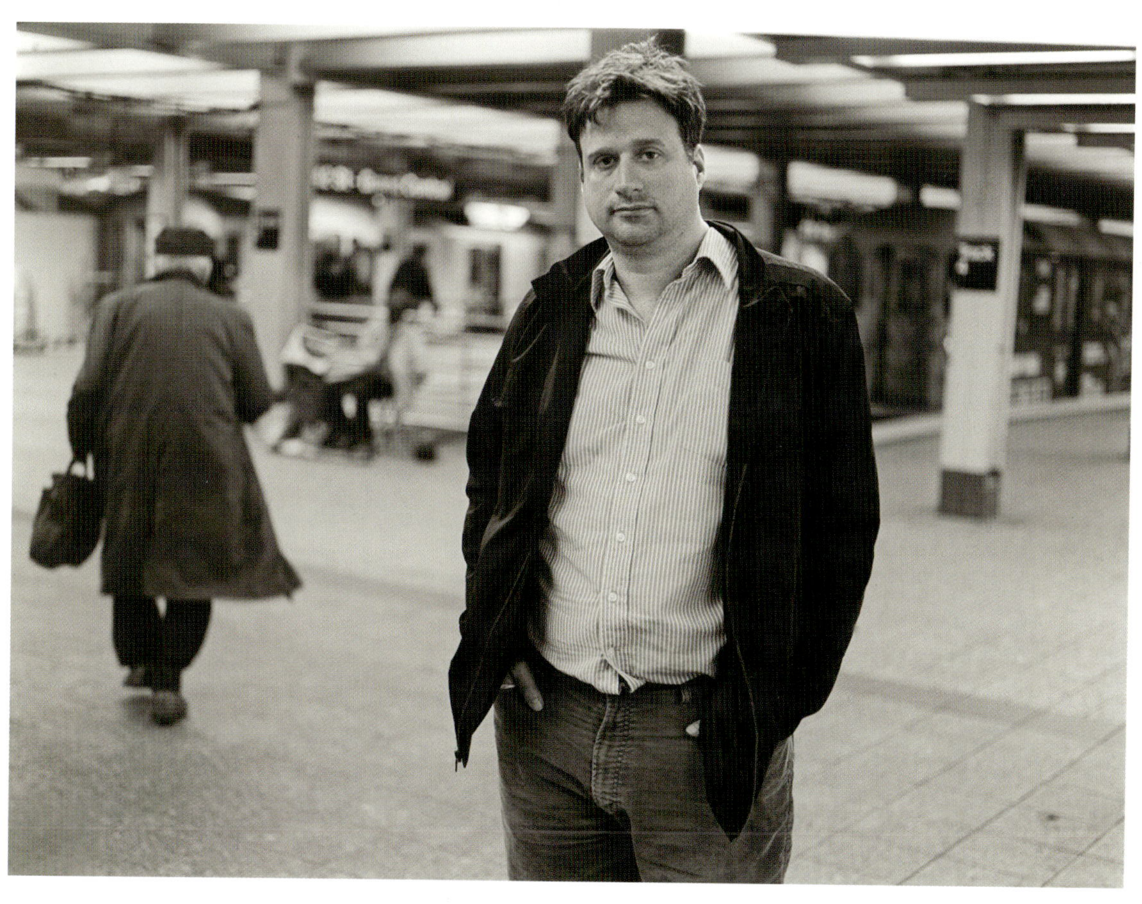

RYAN NOWLIN

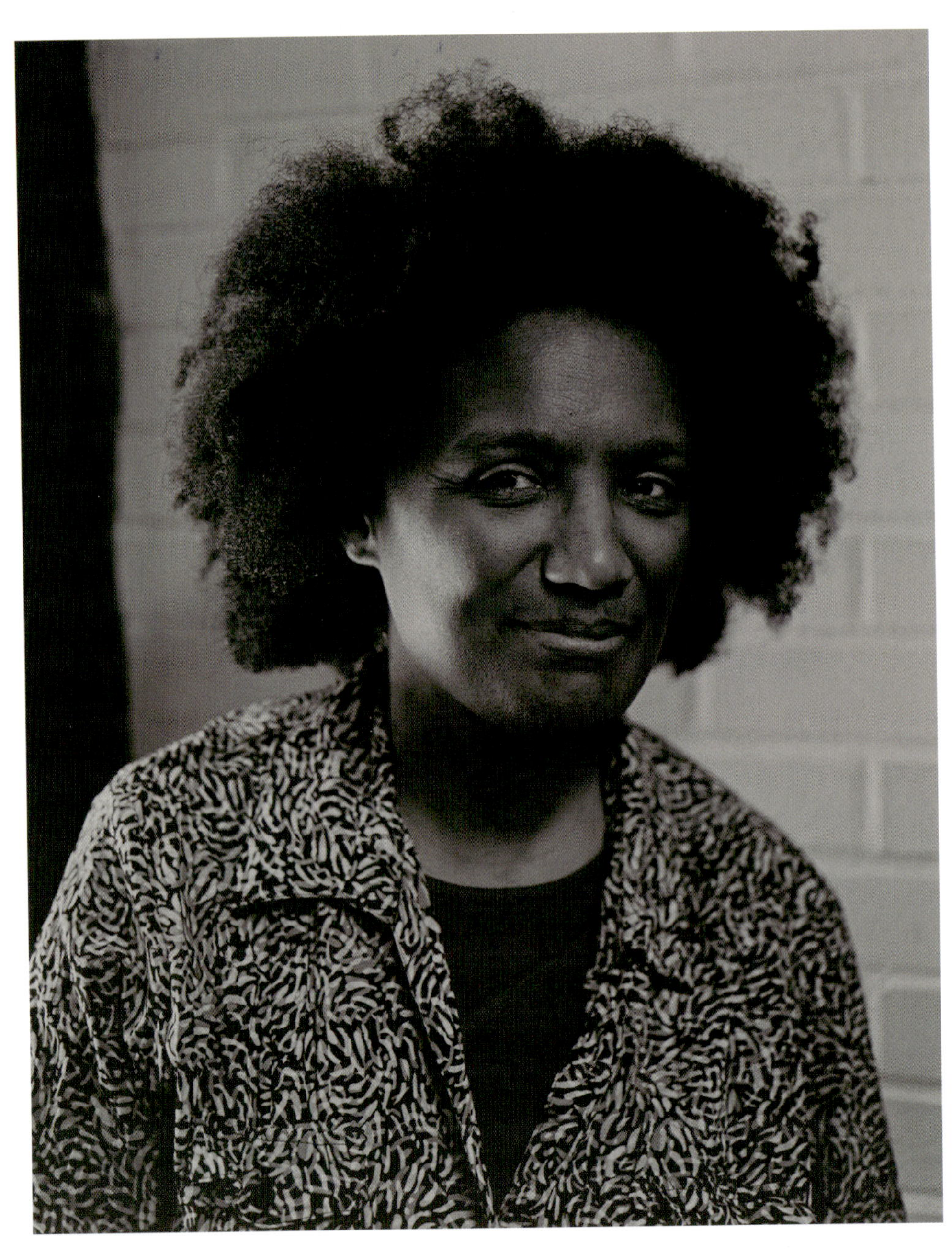

HARRYETTE MULLEN

SLEEPING WITH THE DICTIONARY

I beg to dicker with my silver-tongued companion, whose lips are ready to read my shining gloss. A versatile partner, conversant and well-versed in the verbal art, the dictionary is not averse to the solitary habits of the curiously wide-awake reader. In the dark night's insomnia, the book is a stimulating sedative, awakening my tired imagination to the hypnagogic trance of language. Retiring to the canopy of the bedroom, turning on the bedside light, taking the big dictionary to bed, clutching the unabridged bulk, heavy with the weight of all the meanings between these covers, smoothing the thin sheets, thick with accented syllables—all are exercises in the conscious regimen of dreamers, who toss words on their tongues while turning illuminated pages. To go through all these motions and procedures, groping in the dark for an alluring word, is the poet's nocturnal mission. Aroused by myriad possibilities, we try out the most perverse positions in the practice of our nightly act, the penetration of the denotative body of the work. Any exit from the logic of language might be an entry in a symptomatic dictionary. The alphabetical order of this ample block of knowledge might render a dense lexicon of lucid hallucinations. Beside the bed, a pad lies open to record the meandering of migratory words. In the rapid eye movement of the poet's night vision, this dictum can be decoded, like the secret acrostic of a lover's name.

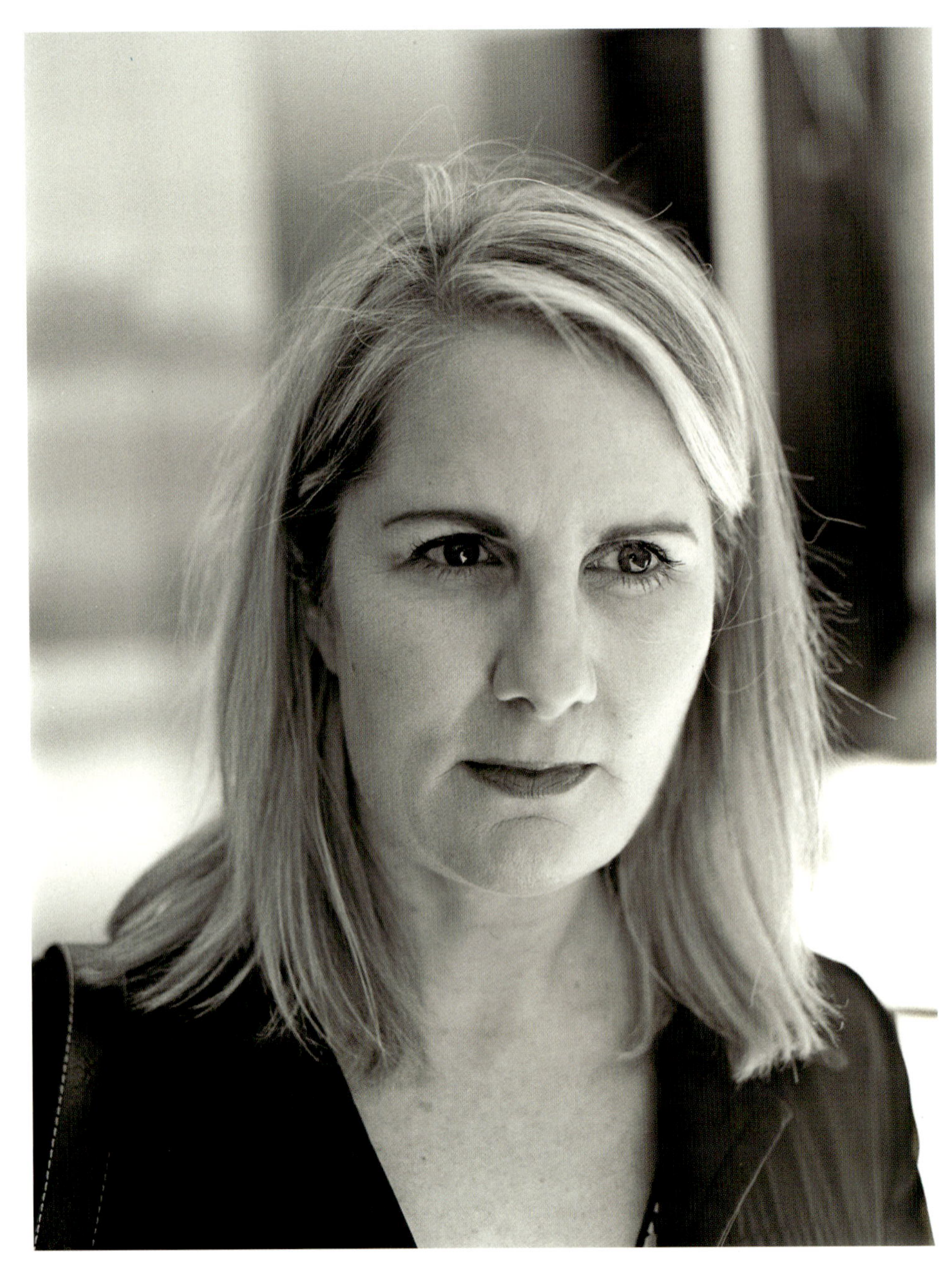

JENNIFER MOXLEY

THE AMBITION OF ART

This poem is dedicated to A.B.

We are, both of us, part of the freakdom, our indecorous
attempts cast distorted shadows when backlit by the light
of the daily grind. I am beside you, without precarious
apparatus or *linguistics,* silent in my kindred deception,
invisible self annihilation, I do not trust
the natural course of things, nor call this pleasure,
the sensuous election of certain despair, exile to the sober
outskirts, small punctures meant to free the false entreaties
of a cheat, where every little midnight laughs to see us,
you in your cardboard cylinder clothes walking awkwardly
down the street, me in bed with outdated logic and to lights
long since snuffed out, obedient. I do not want attention.
A whirligig run out of steam I bang my head against
the floor, deliciously anticipate the onset of rest,
the brief metrical rocking before I am strung up
and spun out again, there letters will settle the contraband
hush-hush alphabet in my head, *A, B*... lost sight for sore C,
columnar memory, rabbit-hole cunt, aching cock, *deft* fingers,
scotch rocks, constructed oblivion laid-out lettristic
in heavy regular beautiful beats, arc of an entreaty—but I
hate this dream and I hate its vanity. Most of all I hate
its desire, with which the lightest breath threatens
to undermine my disguise. Therein begins the experiment.
The glorifying of abstraction when the plain speak
stratagem beats us down. The extension of time.
The wish to explain a lifetime of rote
within one propitious moment, but for what?
Not a slight adjustment in vision, nor a new world view,
not tradition's exhaustion restored infinitum
nor the same old encoded line but... can I say it?
Will meaning suffice? Notwithstanding our friendships
and family we drift, cut throats in quest of credentials,
yet the mind is the life that will die by consent
to the hand but in strategy held, let liberty's pitfall
engulf us, if the night must fall then...

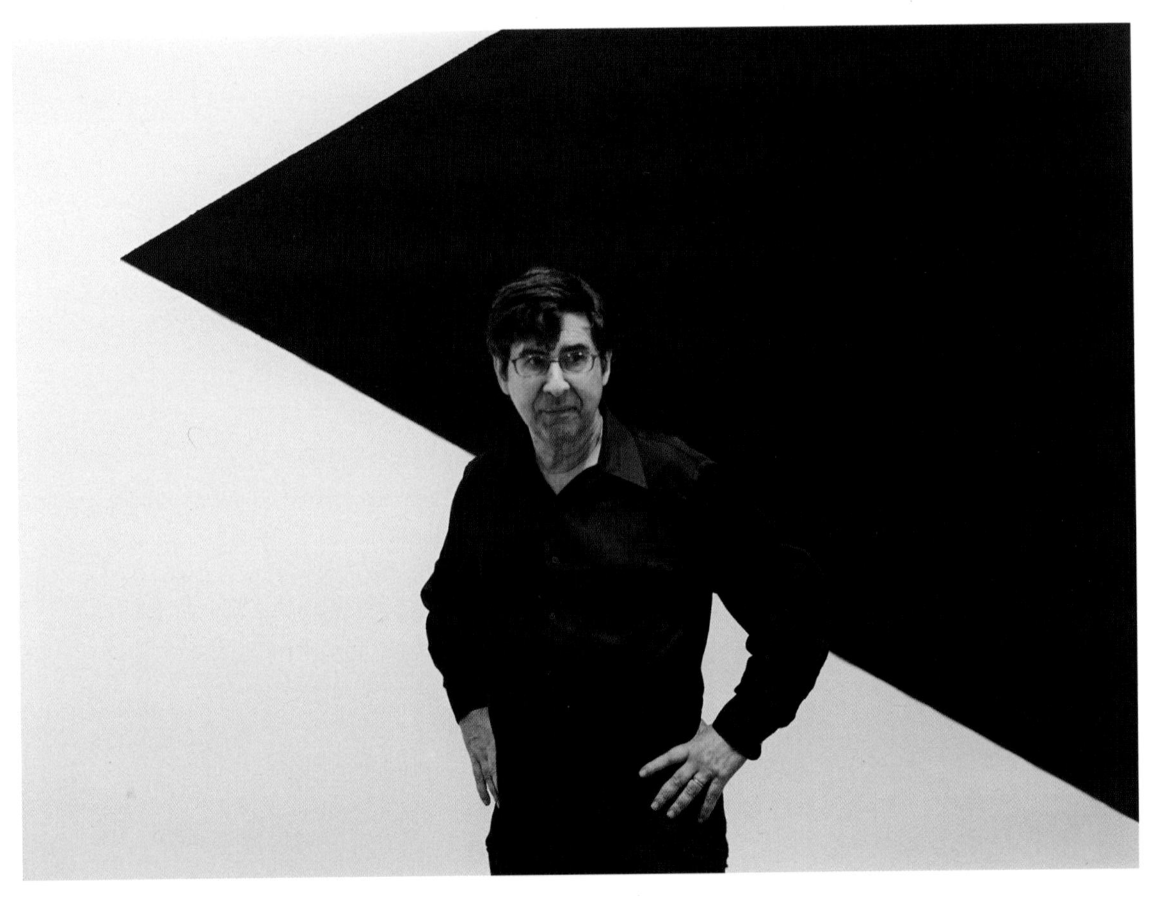

DAVID SHAPIRO

THE BICYCLE RIDER

I see the winter turned around
like pleasure makes the cabinet wail
when I open it, make the girls go
through the curtains again
and fold the shiny parts

The shiny roots are fired, the balls
in the sycamores
are swinging.
A talented bicycle rider
flew out of the winter for a sad party.

I'll stick that man in a tree,
especially without hooks,
without the jocks to meet those horrifying spooks,
like the bicycle rider
irrationally dropping his books.

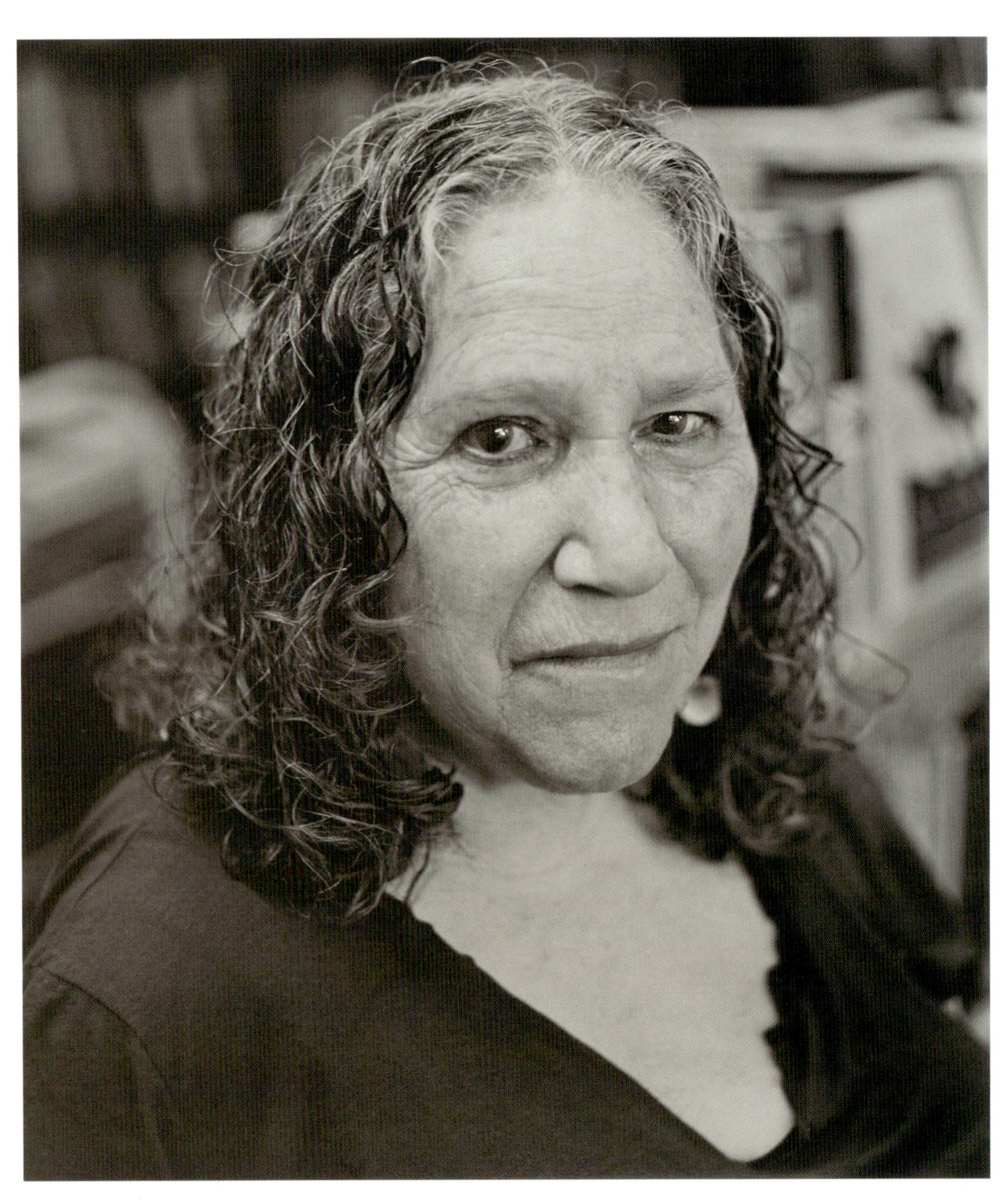

DIANE DI PRIMA

ARS METALLURGICA

A mystery of love lies concealed in the metal—ROBERT DUNCAN

1.
beneath the skin of metals a total love is growing
untapped, except for the sighs of the *cenote*
crystals like teardrops toss in the underground waters
the fruits of the tree of metals

that stretches horizontal
close lover to the magnet
presses its full length
along the lines of force that like a skein
enmesh the friable earth
compact it

for to grow horizontal
from a seed
of densest water
is to call gravitation to account
stretch limbs
crosswise against the Belly of the world

the metals grow
w/their roots in underground streams
they grow horizontal
beneath the hide of the earth
resplendent, radiant Trees

2.
And the form of loves of copper
specific
of iron
clearly its own
tin too, & lead
like a wash of reassurance

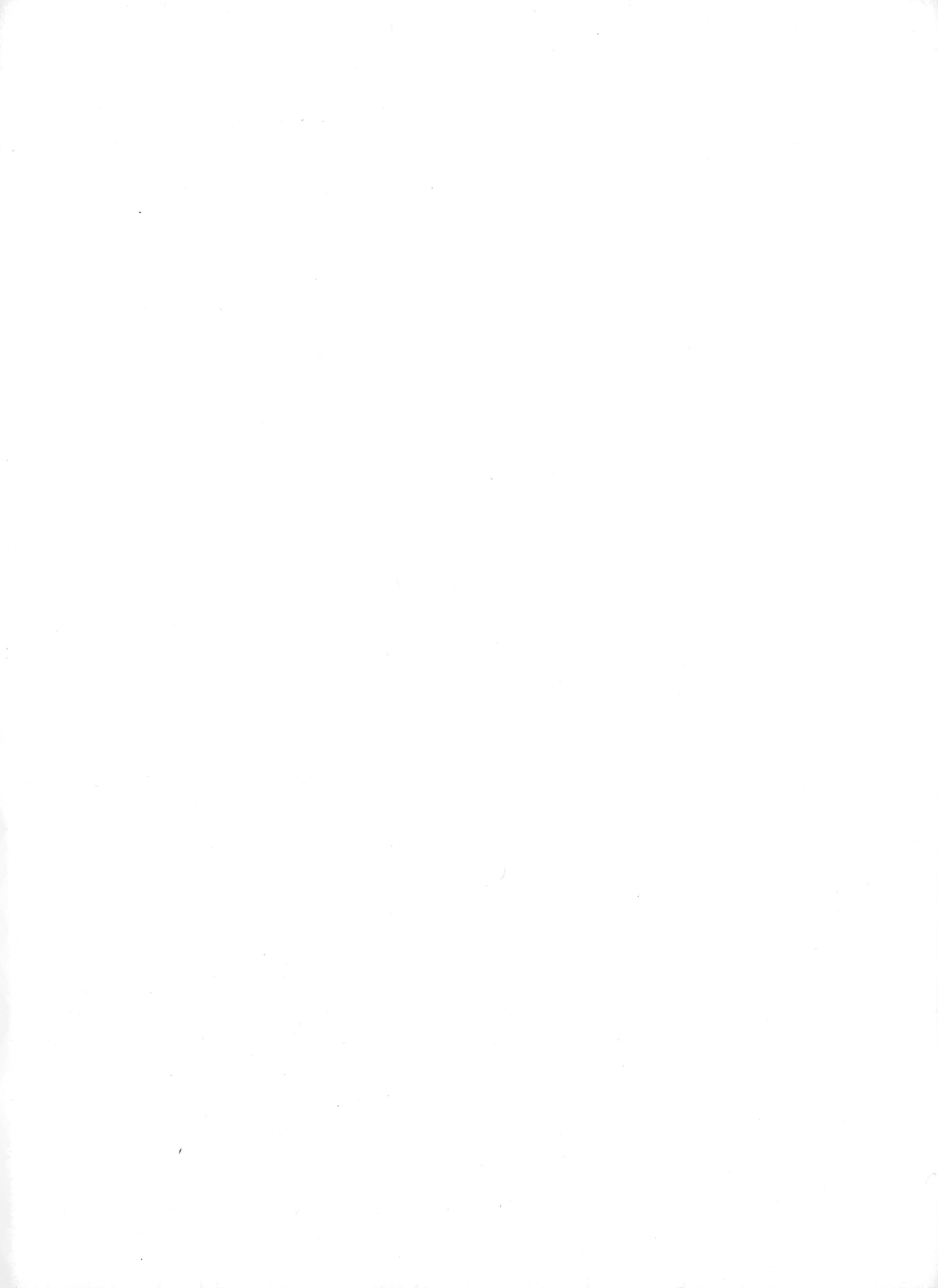

we have all been made aware
of the loves of gold & silver
luna & sol to which our love
is drawn & the scintillating
intelligence of quicksilver
seduction of the grace of eternal
becoming.

                    It becomes us
our delight
the metals bless us.

3.
(The play of them, they divide
& spread their limbs
                  under the blanketing earth
they learn their songs
                  each from the stream
in which it hath its beginning...

HISTORIOGRAPHY

I'd like to hear what you're doing right now
Snow buffers the sound
Good for secrets, bad for suede
A ride home would be nice
Or maybe something frank to sit on
I should think a bit harder before I do things
There are loose bits of paper deep in my purse

I sent my inventory in:
A hole in the dress, button fell off the coat
The shoes will last until tomorrow
I know better than what I've been taught about participation

There's a story that old world Russians would rather
Walk through a storm than wait for the bus
And you should always join the line
Even though you don't know what it's for

I remembered to bookmark your pages
What will you do with your cut of the money?
I hope you keep changing your mind

The new borders are a distraction
I can barely keep my focus
Difficult to know when to begin
Worse when you ask the wrong questions
Fortunately you can speak we can relate
Order is hard to come by nowadays

I have a wrong question for you
I'll write it down on this bit of paper
You don't have to answer it
I'll answer it
The answer is NO
Don't get too close

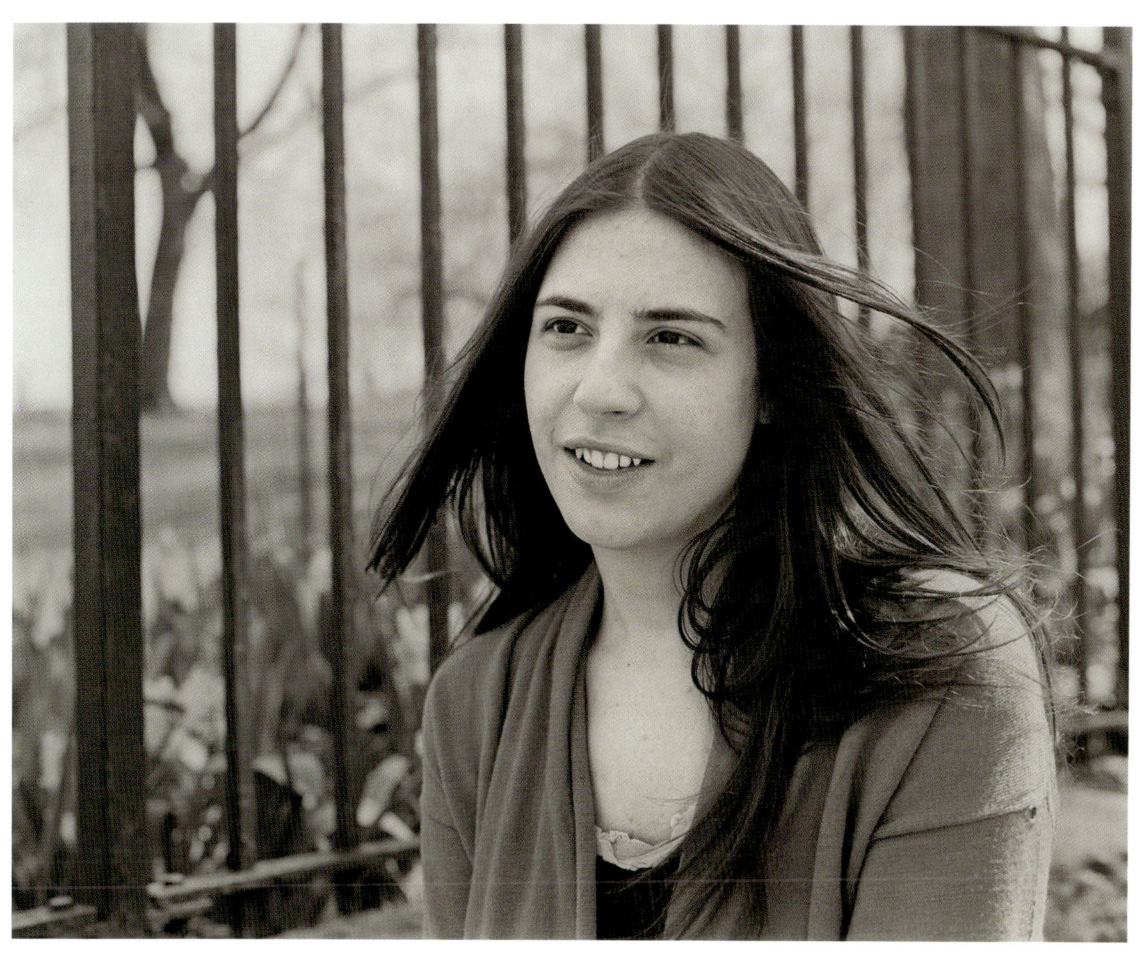

CASSANDRA PANTUSO

It's tiring to be so kind
Grandmother in her babushka
Papa with his fez
Watching people shift their weight at the intersection
I never thought after all these years
I would repair the clothes

It stormed yesterday
It's storming today
Focus on the names
Part mysticism, part science

There are patterns the most vulgar ones
Comrades order and assemble
My dinner is getting cold
Veracity has no known limits
The line was too long
People were exasperated
Candid but there was nothing important to say
Tomorrow we'll know something

Snow is made of other things like bacteria
Expect diminished returns on paper goods
Unless they're novel
What happened to the money?

from VOICES

Oh spring, it's green, isn't it? Oh the spires of two cathedrals are tall,
I walk between the two—why two? Why anything in a life?
You could be Christ, or Mary; there is no Notre Dame, not for this one—
there is no tall woman, though I wanted to be very tall.
How much have your suffered? It isn't just, is it? No it's not,
two cathedrals full, Christ is you: Wear a dress, says your friend.
Christ is a real man, the tall Dame isn't a woman, just structure.
Once I was tall, now I'm uncertain again, like in college.
I'm glad you're wearing a dress: he says it. Patronizing like a jerk.
There's always someone who makes you be feminine, not yourself.
Heaped shoes and small items, clothes, massive barricades, objects for wear,
as of years of usage. Do I have to remember or something?
Do you remember what you've been through all the time? Not even you.
The churches are too big; I only remember them. I'm cold.
I put on a sweater, a long one, but I'm still chilly, fragile.
I feel a great hatred for these shapes I'm in. Become larger
than them...I am larger than you are, am the cathedrals, am I?
Bigger than them, bring it all down, I sure can handle that.

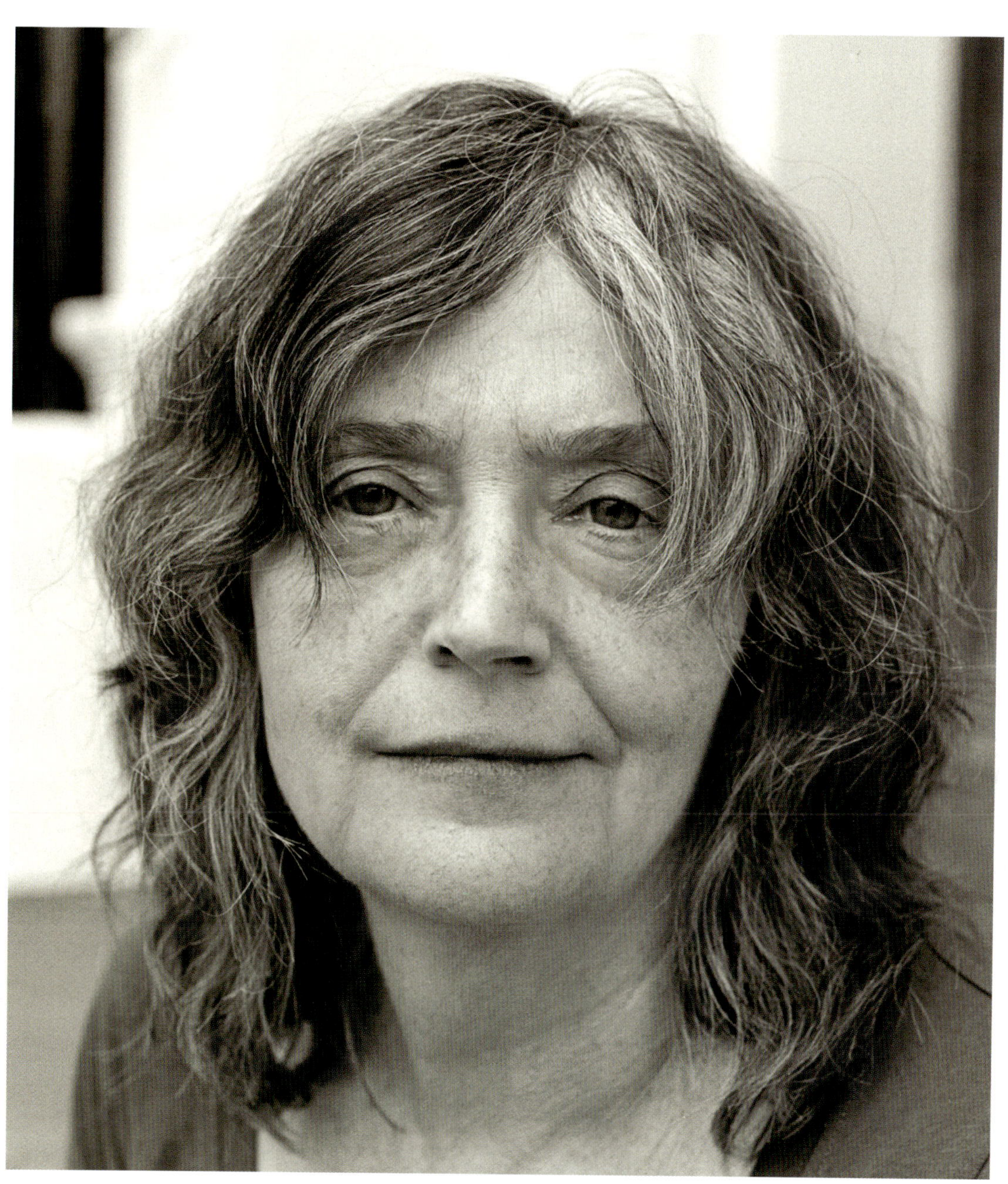

ALICE NOTLEY

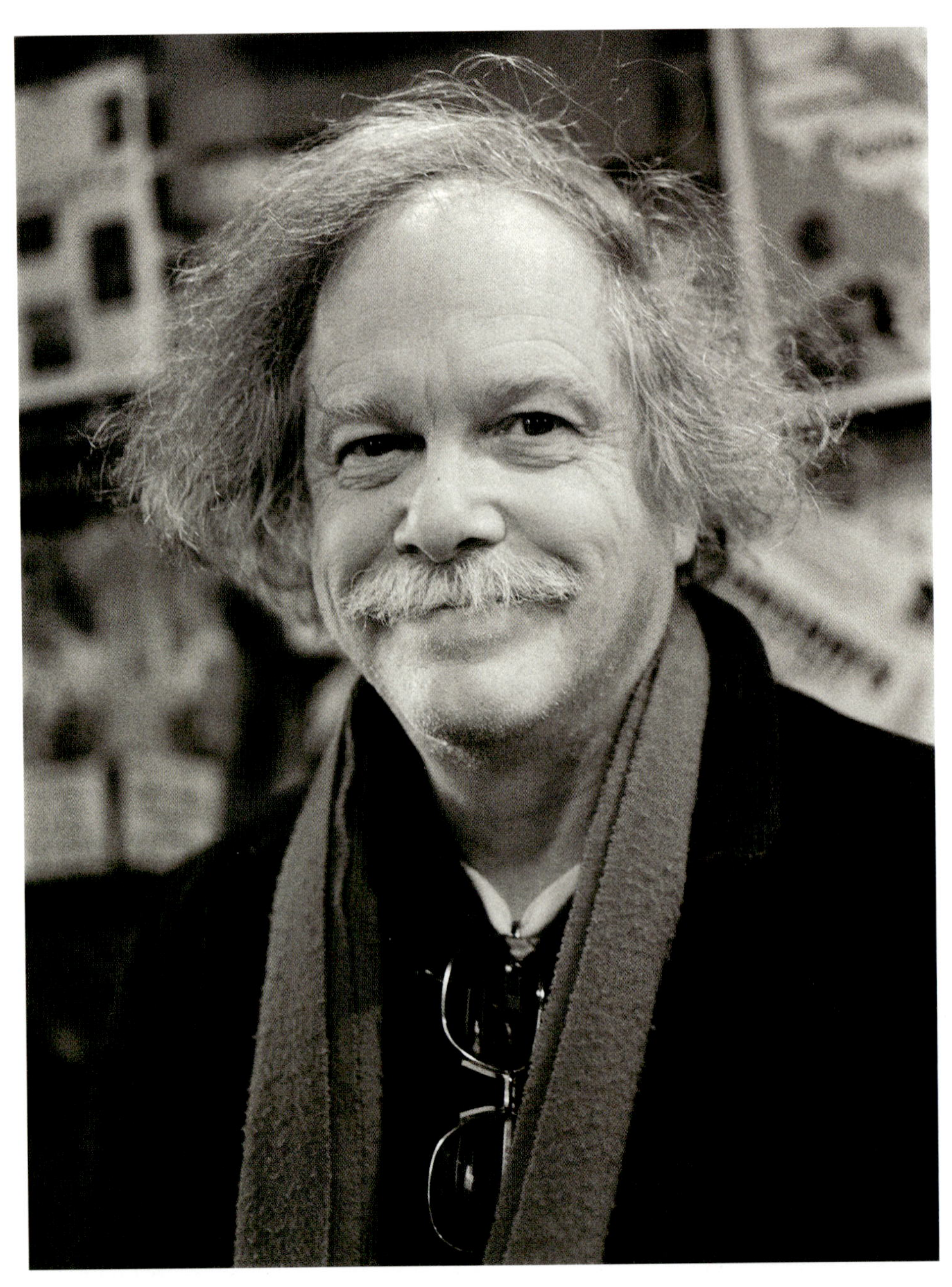

ED SANDERS

QUICK BLACK HOLE SPIN-CHANGE

I don't like it—

two massive Black Holes
each twirling at the core of
                    two merging galaxies

get close enough
to fuse together

then quick as a wink
just as they are melting into a New Black Hole Blob

they undergo something called a 'spin-flip'

they change the axes of their spins
and the fused-together Black Hole Blob
gets its own
        quick as a cricket's foot

Don't like it at all

And then the new Black Hole Blob sometimes
bounces back and forth inside
                        its mergèd Galaxy

till it settles at the center

but sometimes a 'newly' up-sized Black Hole
leaves its Galaxy
to sail out munchingly on its own
                        into the Universal It

I don't like it

Nothing about it
in the Bhagavad Gita
the Book of Revelation
Shakespeare, Sappho or Allen Ginsberg

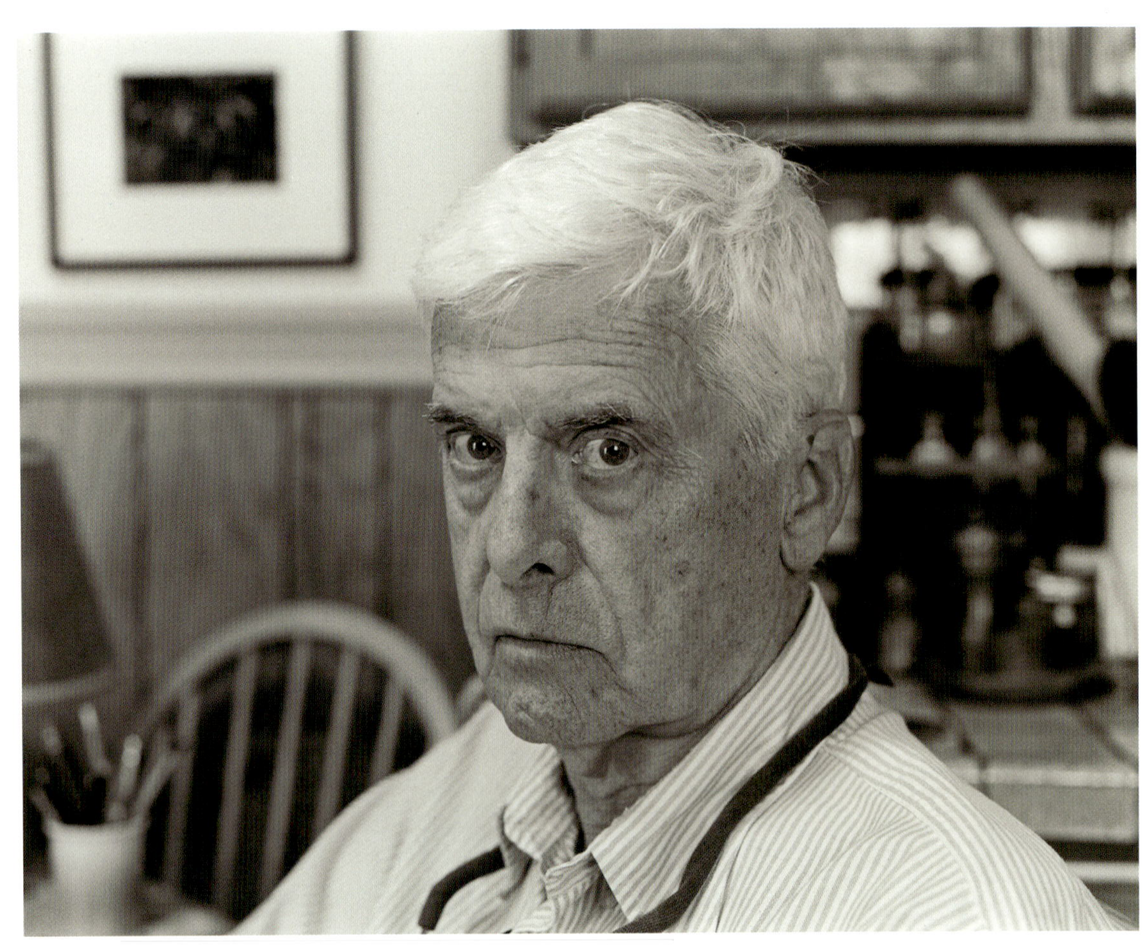

DUNCAN McNAUGHTON

CHRISTMAS MORNING ON THE COAST

You're not kidding there's a story behind that.
George has the sniffles. The best I can do:
imagine a word and its worlds. Harlem,
though ordinarily, because of the
cold weather, you don't associate this
with sentimentality, had two a's.

At supper the young Croatian skin of
the woman seated to my left, I can't
keep my eyes from her complexion, from her
face, her neck, her arms, everse translucence,
Illyrian I would say, tribal in
a way back glacial way, when gods were us
before we devolved. Prior to all this.
Only she hasn't. Of an age before;
another distance too. Each of us is
someone else. Va bene. Crystal eyes.

Dry east wind, doves aloft the rooftops, mild
bright air, pure blue sky. Southwest, beyond the
Moorish tiles of Mission High's tall dome, one
quiet little airplane, heading south. To
summarize, the teeth I like most these days
are those in the smile of Raoul Coutard.

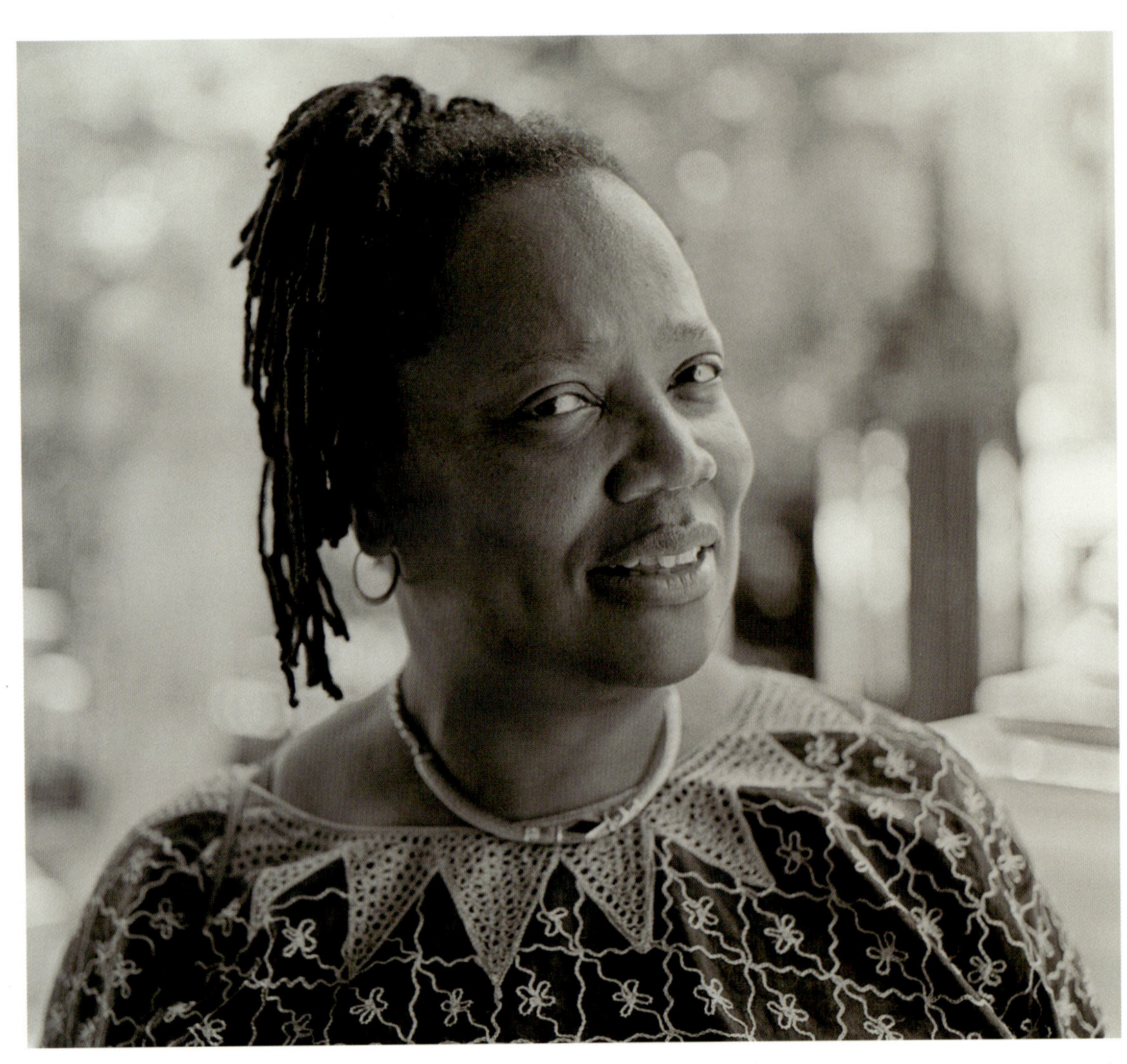

ERICA HUNT

PREFACE

I was thinking that if the ceiling were mirrored we would have to watch what we say about what we feel. That we could not use curtains to conceal what we know. That we could watch without leaving the room or the chair. We could watch the sun take over or the sun pulled up short. Watch the hard stream of current events proceed in yanks or lurches.

We could eliminate the ritual of walking around ourselves, meet head on, relying on how pure coincidence transforms trial and error. That we might even live in the same version of the same country speaking the same language at the same time.

No more being thrown off beat.

It must be love if while beside you I think of you and don't fall in. I could throw away my hat, I need the target practice.

We could get down to work. Work as the metaphor for the idea we can touch: fingers and thumb putting matter into fact, and cease being Sunday Sandinistas.

We could argue, get sprained on topic mountain and pass the whole night putting our shoulders to the planet.

We could remove the calvinist and other secret furniture from the language.

Except when the lights go off. Except when the paint comes off the walls. When the calm we've kept comes off in conversation. When they've eaten the last northerner and I'm the stranger in their midst. Or when the bricks of the aircraft we're flying in begin to migrate slowly apart. Except when the exits aren't marked and the busses have stopped running at this hour. When we believe we have no other choice but to run

while motionless.   daysnumbereddaysnumbered and borderless

Until we give up waiting for solutions that will never be given. Until balance is fulfilled by the barely contiguous unfamiliar. Until the texture of rain is wet with visible points. Until the decay in language doesn't fix logic and enormous fuschia fruit grow among the patter. Until we enlist sense to illumination and make room for the blanks.

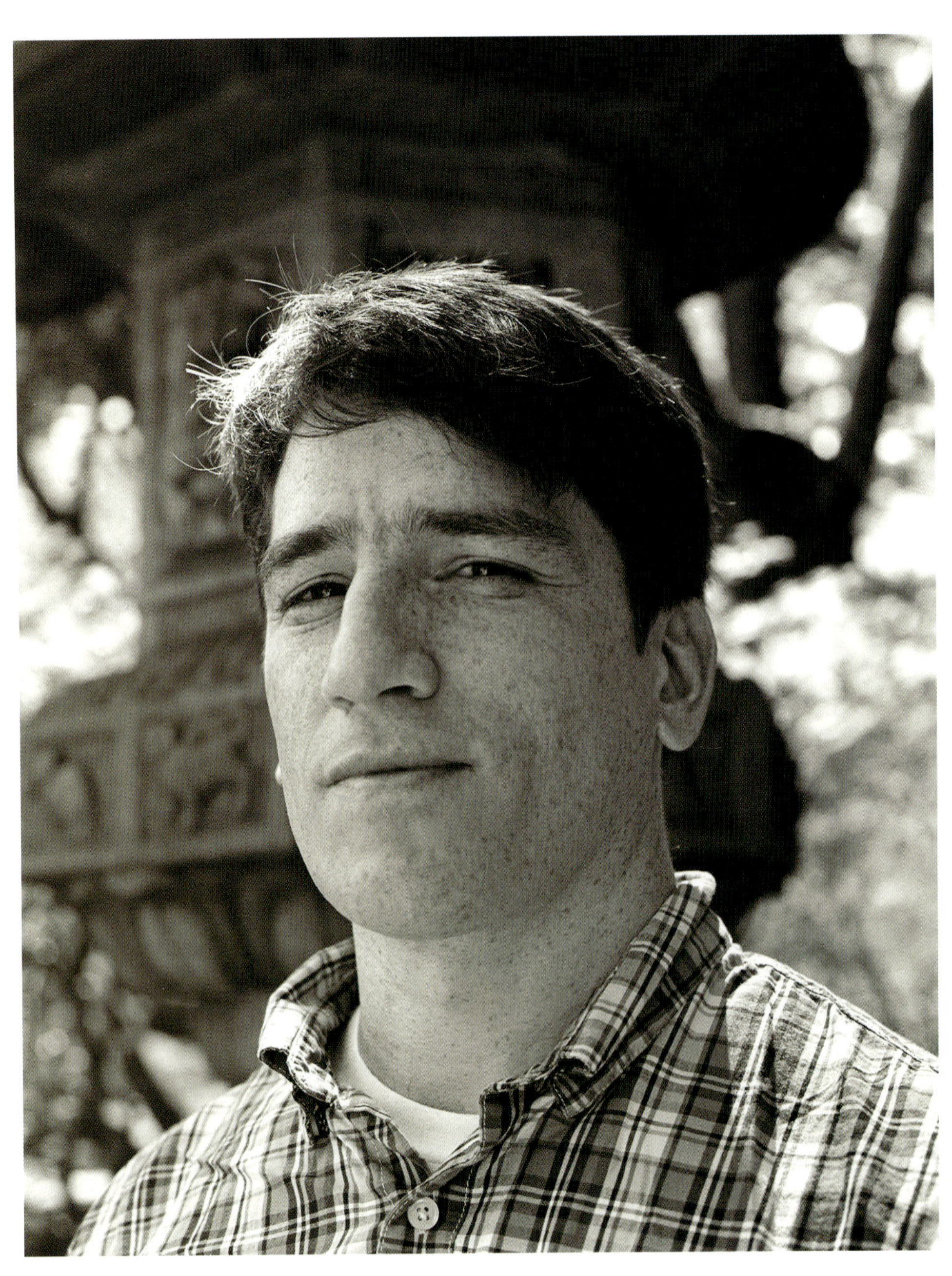

OMAR HUSAIN

SUMMER OF '04

Reading Lear
Where did the Fool go?
Was he funny?
You're not funny
But you're fun
Unlike the king
I think of the two friends who left me in Greenpoint
Laura to stay in her room
With Lucky the Cat who hissed and cursed
And Rhett of the 2 a.m. knock on the door
'A Martini, sir?'
'Jeeves! I'm just dying'
We used to hang out on the roof
With the spirit of Golias
Watching the Pulaski Bridge
Unspool its yellow dialectic
I don't miss it
Now I'm here
And I'm not blind
Rhett the Hegelian fell off a fire escape that summer
Drunk maybe
Dead now
Laura's agoraphobic
So we can never be friends

It's summer again
Again means later
I like all the months except February

CONSCIOUS

The complications of a life, the evening news and a stage play depend on the world's failing memory, altering the course of a prolonged effort to remain present, physical, juxtaposing yesterday and tomorrow, rising with the sun, never noticing the difference. When the freeze comes on, nobody is ready. Brittle. The way the playwright felt when he woke up dead. Peace on earth is acceptable, but only when embossed. Everything else hangs low. The sugar in the tank, the white lie. Selection depends on where one is standing or planning to stand.

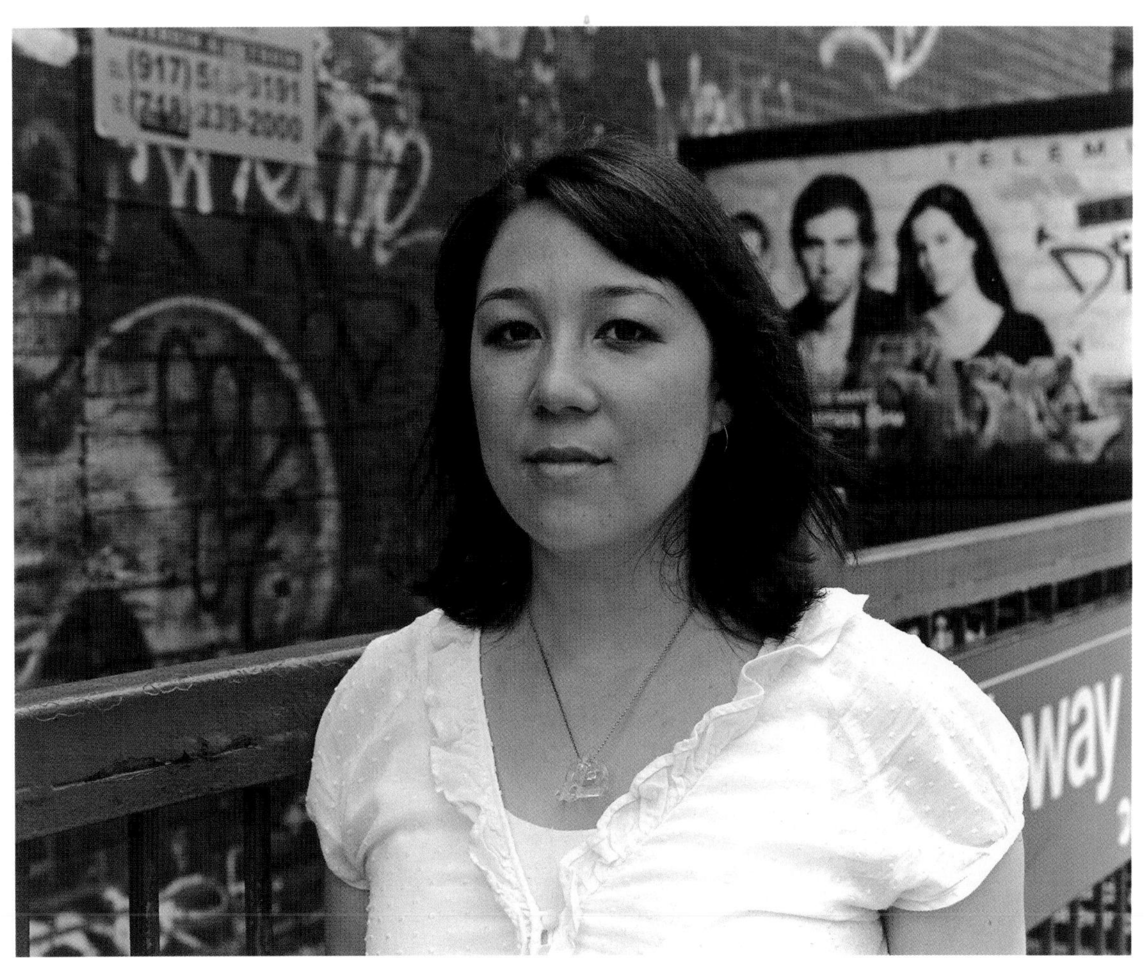

EMMA ROSSI

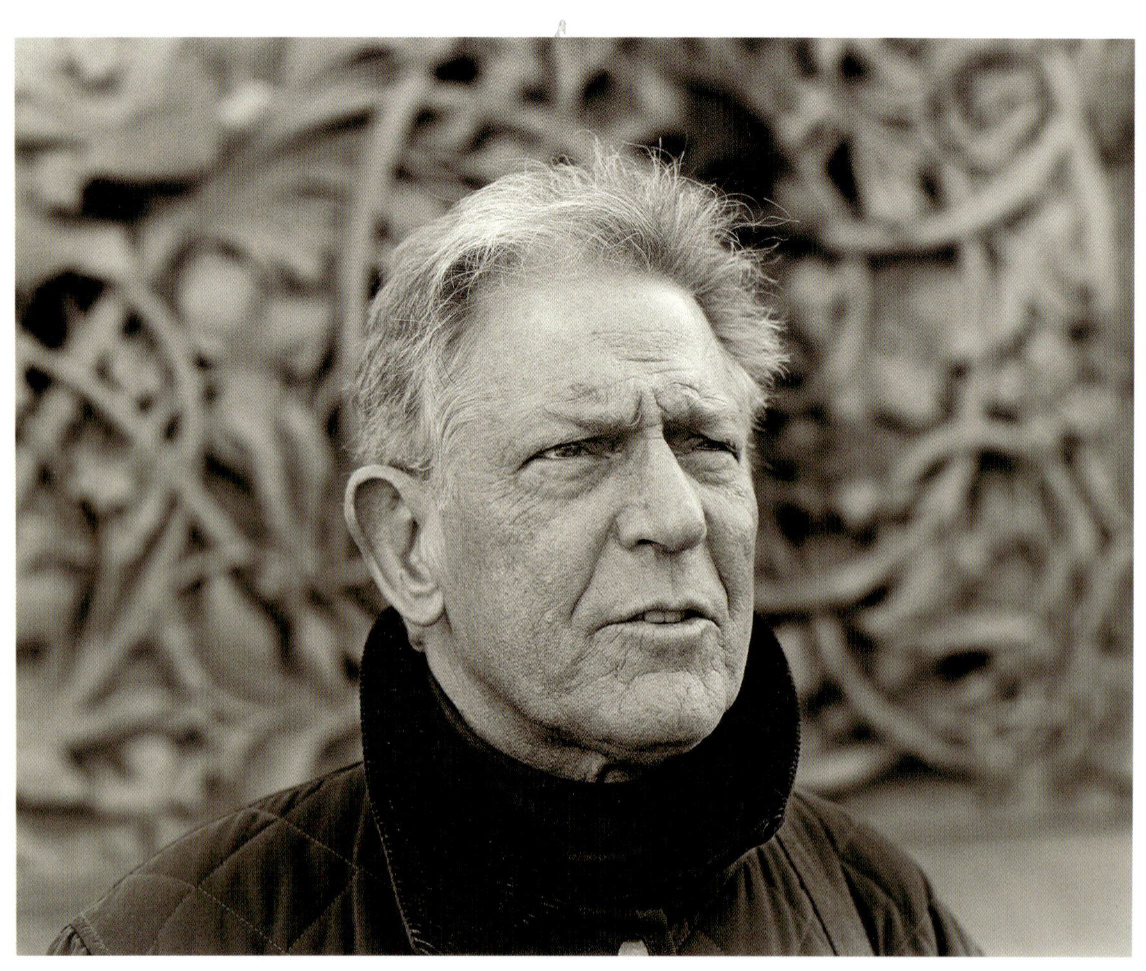

BILL BERKSON

OCTOBER

I
It's odd to have a separate month. It
escapes the year, it is not only cold, it is warm
and loving like a death grip on a willing knee. The
Indians have a name for it, they call it:
'Summer!' The teepees shake in the blast like roosters
at dawn. Everything is special to them,
the colorful ones.

II
Somehow the housewife does not seem gentle.
Is she angry because her husband likes October?
Is it snow bleeds softly from her shoes?
The nest eggs have captured her,
but April rises from her bed.

III
'The beggars are upon us!' cried Chester.

Three strangers appeared at the door, demanding ribbons.

The October wind... nests

IV
Why do I think October is beautiful?
It is not, is not beautiful.
                                        But then
what is there to hold one's interest
between the various drifts of a day's
work, but to search out the differences
                                the window and grate—
but it is not, is not
beautiful.

V
I think your face is beautiful, the way it is
close to my face, and I think you are the real
October with your transparence and the stone
of your words as they pass, as I do not hear them

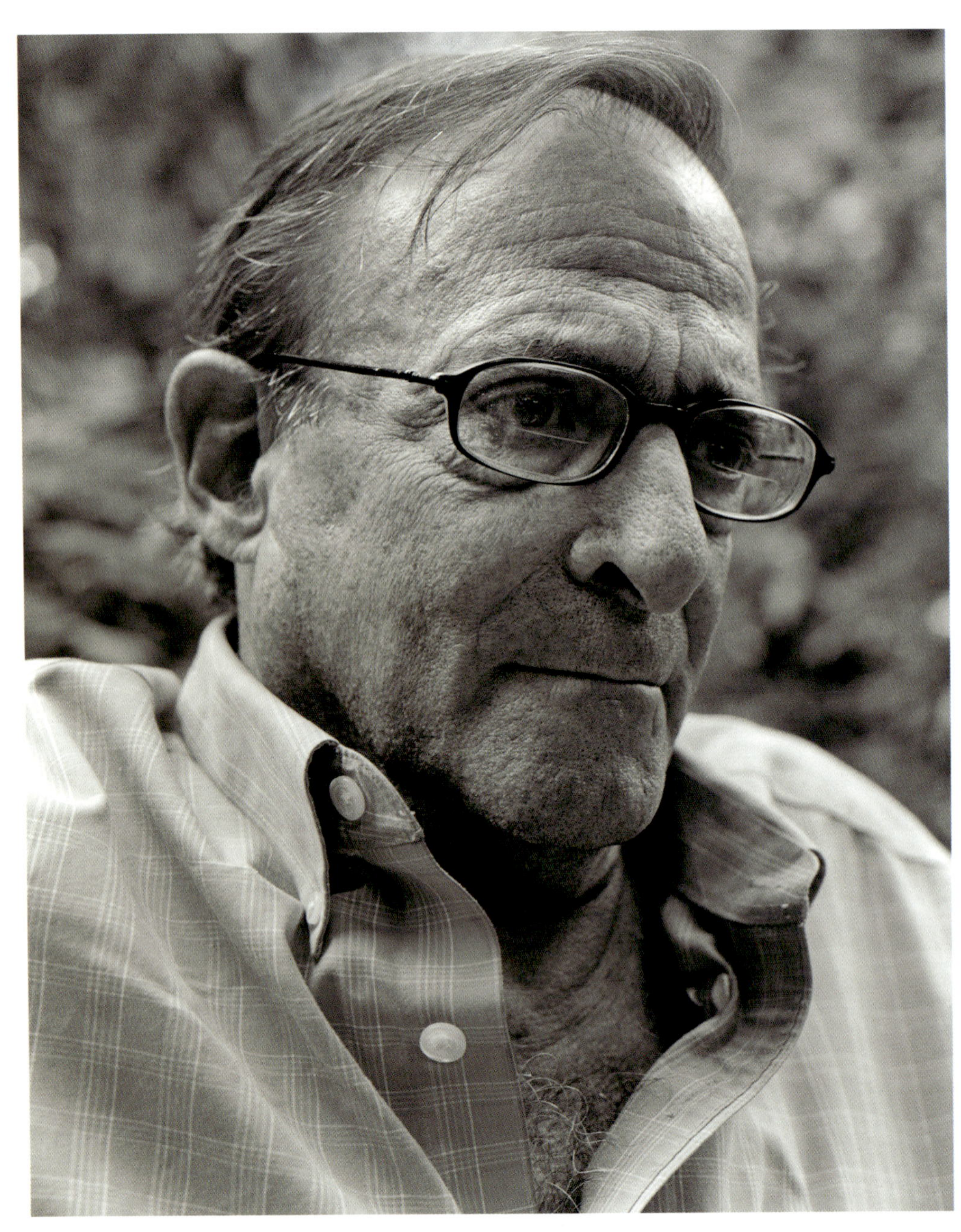

TED GREENWALD

EVERYTHING SEEMS

A faint uneasiness
A shortness of breath
Each little thing wrong I suspect
Of being more than it seems
And so it grows
To be more than it seems
There are no specific examples
Everything falls into
What I've been saying
These are my words

MY LIFE AND BIRTH

In the history of my family, parenthood was always a matter of reproduction by live young. My mother produced only one, tethered and thumping inside her. Had I been an egg baby, drops of oil would have kept me afloat, or I would have been coated with a sticky caul.

On the day appointed for the vignette of my birth, the sky was buttery, clotted, and crowded. Posturing bees hummed in fields fragrant with thyme. My mother put on her travelling cloak and her three-cornered hat, picked up her pilgrim's staff, and walked out along the blue-stoned coastal road. All channels had been cleared, all leaves had been cancelled.

Around noon she went into a restaurant and sat down at a table on the terrace. An aquarium teemed with guppies and goldfish and velvety blackfish feeding in the shadows. A small hose frothed the water, stirring evidence of the unspeakable things that fish do.

And there, against a fusillade of pneumatic drills in the harbor, I steamed out of my weed-sucking muck, followed the buoys, and washed up among a group of tourists, who whipped out their Leicas and began shooting me as I lay gasping at their feet.

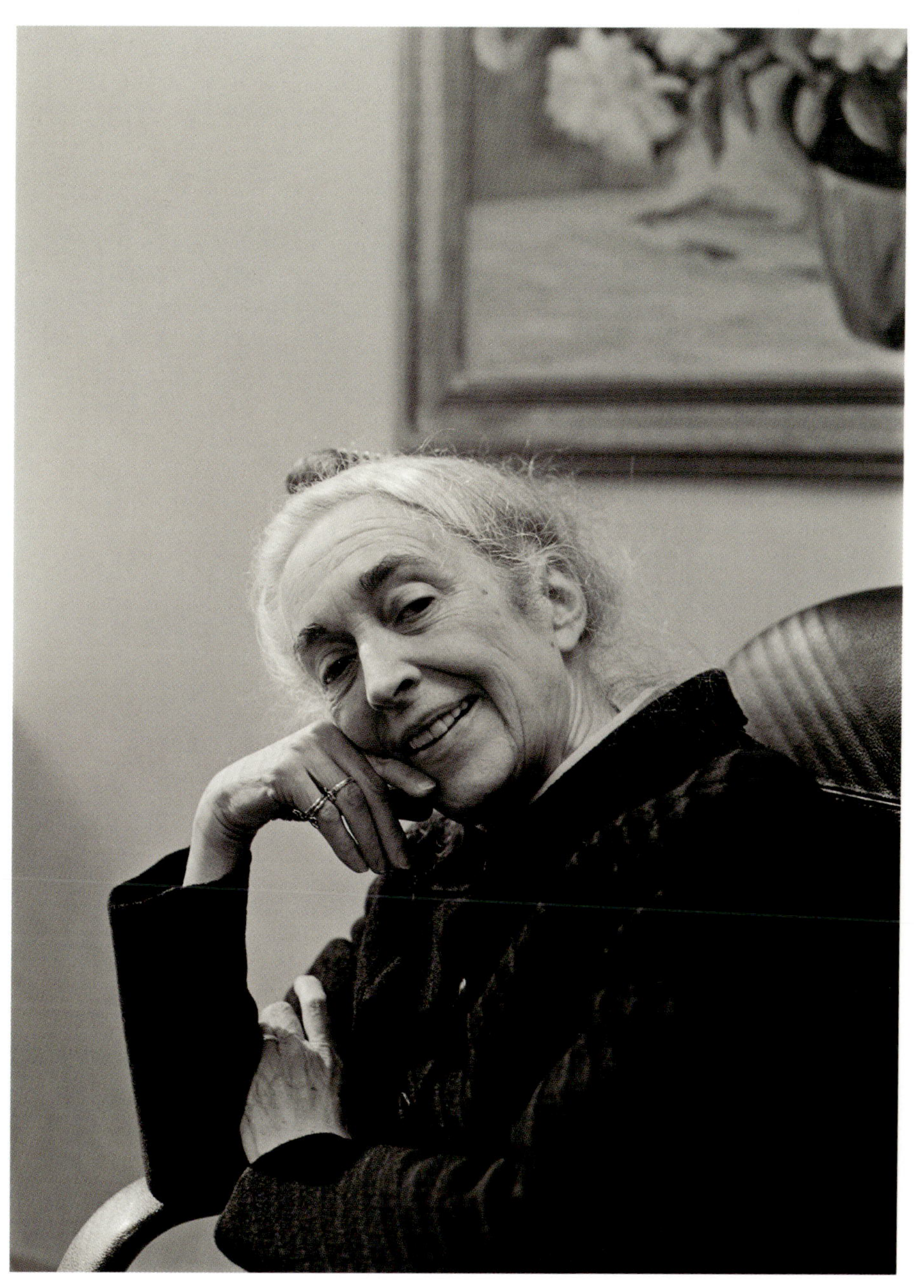

EILEEN HENNESSY

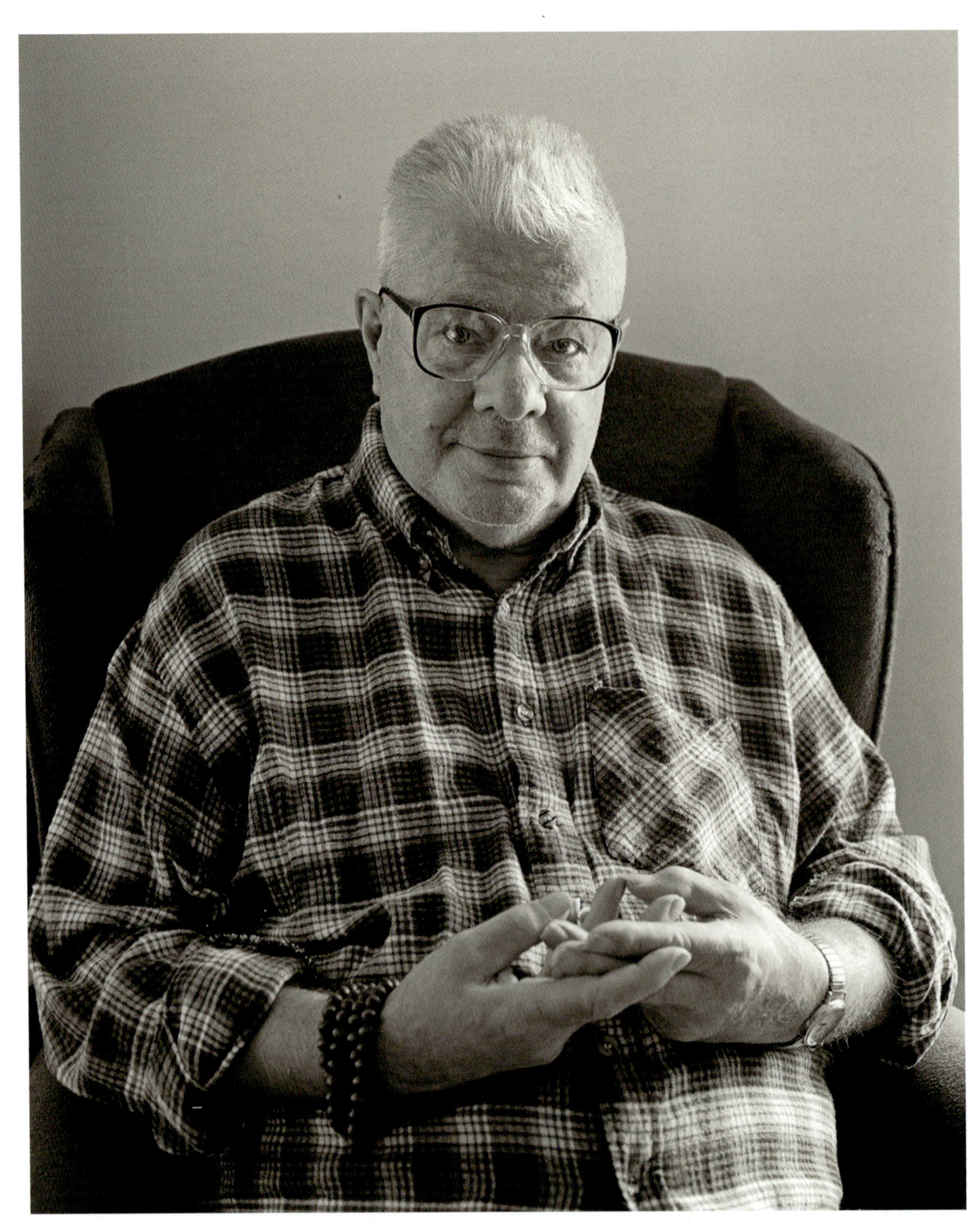

PETER ORLOVSKY

LINES OF FEELING

The mountain bear has a hole in his pants—trouble.
Doctors get free passes to my museum
in return for there labatomies on me
I am not afraid to work—I would love to fly a dirigable.
Nor am I afraid to be a colector of lamps—
provided everone help me.
And as for your cantelopes, 2/29—I consider it dangerous.
My fortune is dedicated to the movies.
I don't go anywhare without my belt
And when ever thers a boat leaving for heaven now
I'll go & never speek another word.
Piano played with tears. Its so easy to jerk off!
Look mister will you give me a pair of pajamers.

There was this fellow I was telling you about
who built something in his room, he built & built
untill it got to big for his room, then he had to move,
then he always had to move, that was him.
Then this new fellow who went out to the store
& he walked & he walked, and one block went behind him,
then another, then another ahead & that went behind him,
& so on till he was far away from home—
all because of the way somebody said
something on T.V.

O science give me twenty feet
twenty grandma meet ball eyes
take me apart in the robot room
do my up right
just give me one thing extraordinary
(I got something going here now
don't rush me, I got this typewriter, right
got this paper here right
all alone, right—)
How much beauty has rolled off the breast of a dying swan?

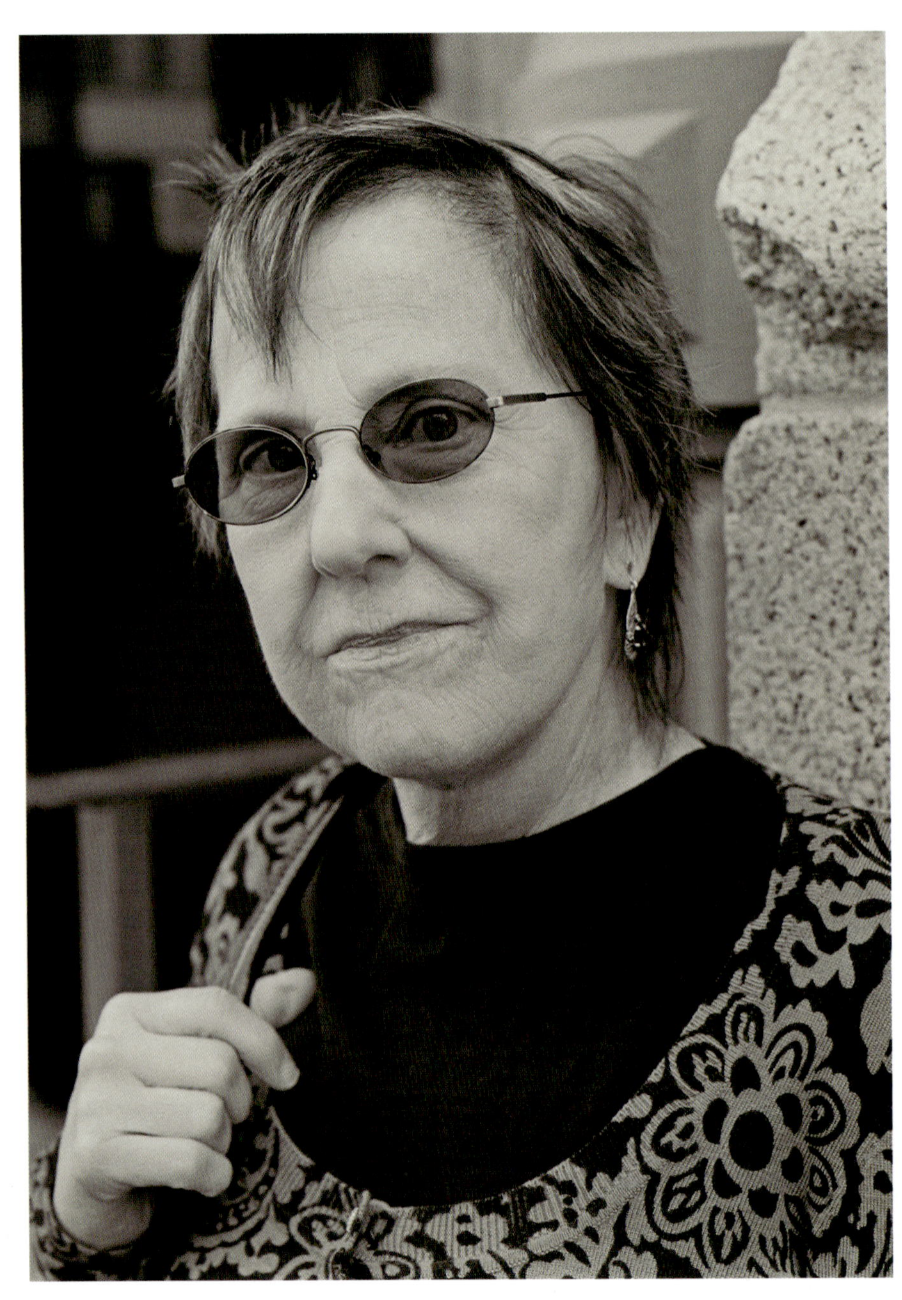

RAE ARMANTROUT

SOFT MONEY

They're sexy
because they're needy,
which degrades them.

They're sexy because
they don't need you.

They're sexy because they pretend
not to need you,

but they're lying,
which degrades them

They're beneath you
and it's hot.

They're across the border,
rhymes with dancer—

they don't need
to understand.

They're content to be
(not *mean*),

which degrades them
and is sweet.

They want to be
the thing-in-itself

and the thing-for-you—

Miss Thing—

but can't.
They want to be you,
but can't,

which is so hot.

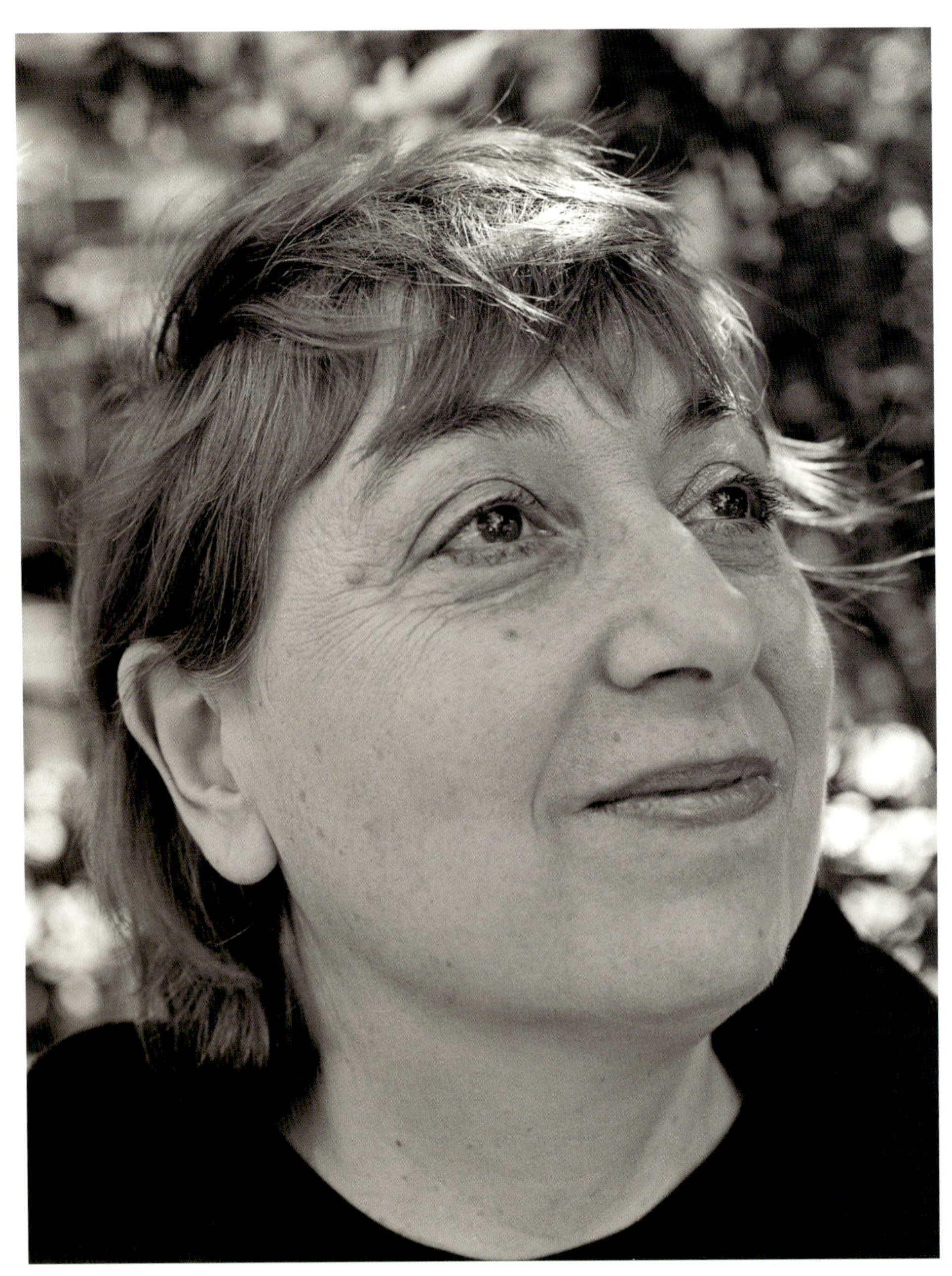

FLORENCE KINDEL

MY ESTRANGED HUSBAND SEES JOHN CLARE ON BLEECKER STREET

The power of emeralds to open the throat
soften water, forgive
bitterns go to the reeds
he records their motions
Rudy follows him to the corner of Christopher & Washington
offers to buy him socks and shorts
you've had a shock to your system
people disappear that way
poems don't
they come at you with things
stand your ground
which is dirt and trees
or come with me to The Spotted Pig
you need meat
but he goes off again
to observe dusk from the High Line
let him go, Rudy
you can't save the world for him
come home
there's pot roast

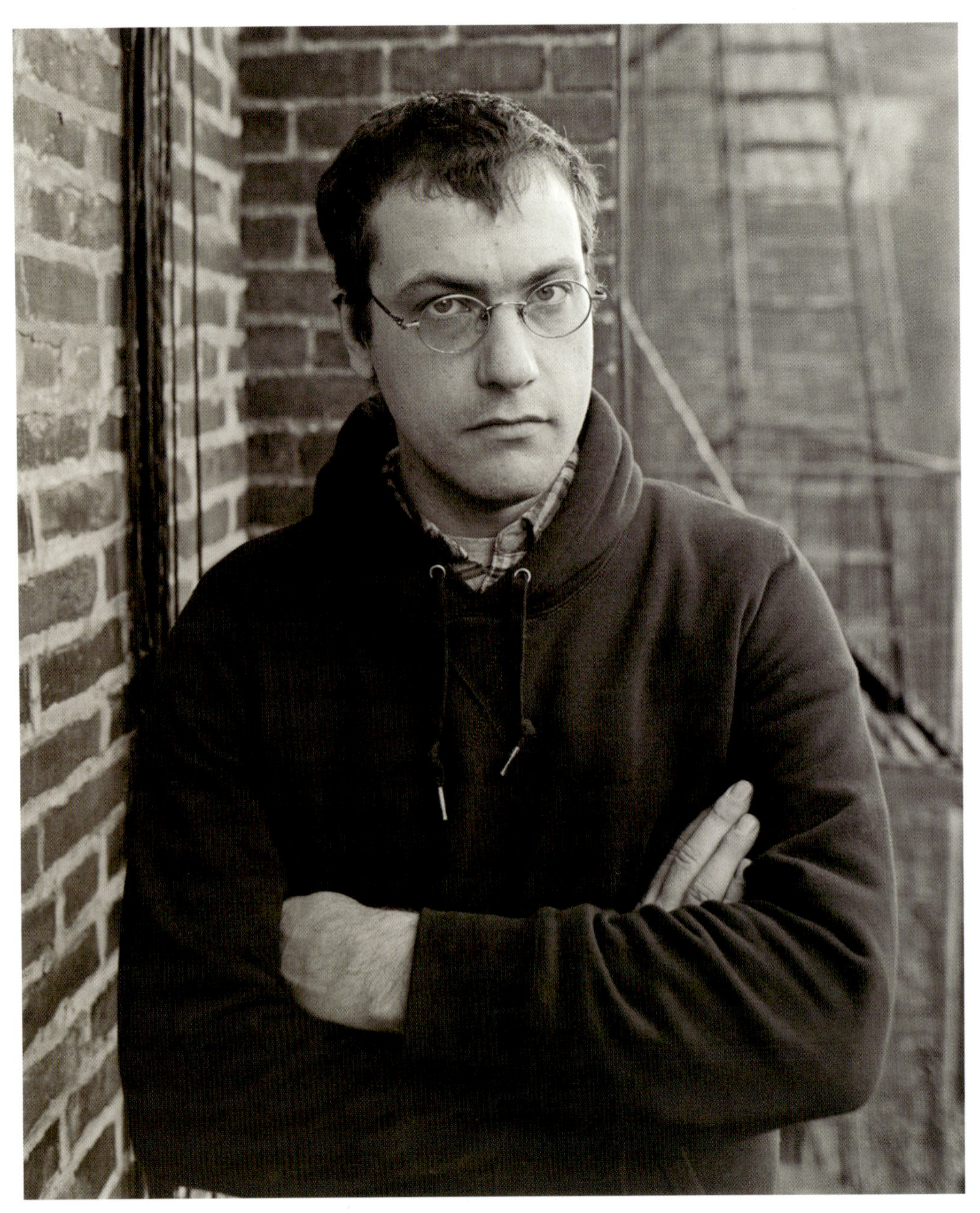

CASEY DROUIN

TIME AWAY

Upheaval
making a hypothetical other
symmetry of time away

As deep felt
deeper still

As in fighting
as in sportsmanship

Deep felt is deeper still

Time away is felt
as upheaval

You are my hypothetical other

‘WHAT ABOUT BEAT FOOD’

What about Beat food?
Was there a special cuisine or was it eat & run or hit Chinatown for
War Won Ton or rice congee at Sam Wo’s dodging velocity of waiter
Edsel Fong’s wired humiliations & verbal aggression at roundeyed
hipsters & tourists dragging in smoky frames for rehab or Green
Valley family style meals in echo chamber
linoleum vault plastic ivy creeping over faux
wine grille bricabrac ceiling grate or deep grease
to soak Anchor Steam saturate carafes of red wine castanets at
flamenco floorshow or mooncakes thick suet gut paste or bagfuls of hazelnut biscotti
or tubfulls of fried onionrings at Mel’s Drive-In
after it’s all over the bars closed need flight fuel
or Yosenabe J-Town slurped with sake & constant
wisdom burning the air between us or North Beach
sourdough fresh from the bakery oven before light
breaks night off like smoking memory hunk or all
the awful great fried breaded brains smog air & layer
oilslick of morning mouth clothing stinks of after
& we ice nostrils with powder make us talk louder
& longer crave sushi especially wasabe bullet train
blasting eyes into inland seas of kelp hurricane weep
or shrimp cocktails at Swan Oyster Depot on Polk
dip pink volt into red horseradish tomato karma lemon
after rye toast soaked in Blum’s sweet butter or linguini
dreamy shimmer glazed with green Pesto paste shiny
at family-style dive long tables raw red in recycled bottles
throttle adam’s apple with w/ laser precise burn through olive
oil veneer or ketchup drowned fries Juanita’s crowned
with pepper black & white bite to soak up tequila shots
lime & salt open tongue’s edgy ridges or a parade of
Martinis at Vesuvio’s getting Ollie to load toothpick
w/ shishkabob of olives & onions w/ LeBlanc waiting to
carry me home to Tina who reminds me for weeks how
lousy I am w/ liquor or after-gig pizzas at Sorrento’s
or questing for kosher dills at David’s or chewing steak

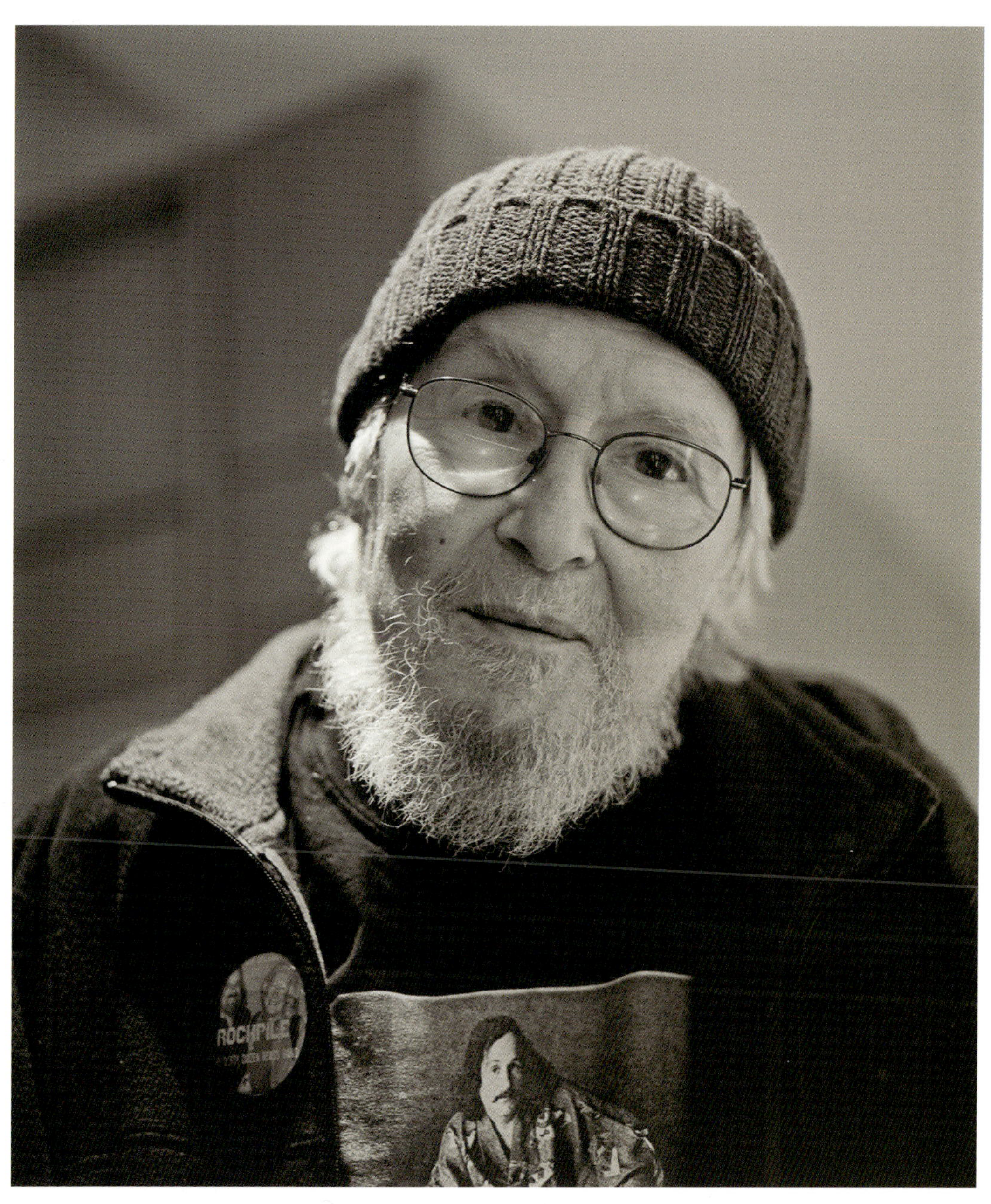

DAVID MELTZER

wallets at Tad's w/ stuffed potatos erupting green onion
carpets of steam table redlights or Mike's Pool Hall
minestrone at the bar w/ Nureyev in trenchcoat
& the sharp blur backdrop of pool hustlers rustling
tourist marks or crunch sawdust crackers stuck w/ tough brie at
gallery openings balance acrid white wine in plastic cup or ardently
overcooked chili sludge leaking out of
rubbery tortillas at potluck party in a basement car
wheels hum overhead & beatniks slump into black
wallpaper spackled w/ splatter of red lights & pot
luck spine tuningfork jazz maybe Monk or Twardzik
or machine slicing thick corn beef yellowfat edged slabs on corn rye for
George & Polly at the Berkeley Bagel or tofu cubes float in miso fog up
glasses or down at the Wharf w/ Judy J scarfing calamari or bologna
discs slapped between Wonder Bread glued shut w/ mayonnaise
or desert mudpies you always rolled your eyes before
digging in or baked salmon at the Roscoe's Bastille Day
feast or fasting in white walled flat or ground round steak tartar we ate
in life w/out a hotplate & no care about spasms of microorganisms or
stew up at Jules' while he was at work & we were at work smirching
his bed before he threw you out into my arms or cold raw red potatoes
sprinkled w/ Vegesal or sourdough cubes dunked into fondue sludge
smudged w/ green eyelashes of dill or

bowls of bar popcorn & beer in the afternoon look out
the window at tourists furtive up & down Grant Avenue or
tostadas & chili rellenos in Mission tacqueria late at night
when mariachi trio walk down narrow aisle breaking hearts
or Sabicas enters La Bodega camelhair overcoat draped over his
shoulders while we stuff our faces w/ paella or into Adelle's Let's Eat
Right to Keep Fit book of revelations revamp our rations go wheat
germ brewer's yeast blackstrap molasses Tiger's Milk chinquapin honey
from Farmer's Market organic soyburgers feel surge of immortality
turn beatnik skins inside out or feast of pickled herring eaten out of
the jar boosted from Safeway or
Rand's Roundup in L.A. where hungry wolfish writers ate all-you-can-

eat for $1.99 or square-shaped burgers filled w/ breadchunks & onions
fit just right on white bread ketchup-soaked w/ pickle mandalas or
grill-tormented American Cheese sandwich you need Lava Soap to
grind off grease sutured hands or back in the Apple bringing a bag of
hot Planter's goobers (a quarter of a pound for a quarter) to Artie &
Betty's pad & listen to Al & Zoot records & smoke Bronx brown weed
or Stockwell treats me to a Chef's Salad in Hollywood burger bunker
or Kienholz buys me a Caesar Salad at Barney's Beanery or harvesting
Ralph's dumpster cornucopia of fruits & vegetables dumped there
nightly for the slightest imperfection or hotplate veggie broth cube in
tin cup or seeing how much a teabag can be reused or infusing an
orange Charm in a glass of water or organic sunflower seeds in shells
spitting husks into a metal wastebasket & writing haiku while rain
rivets the tarpaper shed roof w/ added water percussion from leaks
into an old paintcan or
early morning coffee & English muffin in Market Street Woolworth's
watching shortorder cook Nijinsky stay in one place & be everywhere
flipping flapjacks sunnyside up eggs rippling crackle of bacon strips
hiss or hashbrown potatoes hits the grill or first crab of the season at
open air steam cart at the Wharf or a bowl of Grape Nuts rising
pyramid out of Pet Milk or Lee Romero springing for chili rellenos or
oysters swimming in lemonjuice w/ auras of pearlshell & a bowl of
white sawdust crackers dipped into horseradish or 7th Day Adventist
veggie burgers at stand off Market near the Protestant Bookshop which
years later is taken over by Scientologists or huge white oval plate of
sashimi from the Tokyo Fish Market & sake shared w/ Bob & Linda
Hawkins at our Jones Street pad or a Deaf Smith organic peanutbutter
sandwich on wholewheat home-made bread for Clark only to have
him recoil & confess goober allergy or Thanksgiving Larkin Street
turkey Tina basted in Vin Rose in first trimester of pregnancy & puked
all during dinner & never drank rose again or dinner at the McClures
pad on Fillmore of k-ration food bought at Army/Navy surplus store or
pot cake heavy w/ nutmeg & ginger washed down w/ black coffee
laced w/ cheap brandy or breaking off a hunk of carob candy or
mashing soybeans into soyburgers popped into fryingpan greased w/

saffola oil or dinner at Gravenites' watching 'The Godfather' on
KRON-TV or peeling off tangerine skin whose oil made our hands
smell of it all night long or sitting for the Schiffrins in Silver
Lake eating everything & anything in the fridge on the shelves all the
veined & moldy cheeses even a jar of capers or frozen Heath Bars we'd
eat at Polk Street Royal movie theater crunching through 'Hard Day's
Night' & 'Sayonara' or mushrooms stuffed w/ garlic & parsley fried
in butter w/ a splash of olive oil or eating grilled halibut at Tadich's as
Carol's date & going through downtown afternoon ithyphallic through
the tunnel to Larkin Street monk space for lovemaking on Norman's
surplus cot or L.A.'s poor poet horsemeat filets or first orange peppery
hit of nasturtiums blazing on cushions of oil-slicked spinach or
endless onion dips at opening & book parties or tunafish casseroles
or meatloaf for nights until it got rubbery like jerky or grilled
American Cheese sandwiches or Ritz Crackers salty straw in toked-out
mouths unable to sing cool clear water or sour upchuck baby milk soft
mashed between limp Graham crackers after the redbird wore off or
baked garlic cloves zit squeezed onto sourdough sponges or chive
colonized soupy eggsalad drools out of finger-dented white bread onto
chambray shirtfront or nutmeg eggnog hip square Christmas party pad
& everyone wants to be home again
or Bastille Day baked salmon for boojy Bohemians gone middleaged &
nostalgic or solo amble down Columbus Avenue walking to work
munching cheapo peanut brittle or Tina's hand-decorated hardboiled
egg paradox of loss & gain in my paper lunchbag or sprinkle salt out
of aluminum shaker onto knish held in waxpaper in lower East Side
ghetto of my forebears or times when anything in the mouth works
whether it's crumbs off the floor or suck on paper just to chew as if
eating food or stand in line decades later at Chez Beat prix fixee grub
dressed up to false teeth roots no longer connected to want or food not
bombs or food not tombs or latkes at Halsey's at New Year's party
nobody else attended or watch Abbot & Costello at the Rugby
chewing jujubes or drinking massive daiquiris at La Rondella with
Diane, Robert, McNaughton, Oppen in & out of Alzheimer's telling us
about Pound or

fries in red plastic basket at Clown Alley in vortex of meth heads
rebuild every square inch of utopia all over again & again or
eating stops when everything inside is blocked
& she sucks on ice-cubes to stay alive

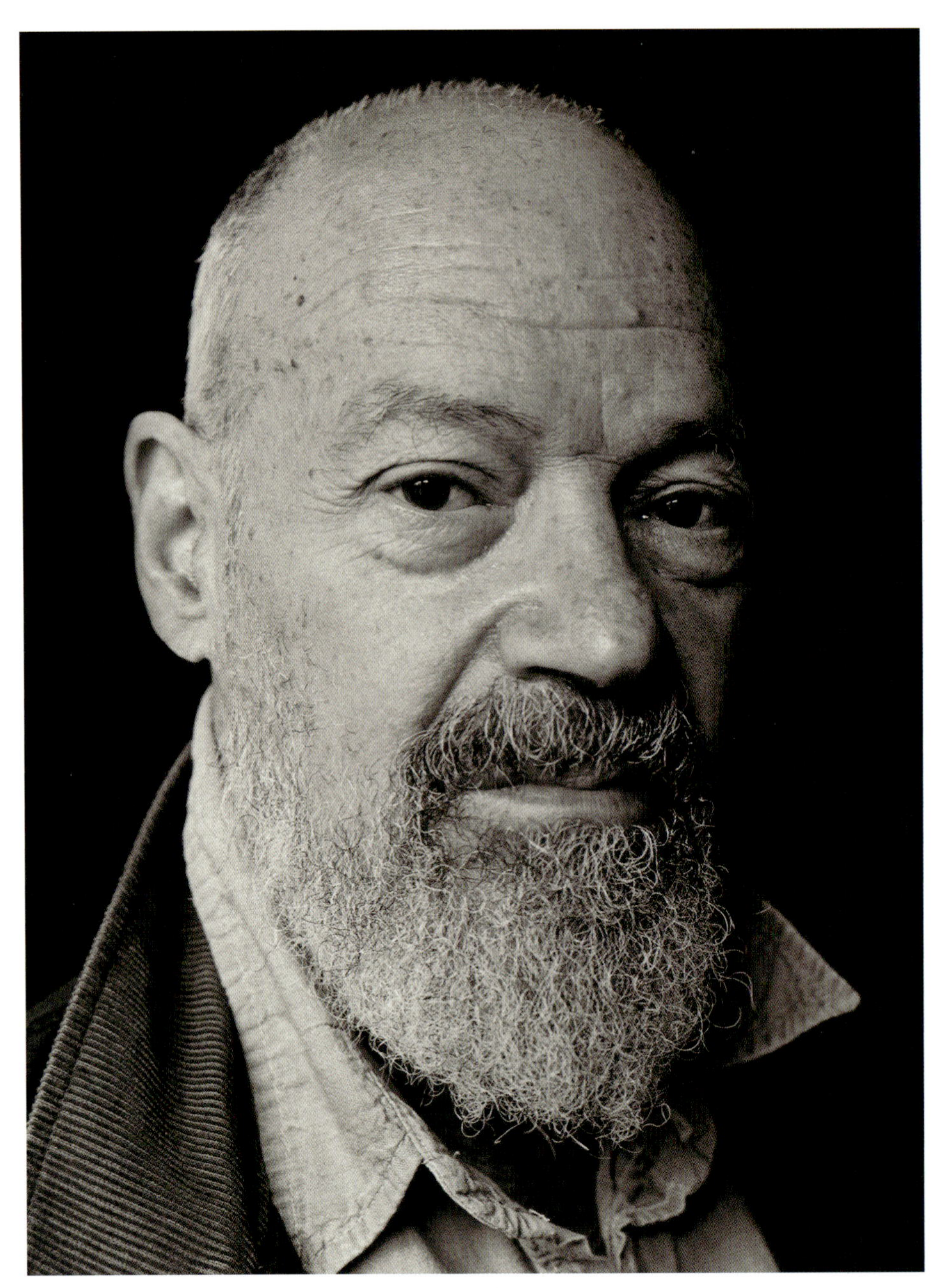

STEVE MALMUDE

POEM FOR MY WOODBURNING STOVE

Goodbye to you!
Freezings and thaws
got to me like applause.
I gave you my shoes

which were velvety twos.
It was grate. Joanne
used every shape of pan,
we swam in flan

corn and oysters in cream
and split-pea soup, oh real!
We can't remember the meal
but we recall the asylum.

I'd say we fried a thousand eggs
with your heat on our legs
and rising up the flue
melting snowflakes.

Pleasamay ingredientheir powening
chasintook chasultook gincorner
pridou fowhe gommon endfriend
materialou, rufflerange.

TYPICAL UMBRELLA FIASCO

test cover
does it weather
a pouring forth
of told-you-so nouns
some graphic
others
cute as a facsimile shadow
I is a solvent
dotting things
with mystery labels
innocent
enough to be occasionally
touching
wood
no
leather
then soap
or vaseline
close to tears
a cloud
gets to exit right
all the world's a tube
next to the heater
chaps emerge
sporting homonyms
the colour of socks
mixed
casual
who gives a bath
pictures just what's
lacking finish
when wet
capsules release time in stages
endings pause to reload more space
actually credited

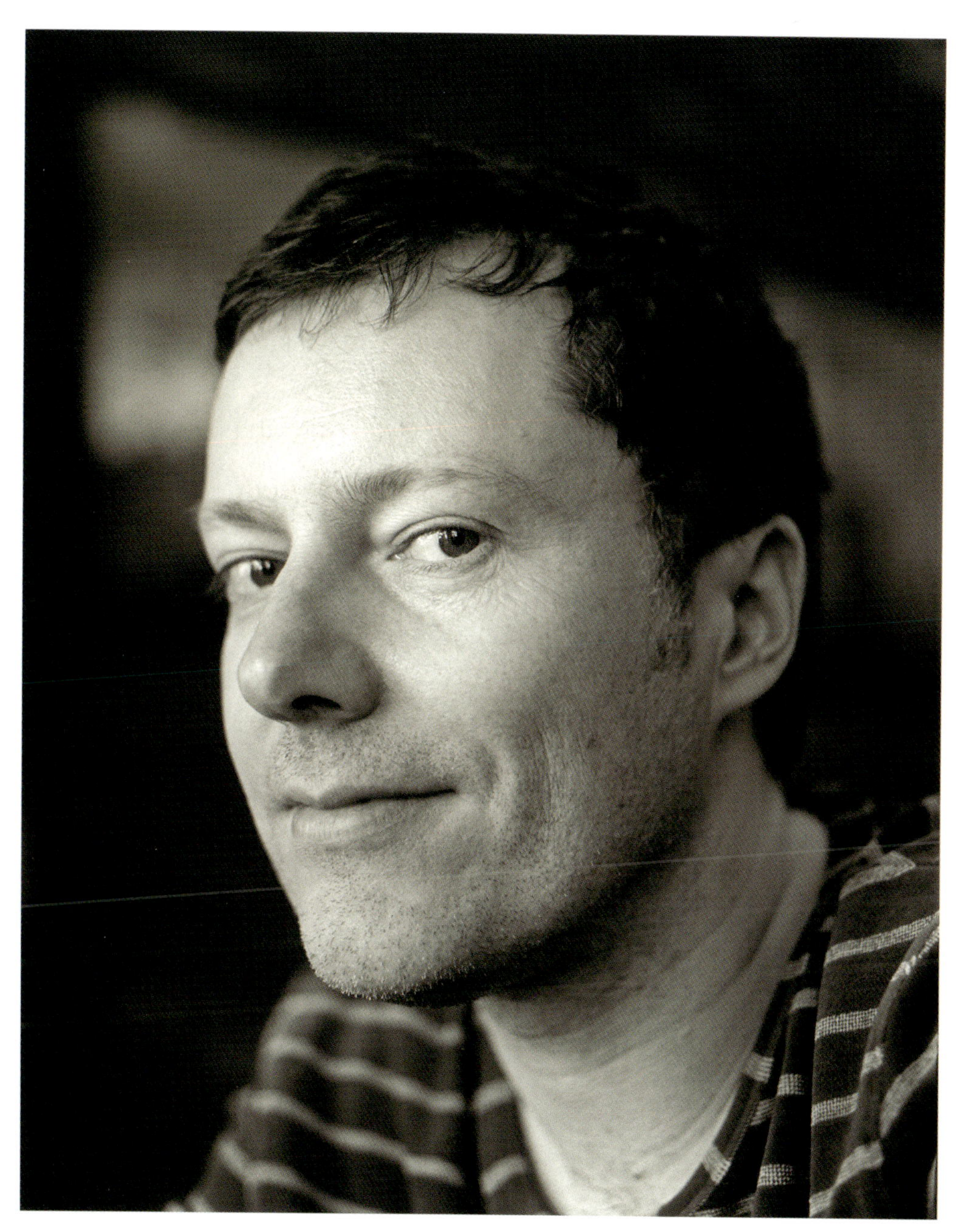

MILES CHAMPION

or lent features
plain enough
to specify or burlesque
walls really

make a room
things come to expect
quite a tap

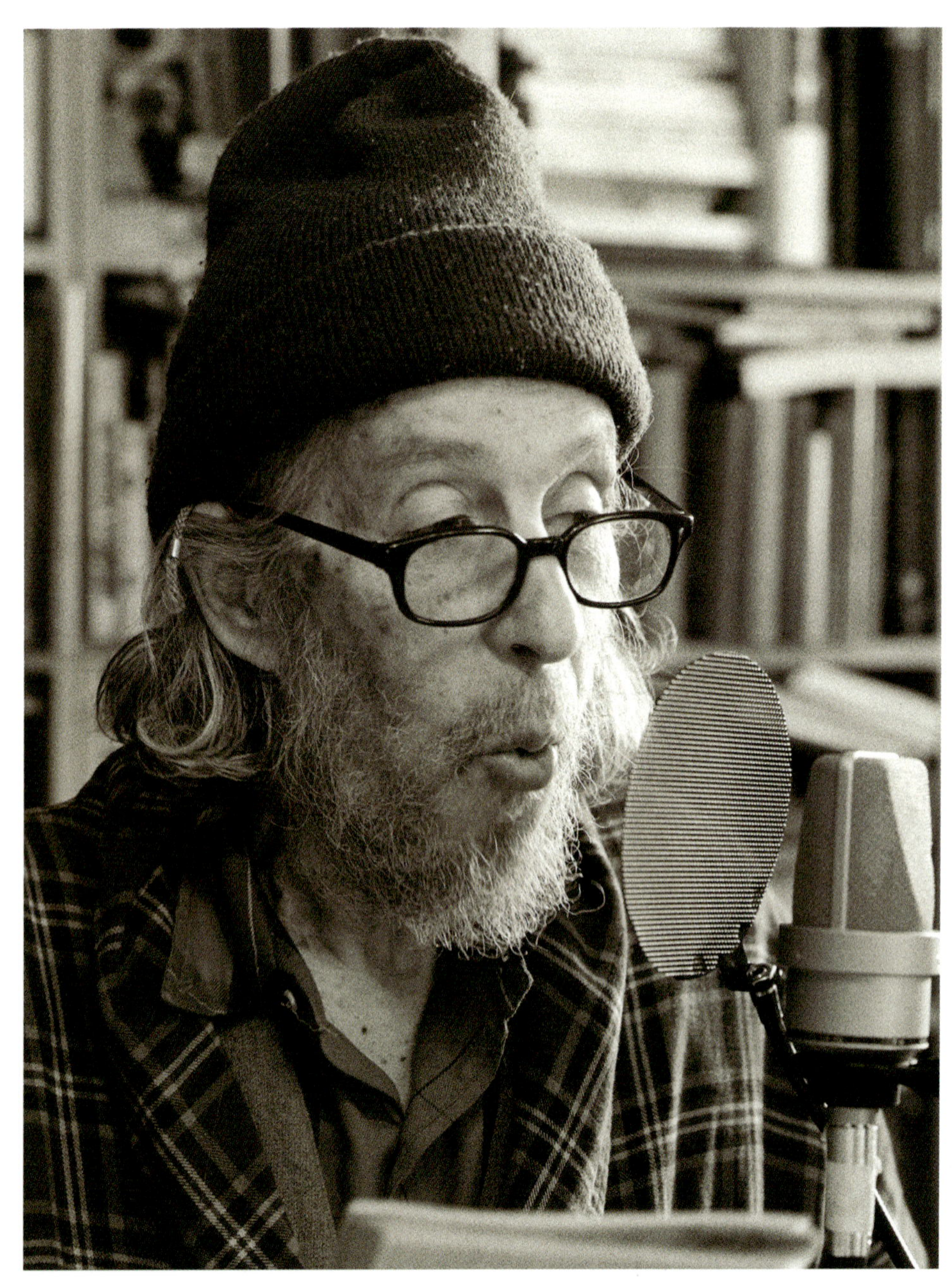

TULI KUPFERBERG

MORNING, MORNING

Morning, morning
Feel so lonesome in the morning
Morning, morning
Morning brings me grief

Sunshine, sunshine
Sunshine left upon my face
And the secret of the shining
Puts me in my running place

Evening, evening
Feel so lonesome in the evening
Evening, evening
Evening brings me grief

Moonshine, moonshine
Moonshine dots the hills with grace
And the glory of the shining
Seems to break my simple pace

Nighttime, nighttime
Feel so lonesome in the nighttime
Nighttime, nighttime
Does not bring me to relief

Starshine, starshine
Chills the moon upon my cheek
Starshine, starshine
Darling kiss me as I leave

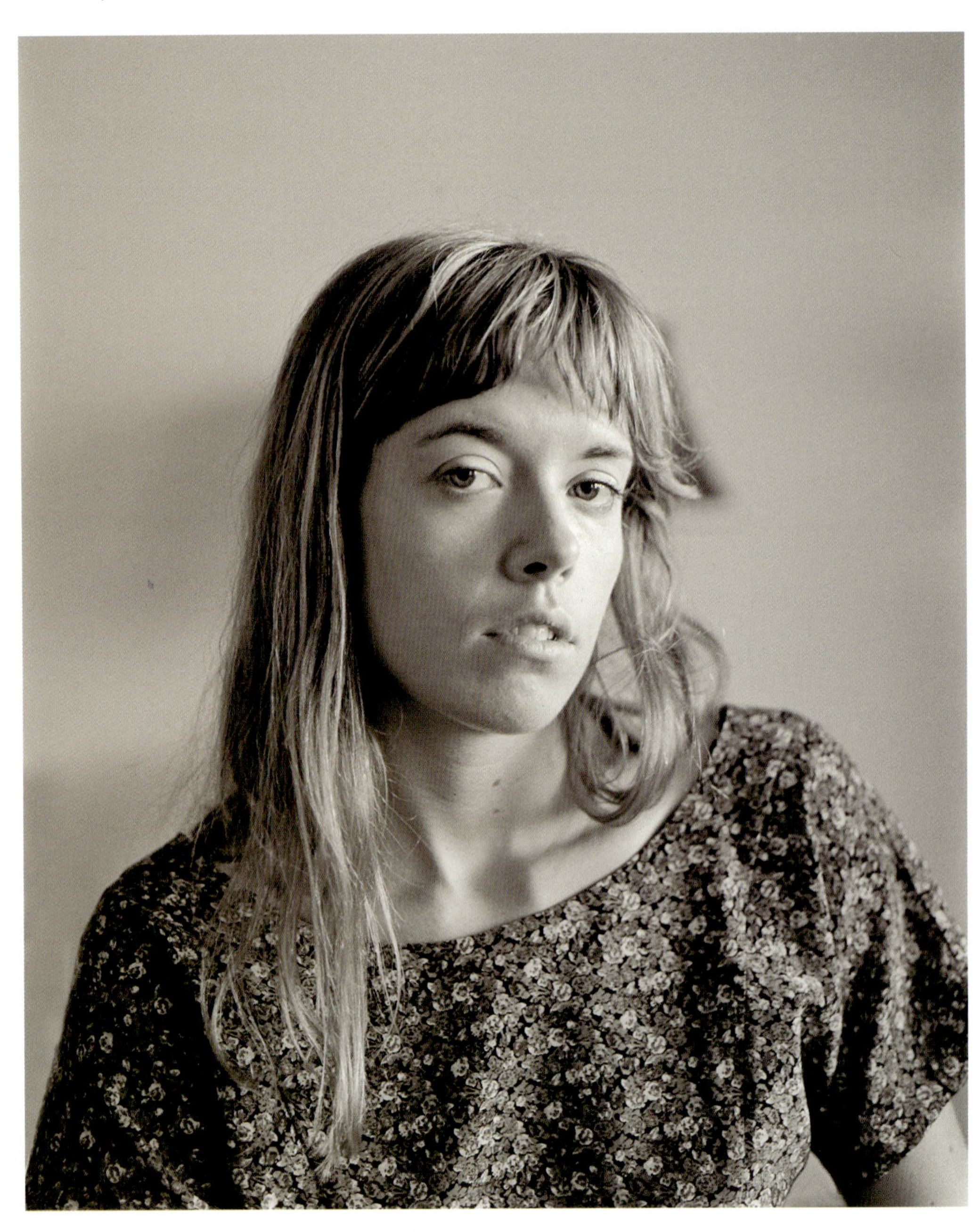

SIMONE KEARNEY

HER CARNIVAL CRUISE

Did we mesh?
I was tumbling down
Touching the walls and windows
Would they make me bright?
Puddles are deep for me
Jump in
It pleased me that you cared
But I was unhappy
Took an ocean liner with a boy
Drank to the gods
Cut out their silhouettes
My boy was sooty, unsymbolic
They oiled us
We liked our pantaloons
One of the ship's puppets looked like me
Full of uncompromised joy
A taupe shade
The crossing shrank me
See here's a nerve tightening
First mate's blood sausage so tasty
But none wanted to be here
Big white interchangeable port blocks
Slimy ropes
At least entertain us
Group therapy can be sweet
Geez, he divorced me
Where's the soda machine?
I can offer you milk rum
Nothing cheerful
I've got to teach lithography
At the crack of dawn
I'll pay for your boob job
We want to be loved very soon
Your hazel eyes like half open doors
I'll be grinding to a halt about now
More olives?
This must be Jerusalem
Their interest in maps is slight

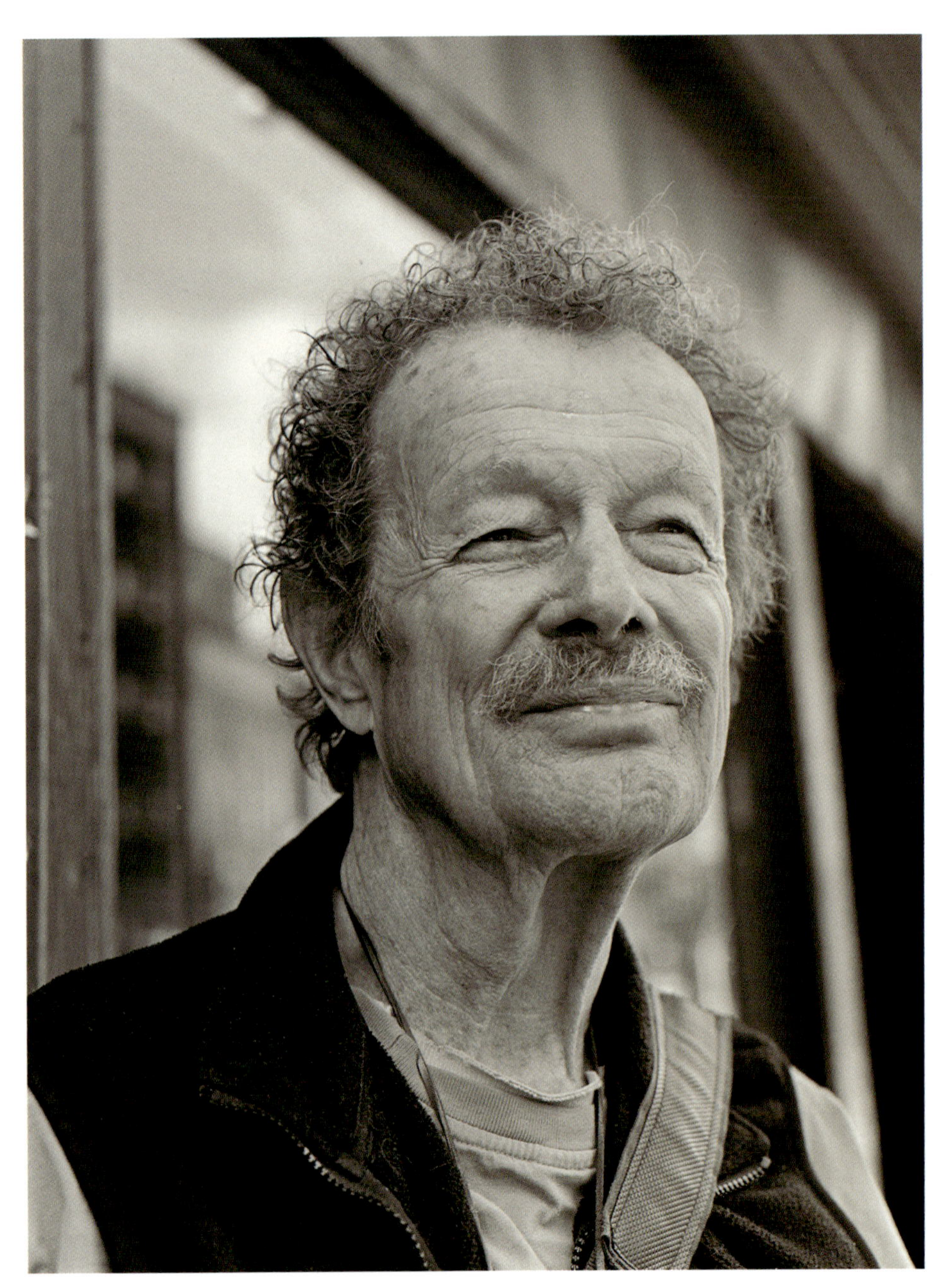

JACK COLLOM

PHONE NUMBER

when I was fifteen years of age
I stepped upon the slow-chapp'd stage
of formal labor. got a place
improving of Cook County's face
by cutting weeds & picking trash
up left by picnics quick & rash.
this work I did for Forest Preserve
District something; I did serve
two men as helper, one named Pesek,
one named something like it: Sebek.
there was a ranger, Callahan,
a lazy, lean-back, pipesmoke man,
who quoted poetry to me,
the following couplet, wild & free:
'The boy stood on the burning deck
eating peanuts by the peck.'

Pesek & Sebek & I rode out
by 9 o'clock, with little doubt,
in District's wornout pickup truck
detritus of the woods to pluck
each day. we'd stop & drink a cup
of coffee or a sodapop up
along the way. we'd work a bunch
(about an hour), then have lunch,
a nice, long lunch among the stubs
of weeds we'd chopped, while watching flocks
of 'hoppers, work some more, then Cubs-
time, on Joe's radio, maybe Sox-,
depending on which team was home.
late afternoon we'd start to roam
'homeward,' motors fixed & tools
cleaned up—we tried to 'bide by rules.

one day, at District, Eddie Buric
called some broad about some whoorish
assignation. first he chatted
with the maid, & then the fatted
calf herself, a dame of rings
& social fame in Western Springs.
this I gathered from the jokes
the men would mutter, envious pokes
at Eddie—he a Bohunk lean,
to screw a lady rich; I mean,
I wondered greatly at this stuff.
& then at home I had the guff
(since I had heard the number spoken)
to look through all the terse & broken
language of the phonebook for
the lady's name who was a 'whore.'
or was that Eddie? anyways
I found the name, & great amaze
filled my glowing teenage mind.
next day I blurted out my find
to Eddie, thinking he would bless
me for my clever doggedness.
he was my friend & very warm.
but now a sort of purple swarm
suffused his face at what I did;
the others cried, 'he's just a kid!'
& slowly Eddie let his rage
die down—till on this page
some squiggle of it now appears
after an ice of thirty years.

it was a magic job I liked;
I used to get there on my bike.

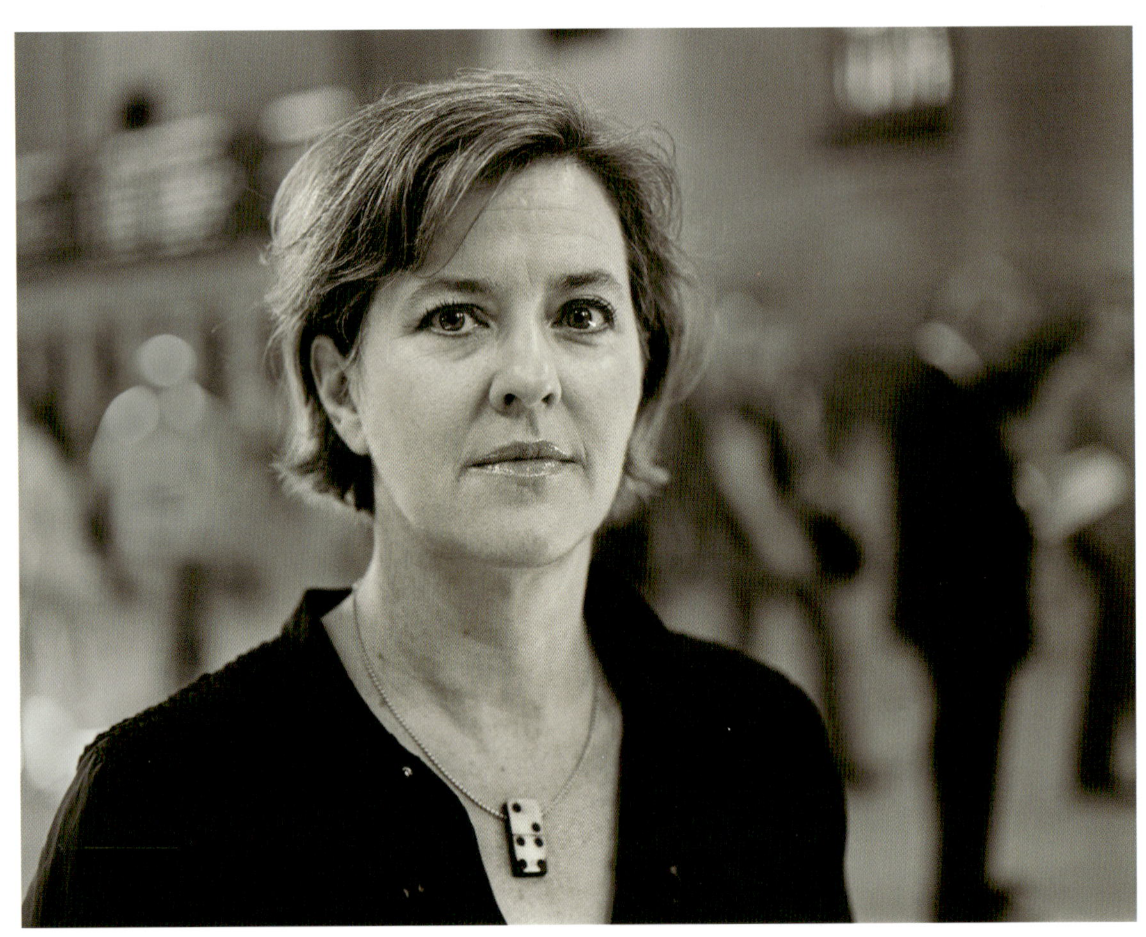

ELIZABETH ROBINSON

'a deeper breathing with other lungs'

I knew air was a collage
and my body a rebus that drove
my breath through the maze of symbols
until I stood
dizzy
at an intersection.

Strange how the sound of images and
automobiles whirring by was muffled.
Now I hear nothing but the oceanic slough of air
in my ears as I inhale
and inhale. I hadn't

wanted my solitude interrupted,
and solitude's own refusals
protected me, a parti-colored
screen that makes, ironically, white noise.

I knew these other lungs
abetted me in the crime of breathing
where I could be sucked whole
into the spongy tissue, surrounded
by world, yet still alone. I didn't want
the womb which is a blank screen; I wanted

this endlessness, someone else's air pinned to
my own breath.

I wanted, endlessly. And here image
after image obliged me with
a pictorial sequence that leads not to sense
but words:

a mute, endless gorgeousness that neither eye
nor ear nor puzzled lung can translate.

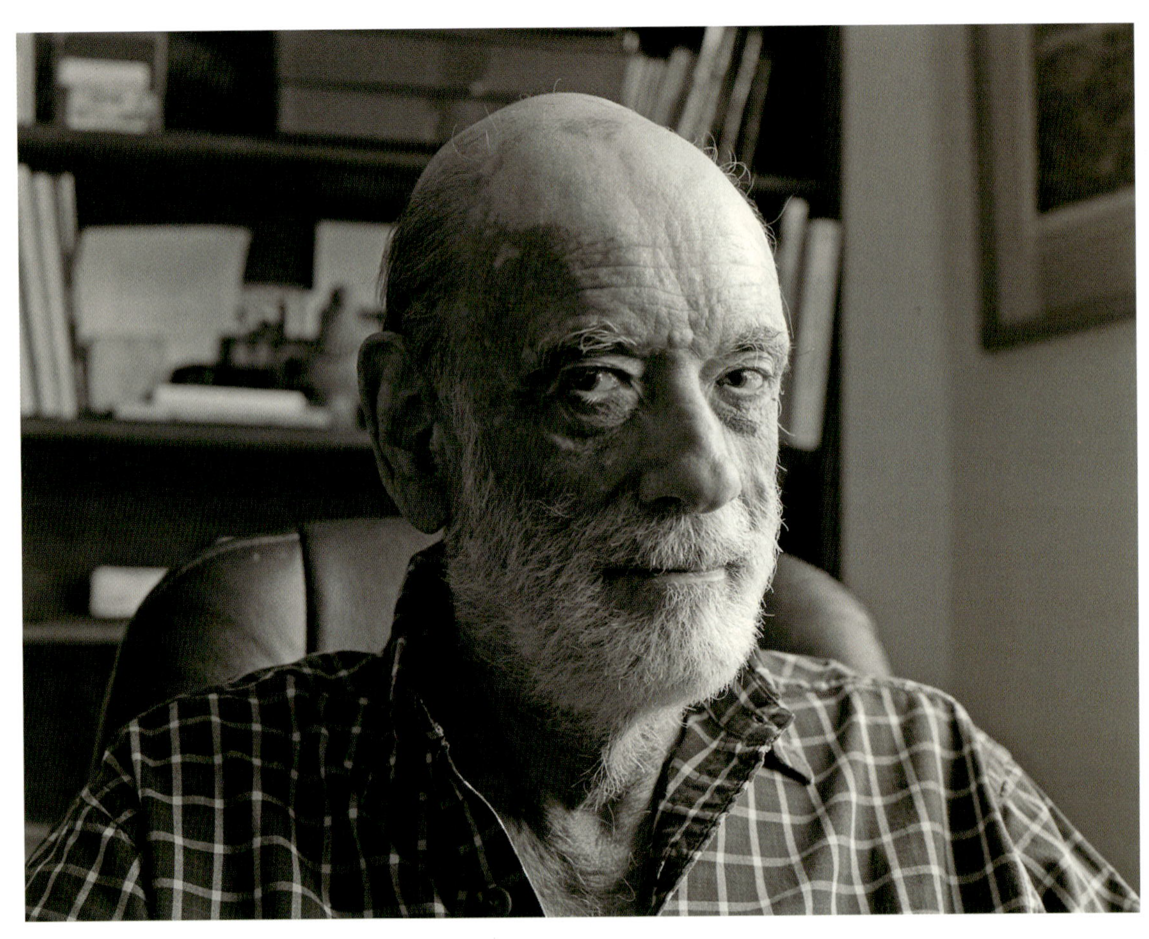

ALLAN KAPLAN

HERMES' DESCENT

While Hermes awes
the junior gymnast
by balancing
on one foot tip
toe on a
whistle of wind,

Excited by
the swiftness
of thievery, slyly
the boy's mother
strokes the well-
turned ankle.

Viewing
the helmet as that
very fruit bowl his
fraternity capsized
over his
head while

He danced
naked on the roof,
father reaches
after a thin wing
of the past—when
a guard forbids.

'Emily, oh Emily, salt
fingers will rub
my ankles raw,'
a 13 year old
hears, 'the ankle of
heaven's word.'

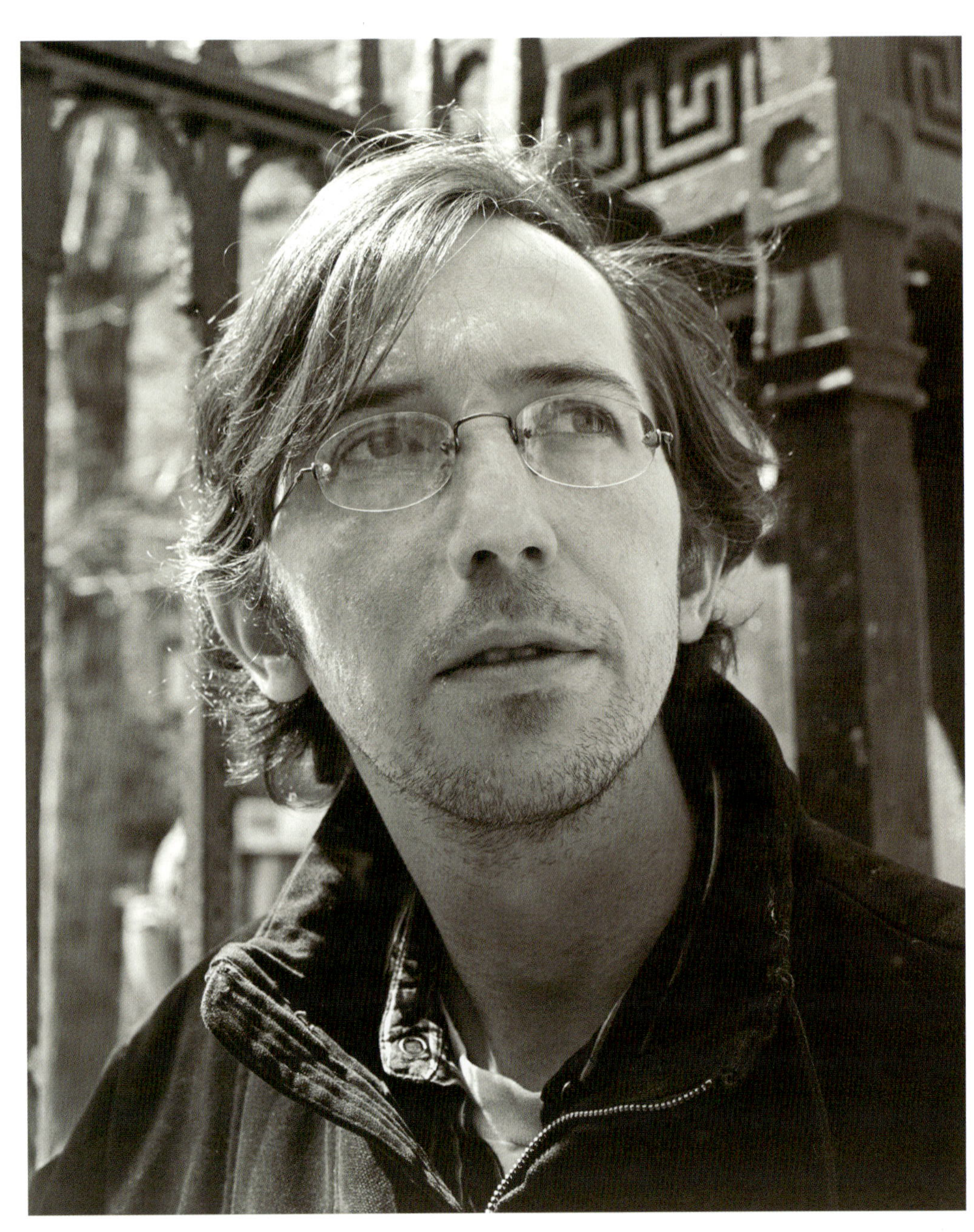

EDMUND BERRIGAN

LITTLE PIECES CONTINUE AS PIECES

A man says I am this, standing on it
a woman says this is unforgiveable
this will be destructed or not
a style of moment we have
sometimes we share this
I talk to the taxi driver offer
some directions 'I can believe
50% of what you say' he says
and laughs we are both named buddy
great cabbies mutter in foreign
languages and sing to themselves
I keep thinking I am 2 years older
than I am getting farther from
my youth but I am also just in
one extended moment I hope
when I close my eyes you are
still there and so am I
I find you on a street corner
another one is chasing his kid
in that playground the gray kitty
rests nearby how is your extended
moment I asked but now we are
just words going over a bridge
whose shadows make us more
and less clear this grammar is
not something I will pretend to
control or master I have no
project but contention
and the monument is already
there as we fade into it

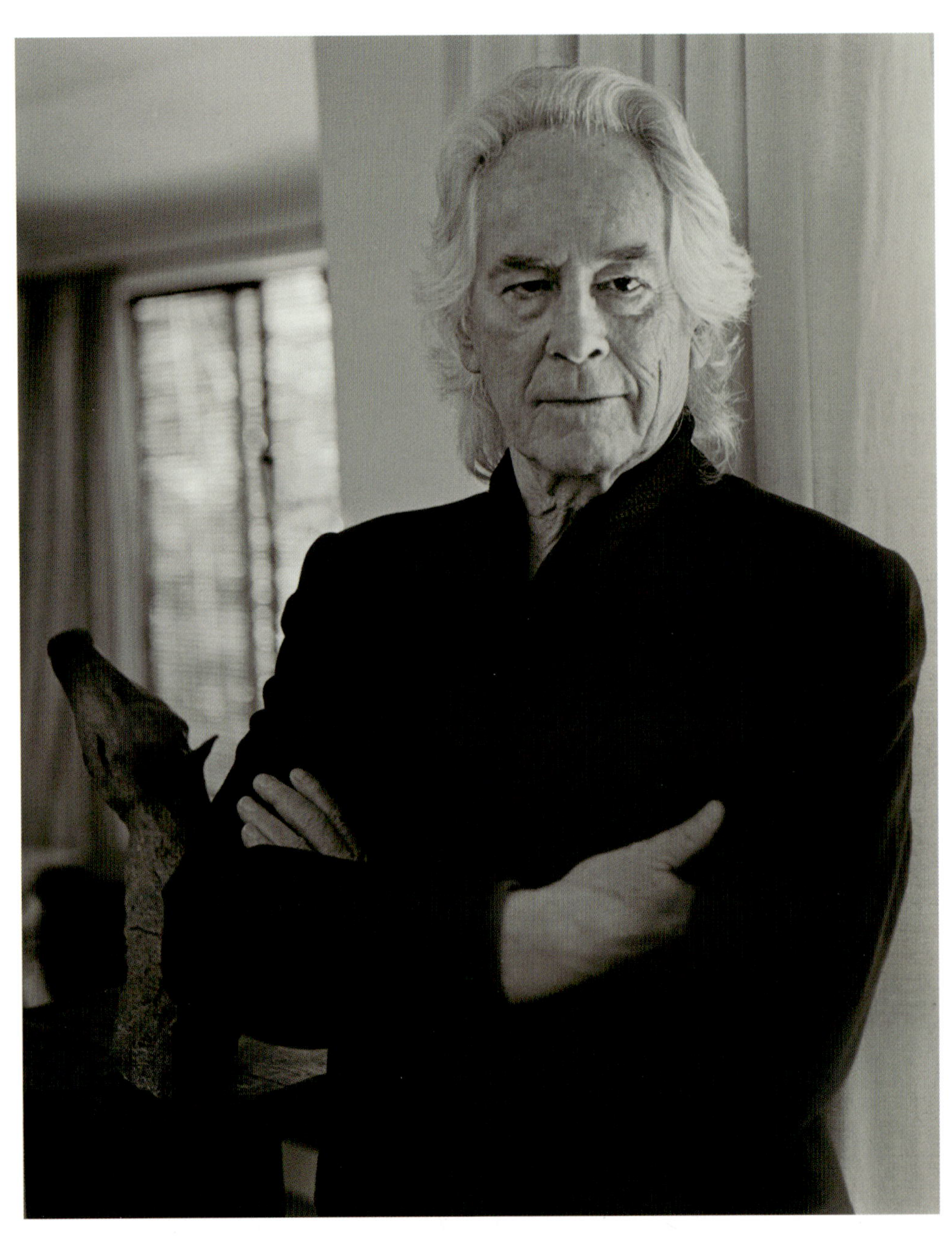

MICHAEL McCLURE

MEPHISTO 32

EAGLES SEEN ON ACID are the rules
that are broken in old poetry. The fierce eyes,
the naying hand of the boy
are the imagination
SHAPING
INSPIRATION
from an edge beyond senses
and made wholly
of reflections in qualia.
NOT true!
Translucent red-orange of the indian paintbrush,
smell of gasoline at the pumps,
are not much
and the train wreck of tradition
is seen in the breath
OF OLD MASTERS.

ALWAYS

THE
CENTER
is a naked statue
of gold and ivory.

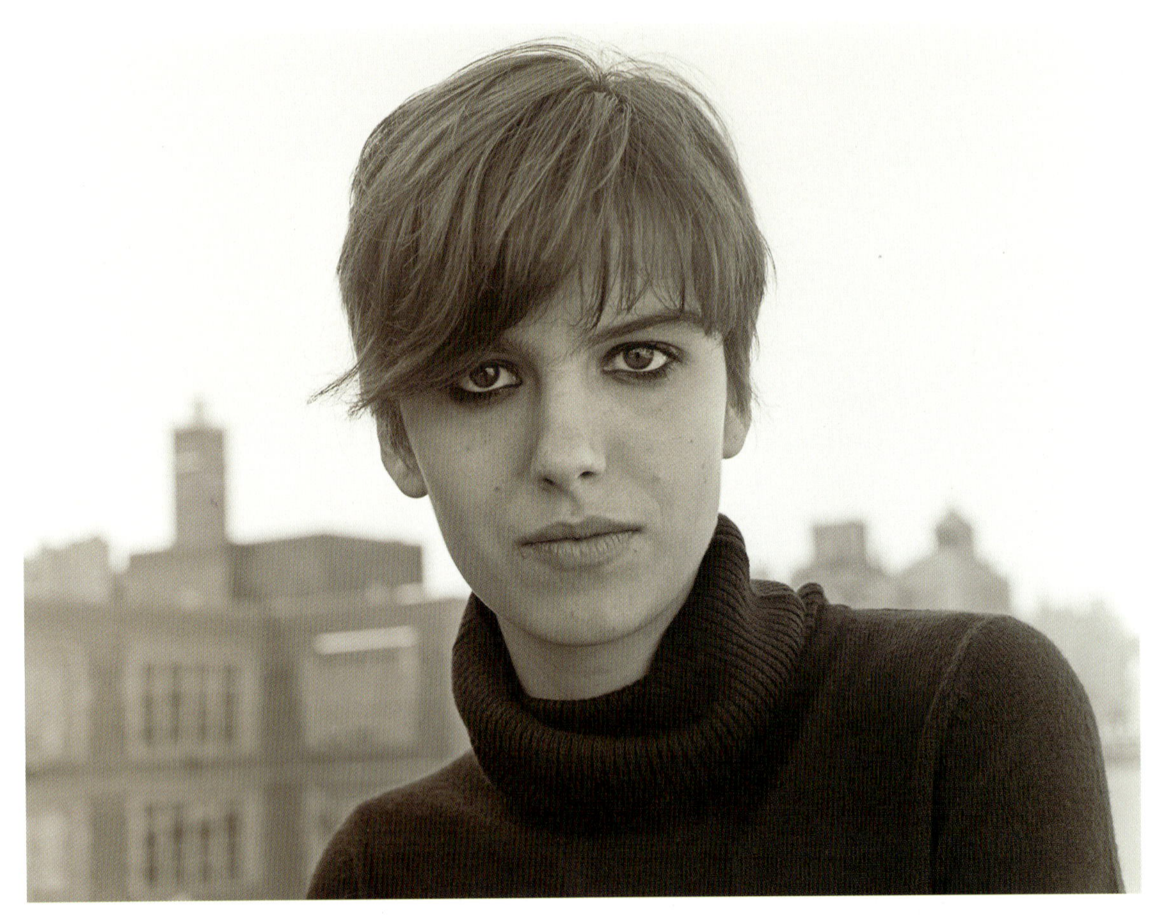

SYLVIA MAE GORELICK

BRIEF NOTE (10 AM)

invest in emptiness
and wake up in the chelsea
where everything tastes
like musk and bridled morning

at the ready and wailing
for it
because four consecutive
piano keys are broken stiff
and an arm of the chair
falls off

I fancy
I will never be myself
again
but I must!
and go on living
with muted poise
to explain: there are no
mementos

but charm enough
in this city for one person
and no one will take it
from her

being angled & limber
isn't being
alive
I insist
and hit a
bull's eye with jackhammer
precision

& the idols fall

TONY
TOWLE

THE SEA AND THE WIND

There is no light, and no quiet;
some areas are smaller than others; a shout
is not heard at once,
but makes a way in leisure to your ear,
and in a moment of leisure you hear it,
with the sound of your voice.
I do not know clearly what it is,
but now in the lime dusk I write about it,
enveloped like time in a larger facsimile.
And soon it will be louder,
until there will be no further need for notes,
or even for an end to it, having multiplied as children
within their boundaries of sensitive particles,
in generations to languish in the respective arms of civilizations,
coming of age in China, ancient Greece, or the fabled Levant—
French for getting up, going to the bathroom
and back to bed, beset with Parisian dreams,
adrift like islands amidst our American ones conceived in English,
all of them together irrigating the wide basin of simple life.
Children learn to deal with the local merchants,
and become used to it;
they go outside and give themselves up to it,
in series of events that rival an eclipse of the sun;
they go alone or with a guide far off in the night,
passing our monuments and tombs
which reflect their obviously transitory state.
Children eat too much, too many cakes and too much candy;
they have vacations, drive to the mountains and beaches
and come back; travel through forests and over boulevards,
until finally there are the continents, the oceans,
and the vastnesses of outer space
to make up the eyes' foreign vision.

In the meantime they find flowers together, fences, stems,
marble, exalted feelings, and ornate cornices;
there are excursions to museums, pursuing
one another down corridors, grapes, underbrush, memories,
and Mozart concerti among the dominant points of interest,
and a gabled roof, a swooping hawk, the silver flash of a trout,
dramatic but nonetheless minor points,
rejoining always one's generation at the elevator,
or elevation, to the combined hallucination and dream.

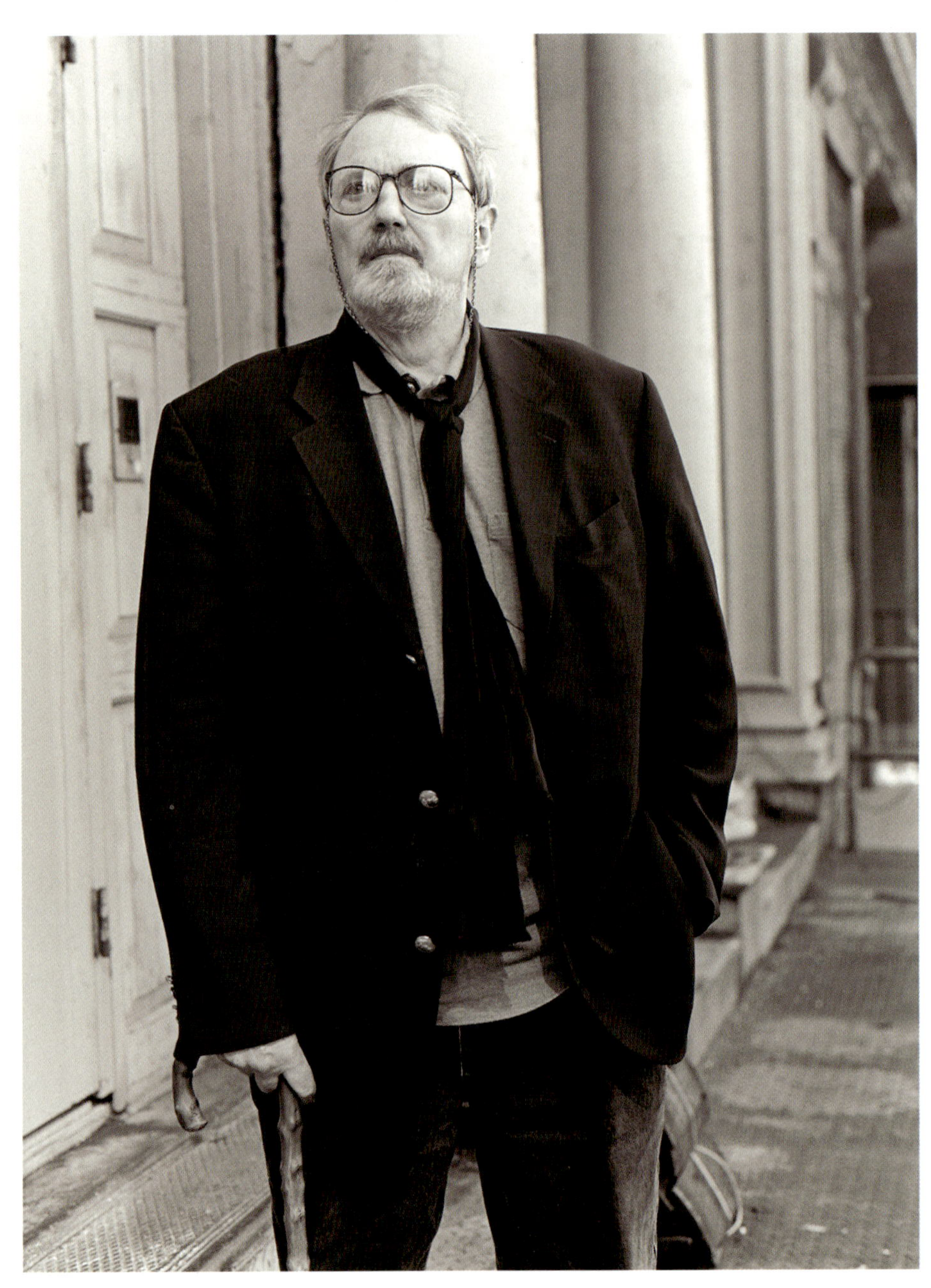

TONY TOWLE

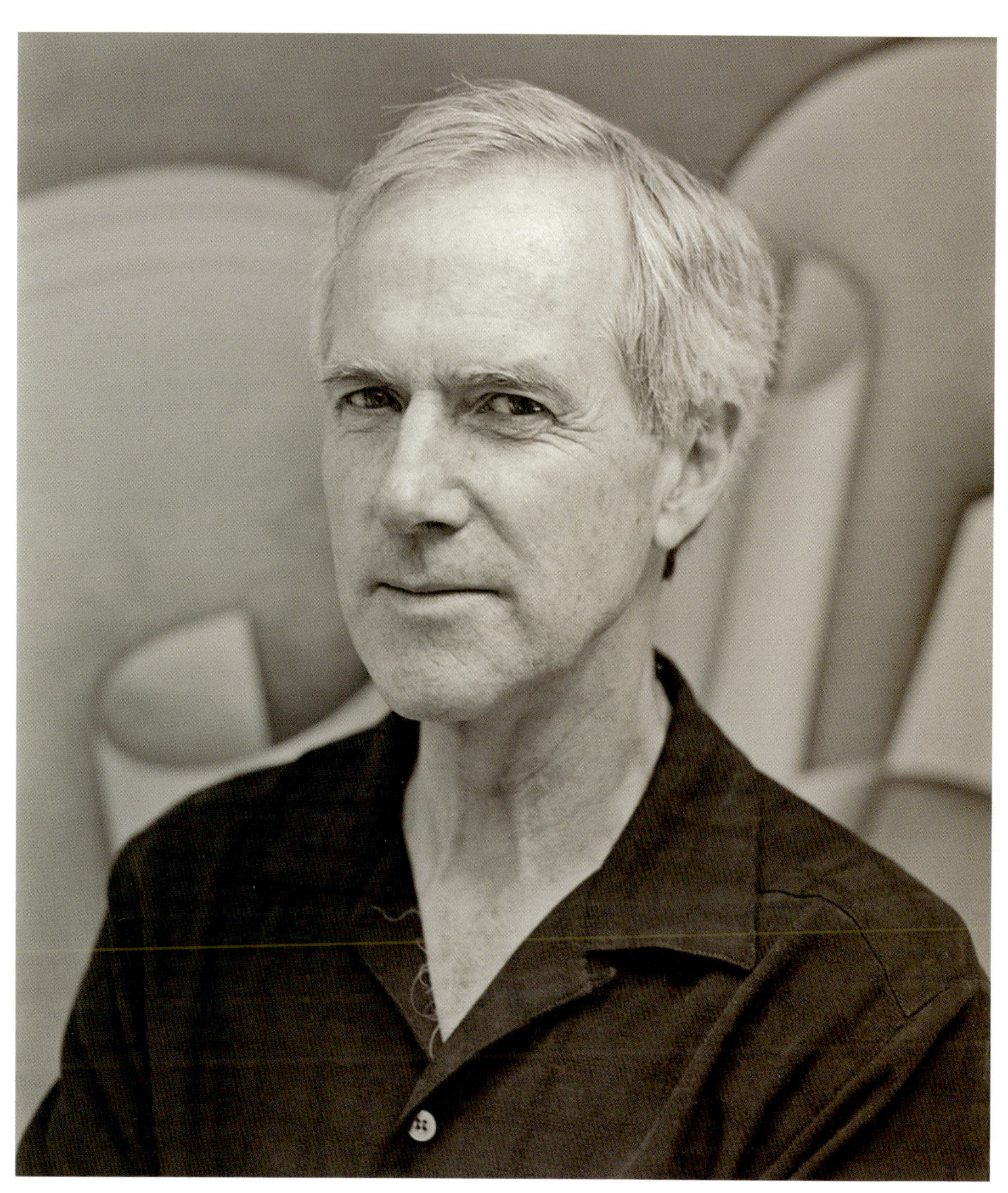

REED BYE

REED
BYE

BEFORE RAIN COLLAPSED THE PATCH

Snug in a parquet of clues
Worm rolled his blown nose toward
a pinch of savory
and sighed back into his cast,
rototilled.

Snaglap came bounding under the sun
drawing up something from the mill
at Hollow Stump where he'd rolled
and stained his beard in the escutcheon fold's
piscine corpse.

And every morning *Fabric Softener*
wafts through the cedar fence
'I think we're being poisoned,
dog and turtle.'

Towards evening *Porkchop* escalates
as by her limpid pool our diva
Au Divan, takes a rose lenticule up-nose
like little clouds we haven't seen since fall,
thin weasels.

Lenticular
Shows more through
than had been when
a young one and let in
such pitiful condition
(smelt ash).

Anything Believable's
now gone, winding up the ridge road
on a night bus, reading lights
moving above treeline,
in the smoke and heady fume of scotch.

'In new trucks there's at least a place to park
your drink,' *Tribble Quarry* spoke on phone
to *North of Town* who here has held years.
'What's it gonna take to get it through
that there will be a meeting
of rain and certain items on the earth tonight,
a short hop on wet slate? Ozone?'

'Don't pass the buck, Dream-on. Your boots
may be tan above streamline but
got something in another odor?'

'That it, *Last Limp?*'
'Stiff shoulder and stiff back,
got home and got the sack?'
'*North of Town,* your head is turned
by every whistle call from *Damp Sweater.*'

'Listen, *All I Know Is,*
delight is chief in spite
of the decadence. Don't camp out
in the nose-plot of ancient sheets if
you can upturn the Sun and re-tar her,
and end up with two beliefs popping.'

Memling Clouds swirl in synchronized discs
to the rhythm of 3-in-1 oil
streaming through stirrup and hinge.
When the sky finally closed, wind was the lathe
on which *Coming Rain* turned her hair.

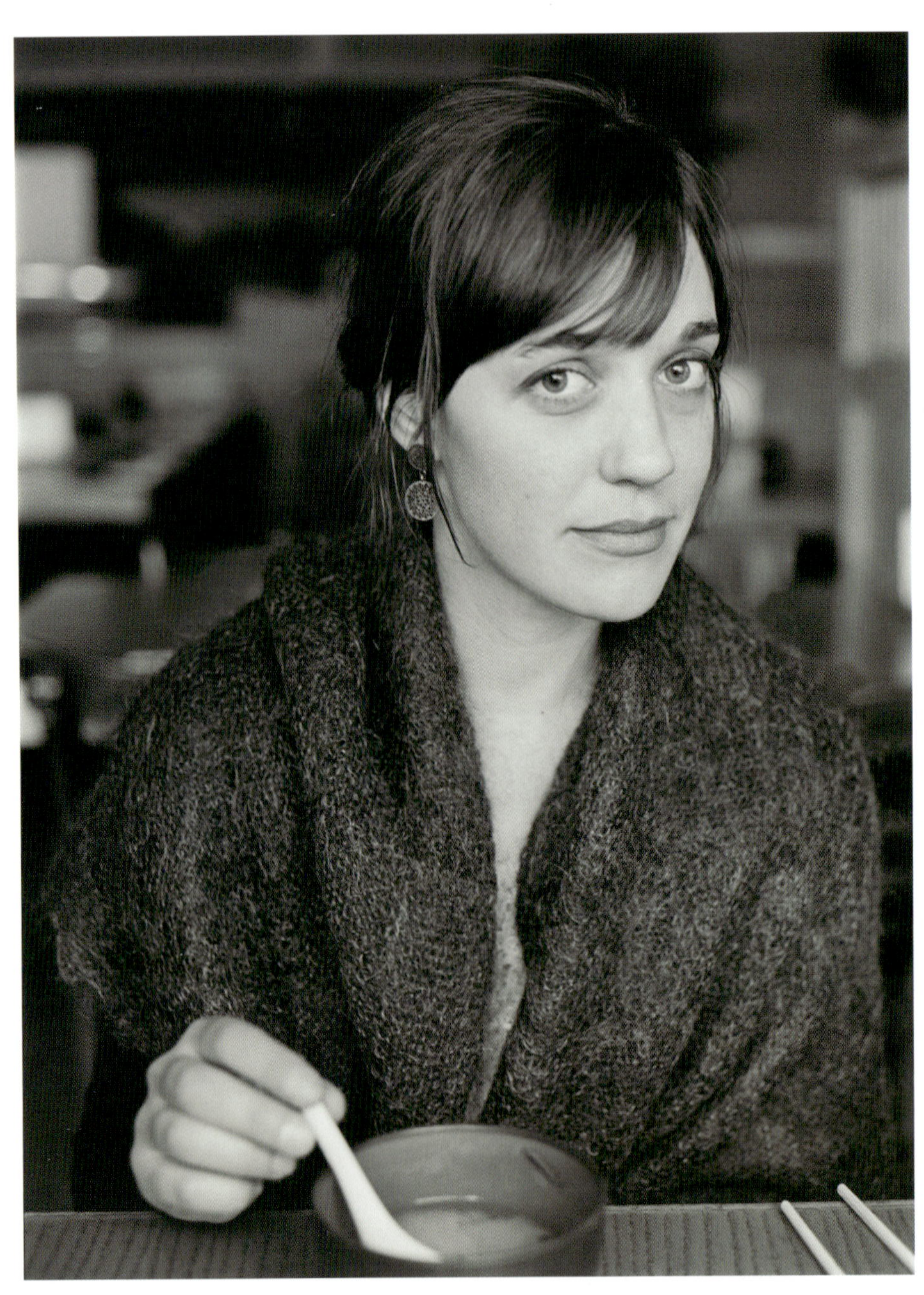

ANNALISA PESEK

HEADLESS

Less listening more talking
That night I went to Maine or talked about it anyway
The state berry is the blueberry
Notice the floor is tilted here the bed is sliding
All the way to Maine in my head
SKETCH FOR KAFKA is taped to the wall
We're both naked
I turn around and around so he can get a good look
Then out the door
Oh Kafka stay hydrated!
These generations of words sour the mood
We're all muddy and sticky it's snowing oh Maine!
Where are your promised huckleberries?
We're purple too
Our words are thrown they may bounce
So many of them why add more
Come back to bed Kafka
Read to me read to my head while I go on talking

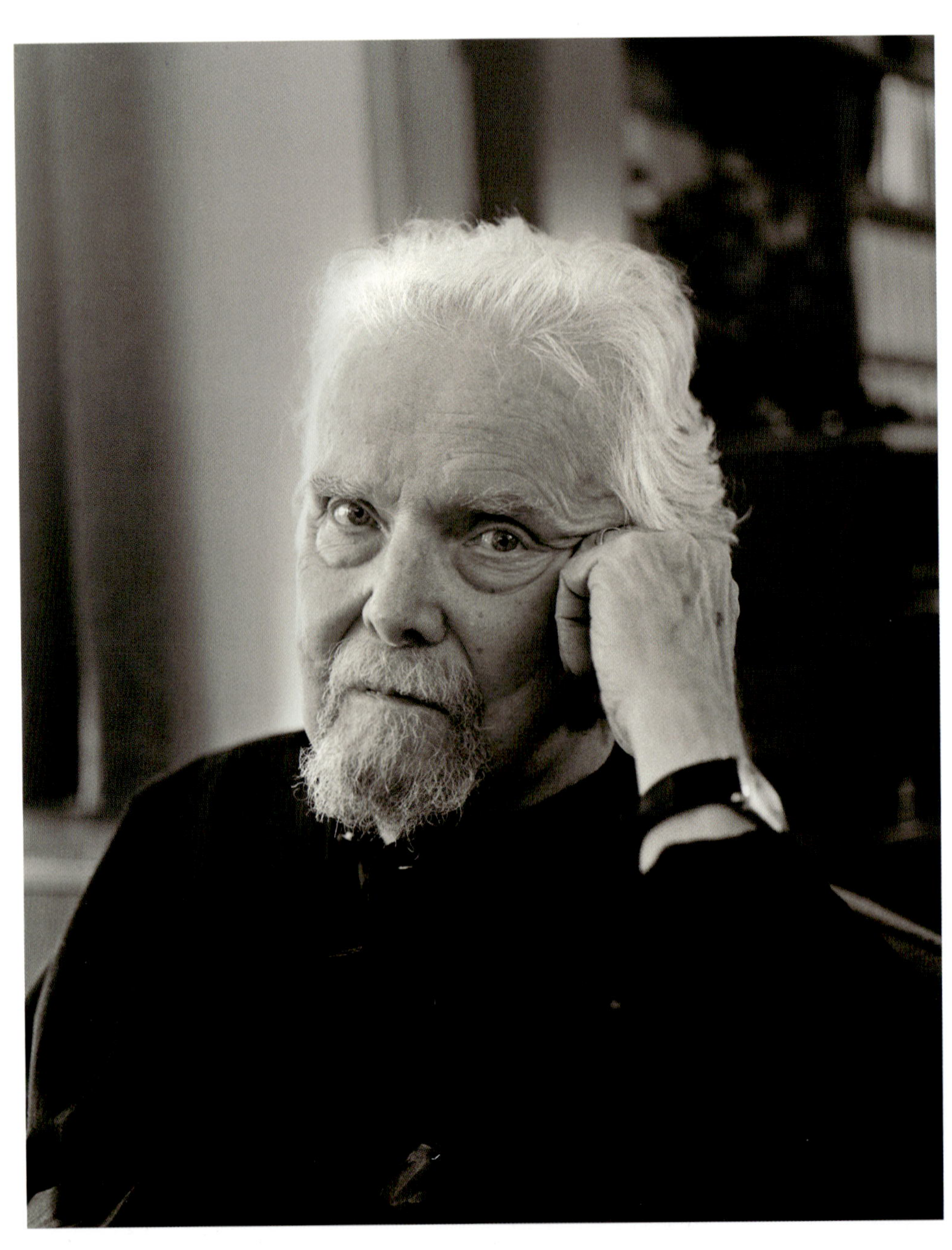

ANSELM HOLLO

'SO THE ANTS MADE IT TO THE CAT FOOD'

so the ants made it to the cat food
but then you scrape them into the compost

one day we'll set out under solar sail
to the systems of fifty new planets
discovered this year

who knows if we'll do any better
than these ants you think
then contemplate vast grids upon grids
shifting and twisting
clashing and jelling flowing apart exploding

shrinking   to this little blob of cat food
in the kitchen sink

oh it gives one the flesh of the hen
comme on dit en français.   cat disappears into bush

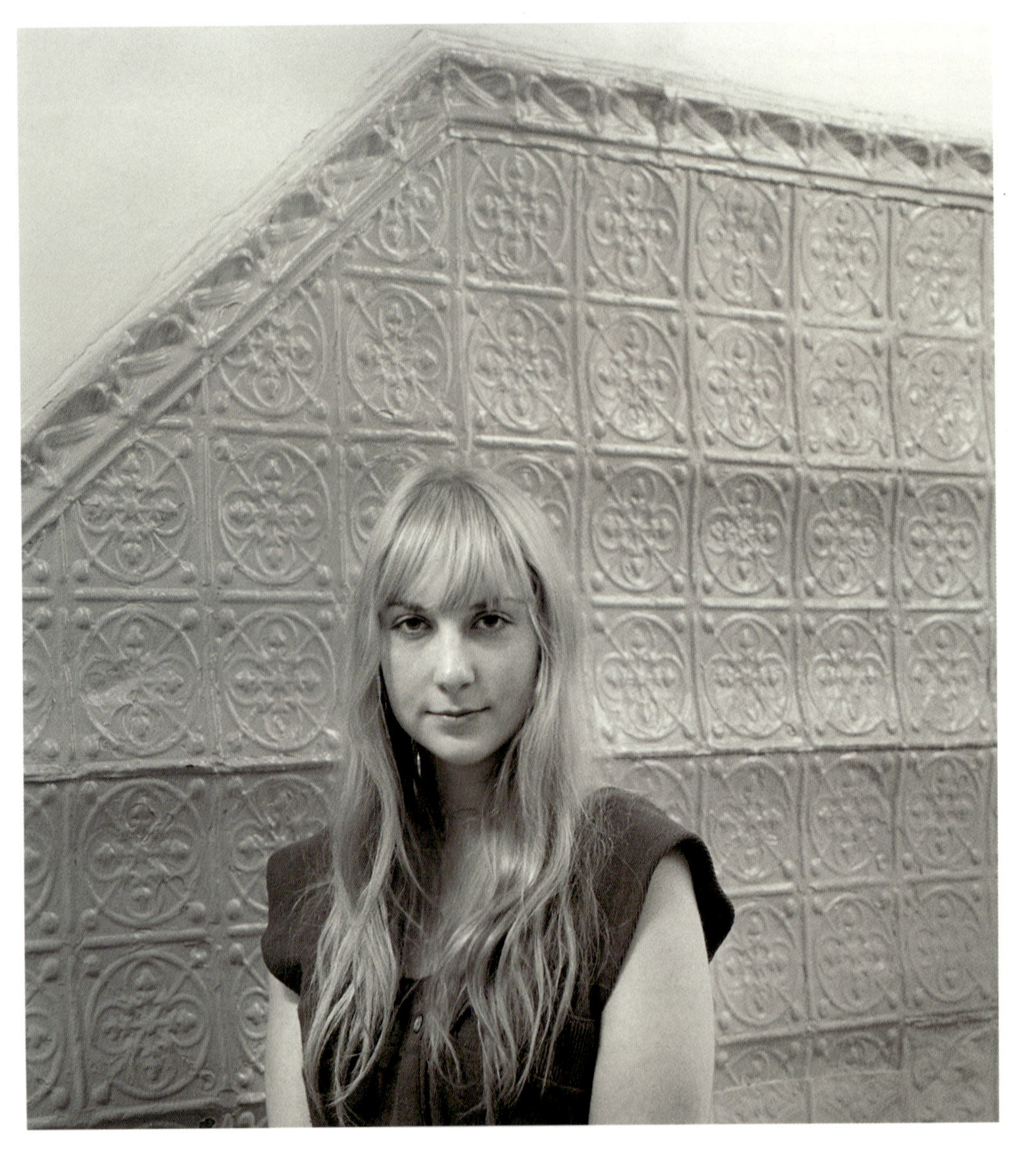

ELIZABETH McDANIEL

OCCASIONAL ANGEL

A dung beetle mistaken
for a petit four
in a box labeled FRAGILE–WEDDING
on a beam above a landing
it isn't smart to touch them

I know a trick
I can catch last year's flu
I view the room through a hat of light
spilling my tea
on a delirious blanket
that wises me up to sleep
overnight
ceramic cats have re-arranged themselves

The window is crisp
from the fire escape
where I may cough
whorls of smoke
as a prelude
to moony the second
they dissipate

Pleasures expire
indifferent as a jar
with no finishing touch
forgive me for mentioning it
as I grow ever more vulgar
adieu
I can't wait to see you here
in warm and normal Paradise

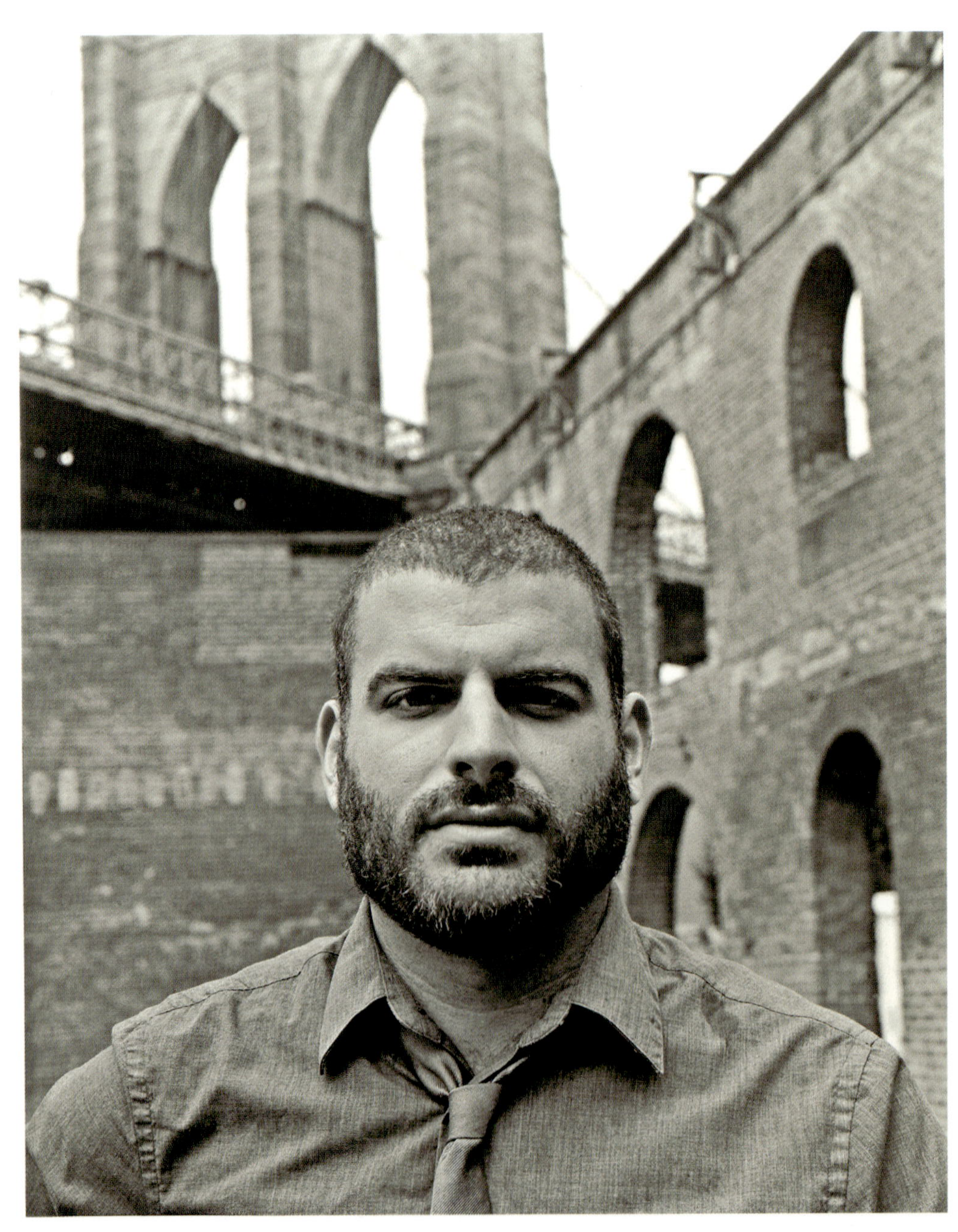

ROBERT ELSTEIN

SEIZURE ON A SKI SLOPE

You would have to be crazy to go along
with the theory that Truth is physical
but I can't worry about you
I've got enough trouble swearing and walking under ladders
jamming my fingers in card catalogue drawers
now here's a reluctant page-turner with beguiling eyebrows
helping to shut out an easterly wind
a mysterious dream figure rummaging through her pockets

Never knew what hit her
knocked out cold in the snow
for indeterminate minutes
until she felt something warm
a hand perhaps
grasping, refusing to let go
I wouldn't mind, myself
I learned early to never stop
not turn around to monitor the recent past
not count the pillagings
because there might be a few more gold nuggets up ahead
what about that guy who never stopped to count them?
some would say he's the one who's ethically deficient
but that logic is like tables turning
in a shadowy beer hall
or across the street in a frozen washing machine

Nah, I can't help myself
restraint's not my bread and butter
why not meet me after après ski
I'll be working on a Topfenpalatschinken
at the only decent Stube in Mürzzuschlag

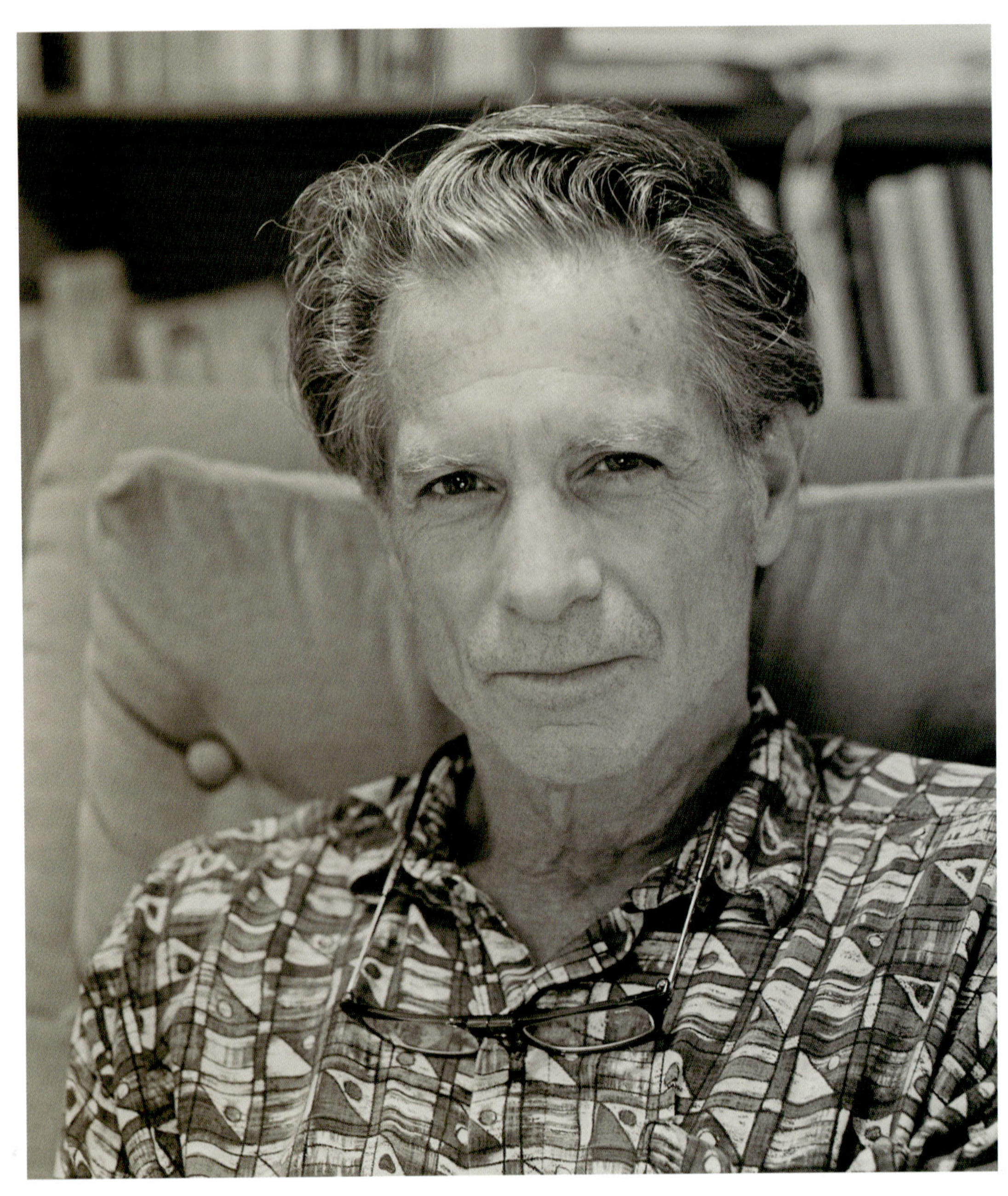

MICHAEL GIZZI

SHUCKS IS NOT ENOUGH

A doctor is sent to the workhouse
now he'll never get well
at any moment a generation
is knowing what's gone—or up!
cut the crap, Winesap
is feeling not family
earth made to pose home
a moving picture house
snoring on the screen?
today it rained a little
and so she loves him great
minds recycle the same carnation
take a rose by the cheek
and banish the word blush
among those arrested
was a how-to book
every time I pick up
the phone it's me again
clowned into oblivion

SHE

I've reached the middle of my rope, staggering around the kitchen before the night turns white hot. Moving boxes, beer bottles, stacks of dishes cover the floor. Volcano rising out of African plains, I will obey. Report to doghouse. List of books and authors, innertube downstream. Medic! Without limiting the generality of the foregoing, needing to see her, I peeked inside myself: rope lowered over edge of cliff into nettles, night turning white hot.

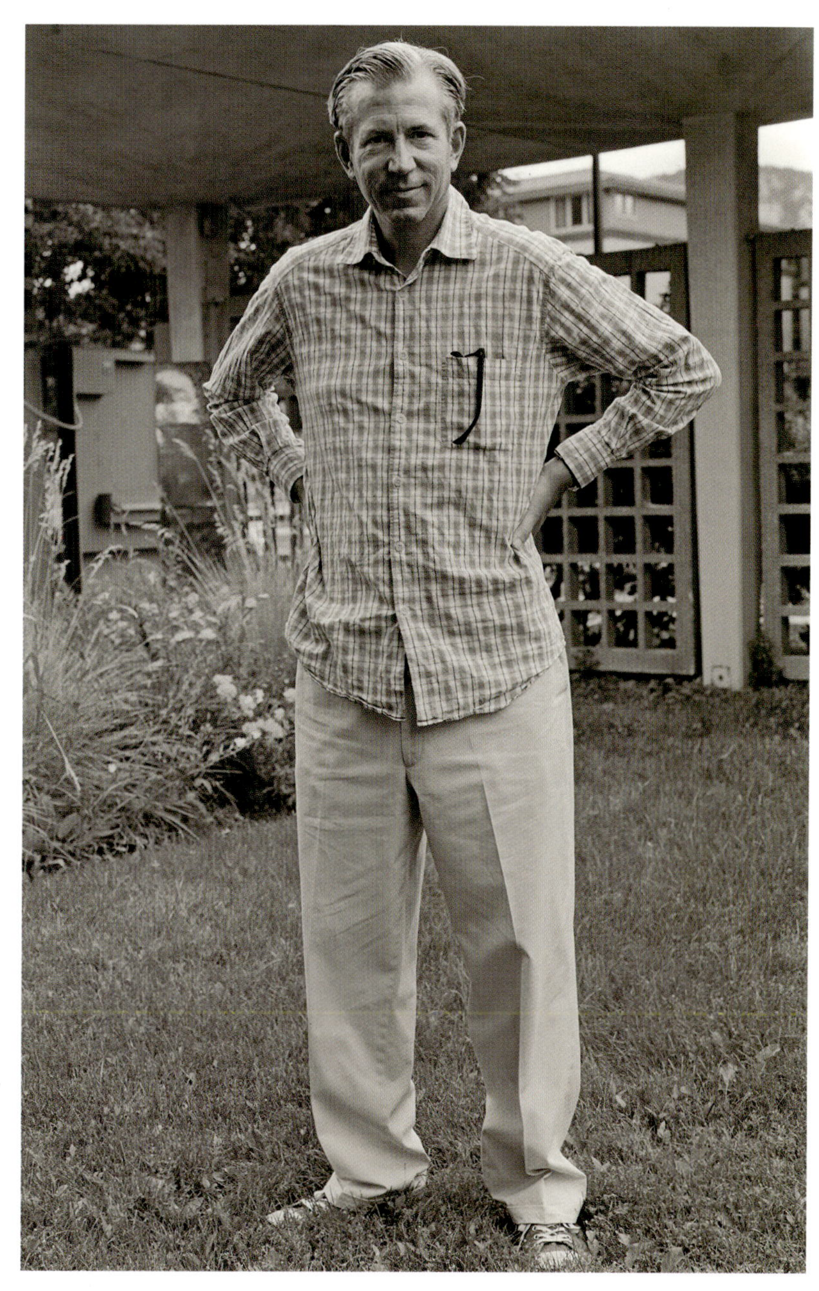

MICHAEL FRIEDMAN

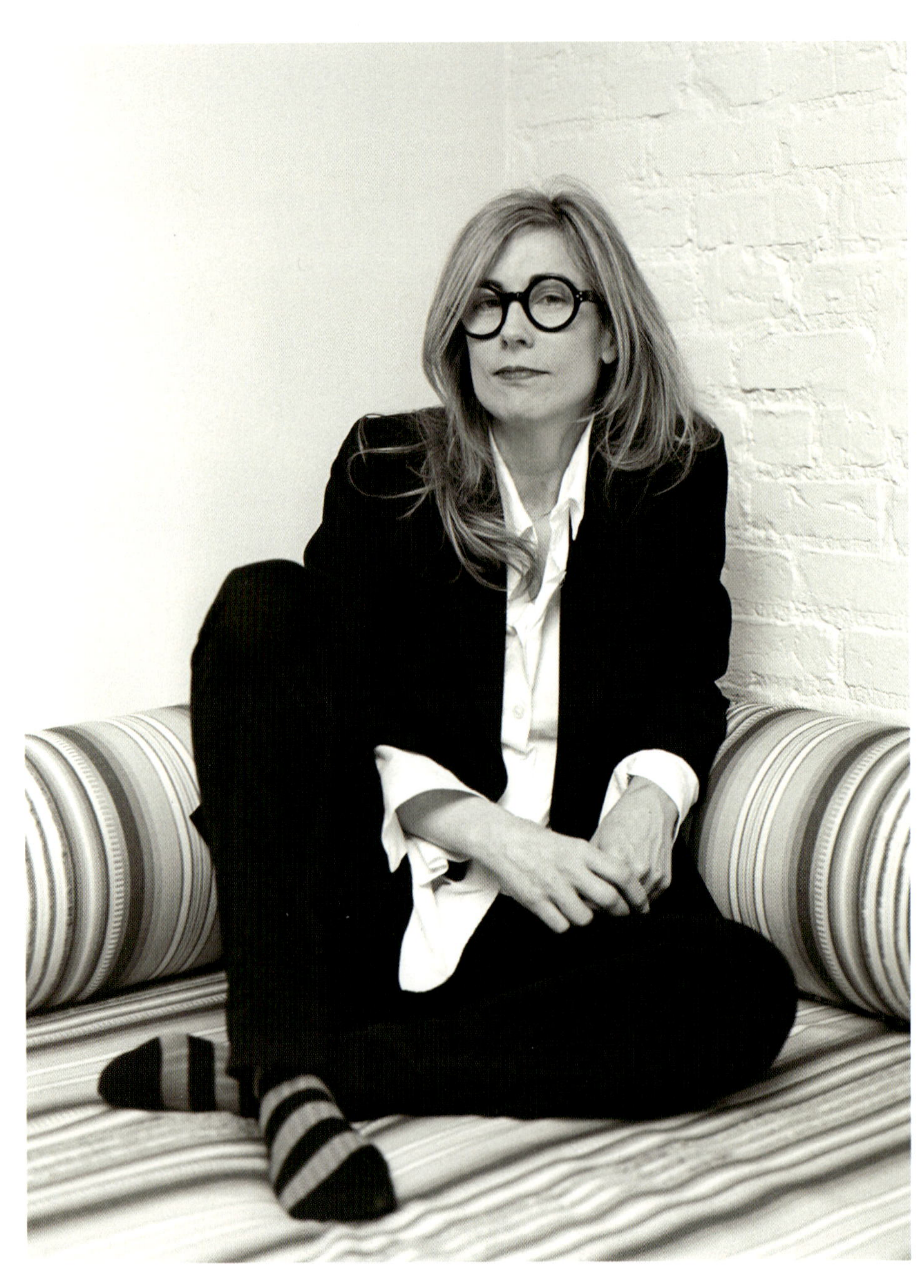

GILLIAN McCAIN

YOU

I'm a hair consultant, color and what not. I want to make a million dollars. I do daily visualizations of an undiscovered hue, a new you. It all passes by in a blur. Once I get the patent, all that remains is board approval. In the meantime, I'm leasing a painting: The Triumph of Marius — wild horses, tambourines and what not. Let's face it, I'm always trying to escape. I thumb through back issues, promises of a better life, common as dirt. My former boyfriend (whose street name means he's the one with the inflammation) says I have to admit I need help. All I know is that I want this stage of my development to be over. I can't change my stratum, no matter how long I keep scrubbing and scrubbing. What's with that fucking board? What would you do if you were I? But you're you, aren't you, the old you, without the pink streaks. Look, I never claimed the solution was water-resistant. What I lack in credibility I make up for in sanguinity. And I have the stains to prove it.

UNPLANNED ACCOUNT

Everyone has a story. The mountain threw rocks at me. I stood up to it. At the top I built a shelf for my record. There was enough sky for another life, an abutment of air. Science itself authorizes blue, whoever comes along may have some. Up here one can appreciate the eye as an exposed part of the brain. That's Helga, the chick who shares my pad. She's not really orange, it's the picture. We're moving the aerial into the hall. I'm an emotional guy who lacks a cohesive point of view, and Helga has an eating disorder. She's a monist. I can dig it. I mean, why did the universe go to all that bother? Bears drunk on honey wrestling with monkeys, electric burgundy odd-toed ungulates, and the two-headed snake—one head for eating and drinking, the other just for thinking.

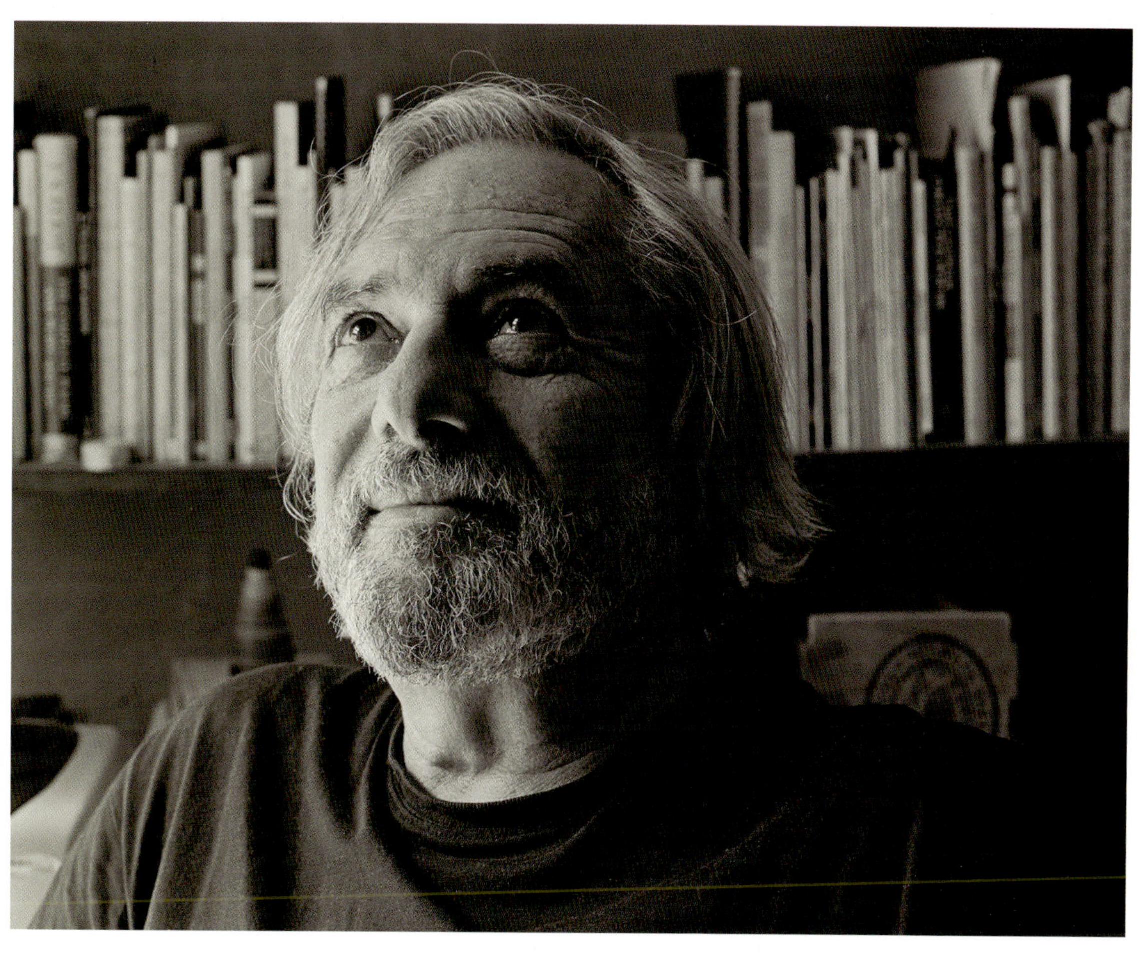

LARRY FAGIN

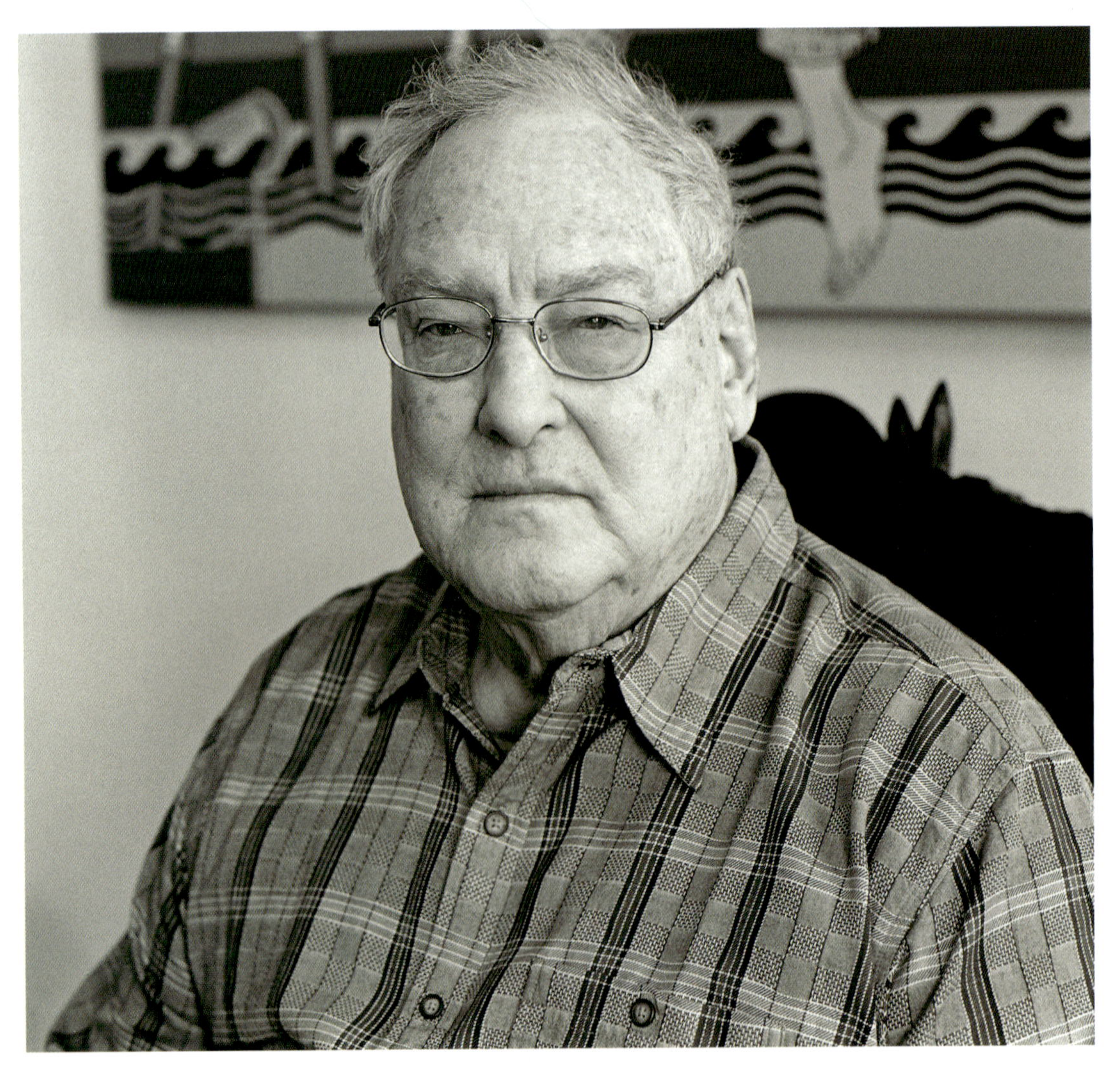

KENWARD ELMSLIE

WHITE ATTIC

The white attic rests
among dripping trees

with unrolling tunnels
and trembling luggage

around were dens
all kinds of dens

and dazzling fruit
to weary the wind

the sun would end
and we'd smoke among the trees

our wary arms
tenderly relaxed

the urn faces a tree
of unequal height

when it came I grew
moved to two rooms in town

where I reach out at night
and bat the far air

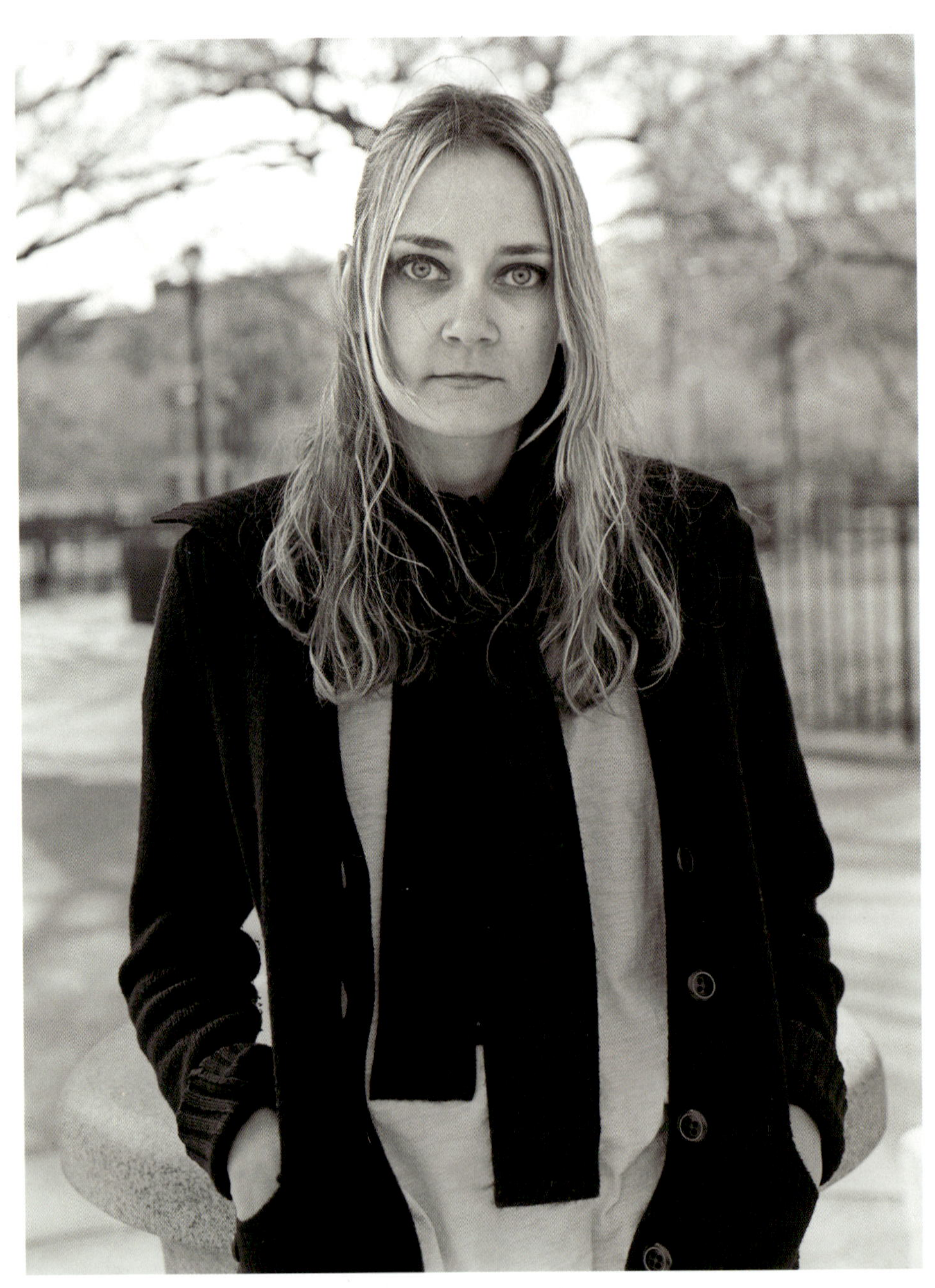

ANN STEPHENSON

STEADILY

I will keep it in sight, keep it on the bedrock
keep it canned, and you will understand it perfectly
I will appear to take part, be included, inscribe myself
on the wall or in the general mood, speaking
out of habit, to conclude that something is the case
loosely fastened

I cut in line, I had a pass
they bit their tongues and complimented my shoes
noted the colors of my head, how I blended in
with the dried catkins funneled from above

On the anniversary of my showing up
recorded what things looked like
emotions as consumer goods, final goods, with regard
to attractiveness, especially when human shapes
were fuzzy in outline, numbered or illustrated in a book

I think of something small, calculate it
with small maths, as in the problem
of the broken arm, or the shrinking violet

Deliberately not seeing the difference
between creeping and walking
with the practice of a lazy eye
the way doesn't matter

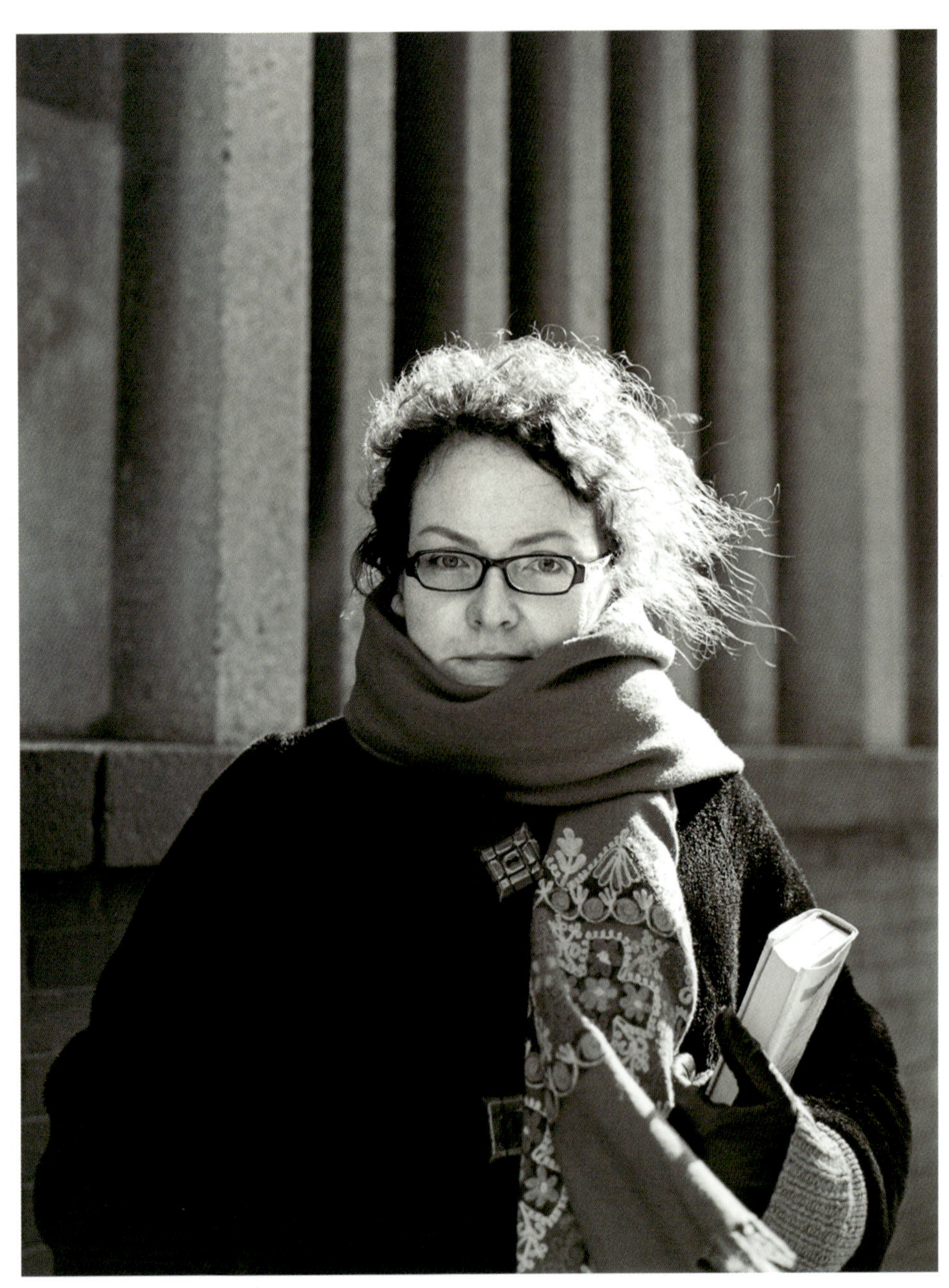

JENNIFER KIETZMAN

EACH DAY BRINGS A NEW PODCAST

When people find me amenable (what I call being a good customer) it feels like an accomplishment though I suspect it of being far less.

I couldn't see my sister's reaction for several days after initially reading it. I felt what I knew as the shame that comes with pity and is difficult to separate from love like what I felt on the playground in fifth grade when Michael Vanderwarker said he was sorry about my father. I might have hugged him had I been older or nudged him had I been human instead I ran away.

Is what I have now enough mine for times and levels of reality to intermingle as my sister suggested? Is that what having the feeling I thought I'd have here means? Conditions might be right for this. Or is it only mine because I can make use of it? Is everyone else likewise concerned with possession? As it does my sister layered reality reminds me of the archaeology that is our common home. What she means by that is Hattusa, Turkey though she might also mean mother's house. She says we work to manage our dirt whether we bury it excavate it or use it like junkies. How did I get down on my knees? She wonders if we're the unbefriended dead. Anne commented that most of my email messages consisted of questions. After 20 percent of the company got laid off it would have been a good day to have stayed home. I nearly fell in the shower and heavy rain and wind made for an oddly close commute.

For Halloween Katya will go as Dracula, Jackson as Iron Man. Mary Jo was supposed to be a rooster in pantyhose but Katya may allow her to be Dracula's grandmother.

When a place is unfamiliar all that can be said are simple things if one is to attempt to say anything truthful. Apple purple mountain dinner.

We both experienced the night dread of having to wake up again. A road trip of some sort is the answer even if it's only to Staten Island (botanical garden). At least the encouragement I gave Katie to spend a weekend with Pete proved beneficial insofaras she had a 'great time.' Personally I can't admit even one more ongoing anything into my life. Open closed open closed. The romance the Japanese have with suicide seems too programmatic. Give me the Swedes.

He crawls into bed naked. I can hear his eyeballs knocking around in their sockets like dolls' eyes. Listening, laughing or scratching are his choices. At the least he deserves to have sandwiches made for him and someone to take note of his comings and goings—the equivalent of saying you are worth saving though no one says that.

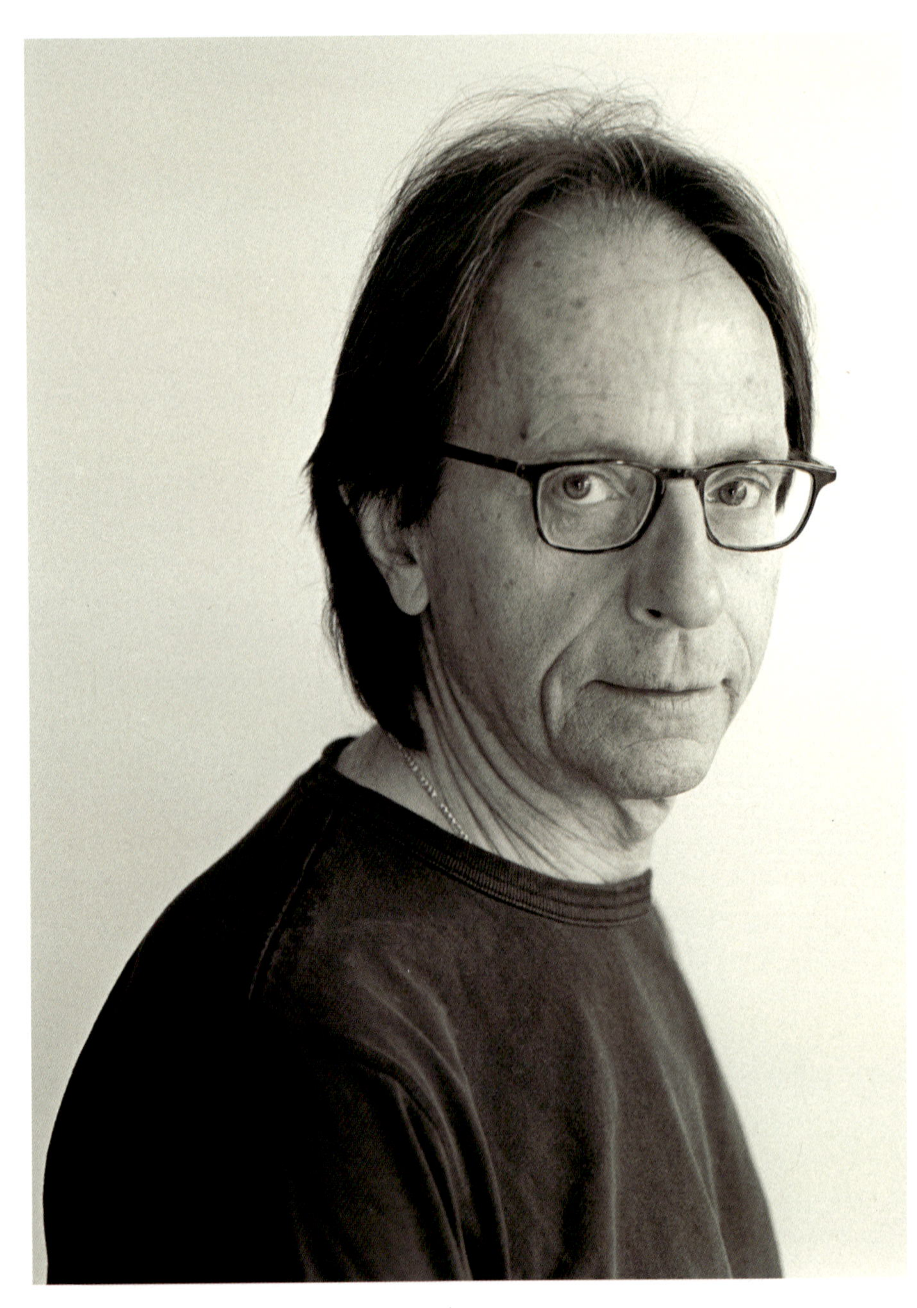

MICHAEL BROWNSTEIN

LIFE

Life is beautiful   However

The only truly human, American expressions
                                        of its staggering rich moments
        (two baby bulldogs in open window, 3:17 a.m.)
Aren't really forms of expression like language, but

The only truly human, American expressions
                                        of its staggering rich moments
        (two baby tomatoes in open window, 3:17 a.m.)
Aren't really forms of expression like language, but

Parallels manifesting themselves right alongside
These moments, like music. It is just
Your specific choice in music, the one when you respond,
Dropping onto my back as I walk past
                                        flinging Tasty Cake...
Your breasts that have chosen their call, for always
        they drift ahead of what you plan on leaving
            in your mind and its musical chair.

Genius, to eat and mumble in peace...

So, the definition of tragedy is
'A waste of time that you stop to consider it'
And not stop to consider this: applying
Force to the mirror which by itself
Already is falling away from self-consciousness,
Nemesis of the 20th century... to do that
Would be a waste of time. Or would it?
Making the right choice is calm laughter
       when it occurs to you except as an idea.

I say 'American' because the universe, all the radar
Technicians of enticement, is American now
Entirely. I say 'nineteen' because
Nineteen is your age, and take
Your life into my hands
And you take mine, we jump into the truth.

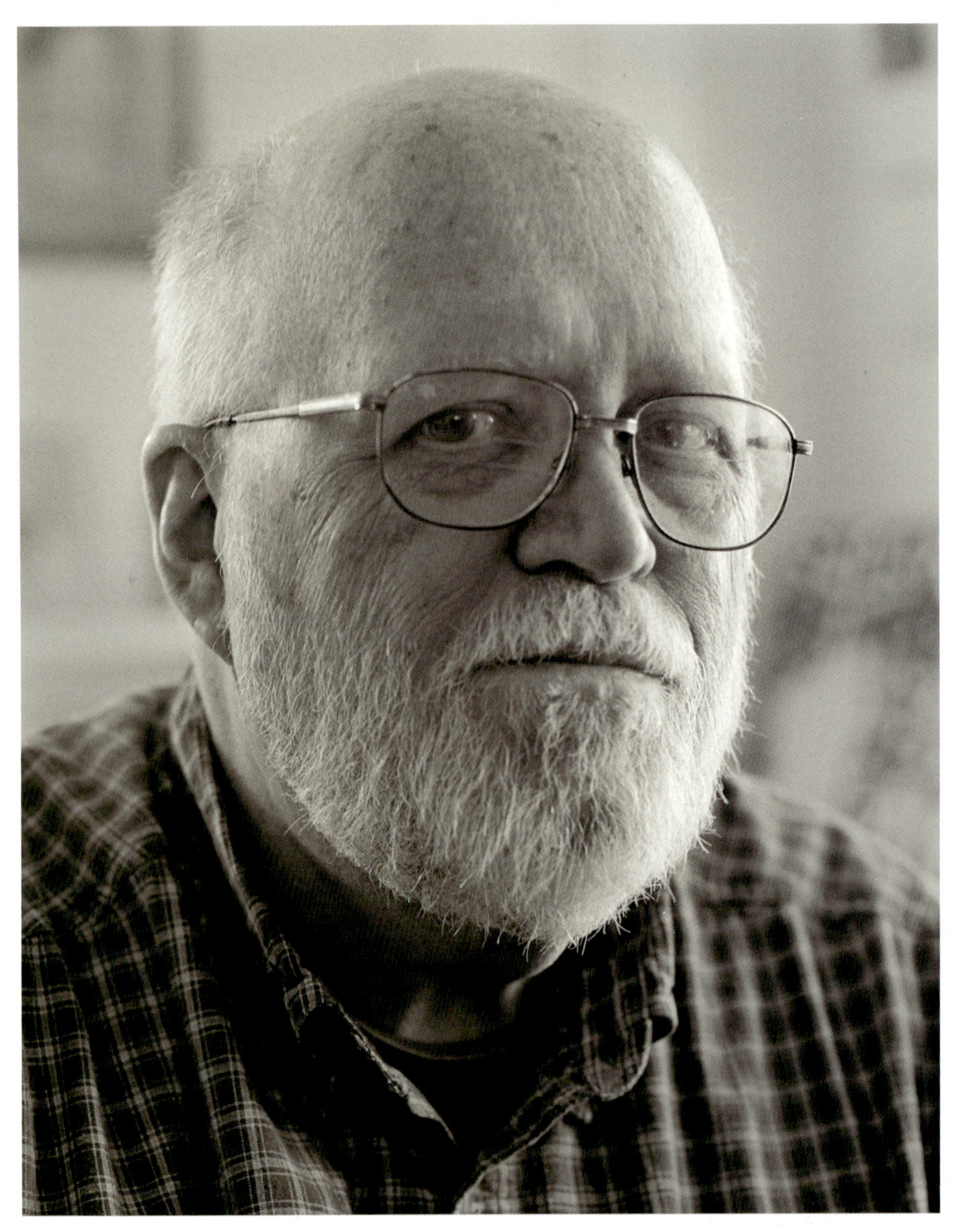

RON SILLIMAN

from SUNSET DEBRIS

Does a word fall into crevasses of recognition? Are the first days more intense? Which is necessity, which coincidence? What does he mean about getting more ass than a toilet seat? What makes him choose a shirt of false leather? Is it true that the gap between known and not-known is the distance between pattern and form? Is pain physical or an emotion which might on occasion have its origin in the real? What is objective cause? What is the mystery of name? What is more powerful than the vague? Is Liz the Whiz? Do we tell Mel? Is there a formal consequence to running out of ink? Do you want to drink? Can you smell sex? Is it six? Is it principled action or just trashing? Is it armed education? In what way was the Civil War not just an extended black rebellion? Doesn't the buildup of artistic images always result in the lie? What is the importance of texture? Isn't it about time you brushed your teeth? In what ways will you change your life? Could you go to a place and not be known? Is it butcher by the dozen? Could you feel the quiet settle in? In this what it is? How could I convince you I'm not writing the words of the person I would like to be? Is the rooster friend to the dog? On whose side are the service providers, on whose the agents of change? Has this house been good for your head? Was it difficult to relearn the art of waking not alone? What is the taste of the underside of your tongue? Does this disprove the null hypothesis? Will the tomatoes survive the rain? What is the life of the mechanic who walks alone on the runway of the fog-shrouded field? Is it that your socks keep slipping? Is that flat, dull white disc the sun? What do they catch in these waters? What is the wrong way? Why is the earth redorange? Is it a question of which questions? Does it require the ingestion of Peyotl? Does my hand shake? How do I recognize my palm? Is it as I see it or is the image mere approximation? How is it that I admit to the possibility of mass noun, category? Why as a child did I choose to tell my brother tales intended to fill him with terror, lying in the dark of our room, his sobs, my narrative? Who would live in the trailer park? Did you get off? Did it happen? Is today safe? Is that the rock quarry? In spite of its gradual windings, do you conceptualize this road as straight, altering the map in your head to conform? Is this the confusion space? Is this the dream? Is this the higher level, the new plane? How do we get out of here? Are those ants? Are you sweating? Is it dark? Did the sirens wake you? Did you emerge from the house, dressed only in cutoffs, into the fog filled with big trucks and the pulsing red lights? Could you see the hatchets chop into the walls? Who were the men in black raincoats? Were those your neighbors' faces in their windows? When is you I? Is it fiction? Is it friction? What is my capacity? Did I mean limit or function? Does it feel more equal, casual, affectionate, to do it on our sides? What is more solitary than a jogger in the fog? What are the berries like? Could you sleep in a net? If you could construct an image of the world, how would you know it? What did I forget to ask? Do not avoid them? Would he

choose to be flat, prosy, slow? Would he bring up the issue of gravel pits? Is he the most fearful man you know? Are our lives merely sequences of constant description? Are you loyal to a form? Do you conceive of secretaries scuttling in the morning fog? What if your kidneys go? Are you cruisin' for a bruisin'? Who thought up corrugated corkboard? What is the perceived need for secrets? Why must they be told?

SLEEP CITY SQUEEGEE

Words have the same
consistency as images
in all their instars

as if sentimental chameleons
lavished thicker sunlight
once the horizon disappears

and powder of sympathy
navigates the real world
made of real words

champagne and salted almonds
over and over again
in a hail of bullets

Nobody knows
what kind of trope is
has your name on it

but glance on a great stir
This then was now
We can screenscrape it in

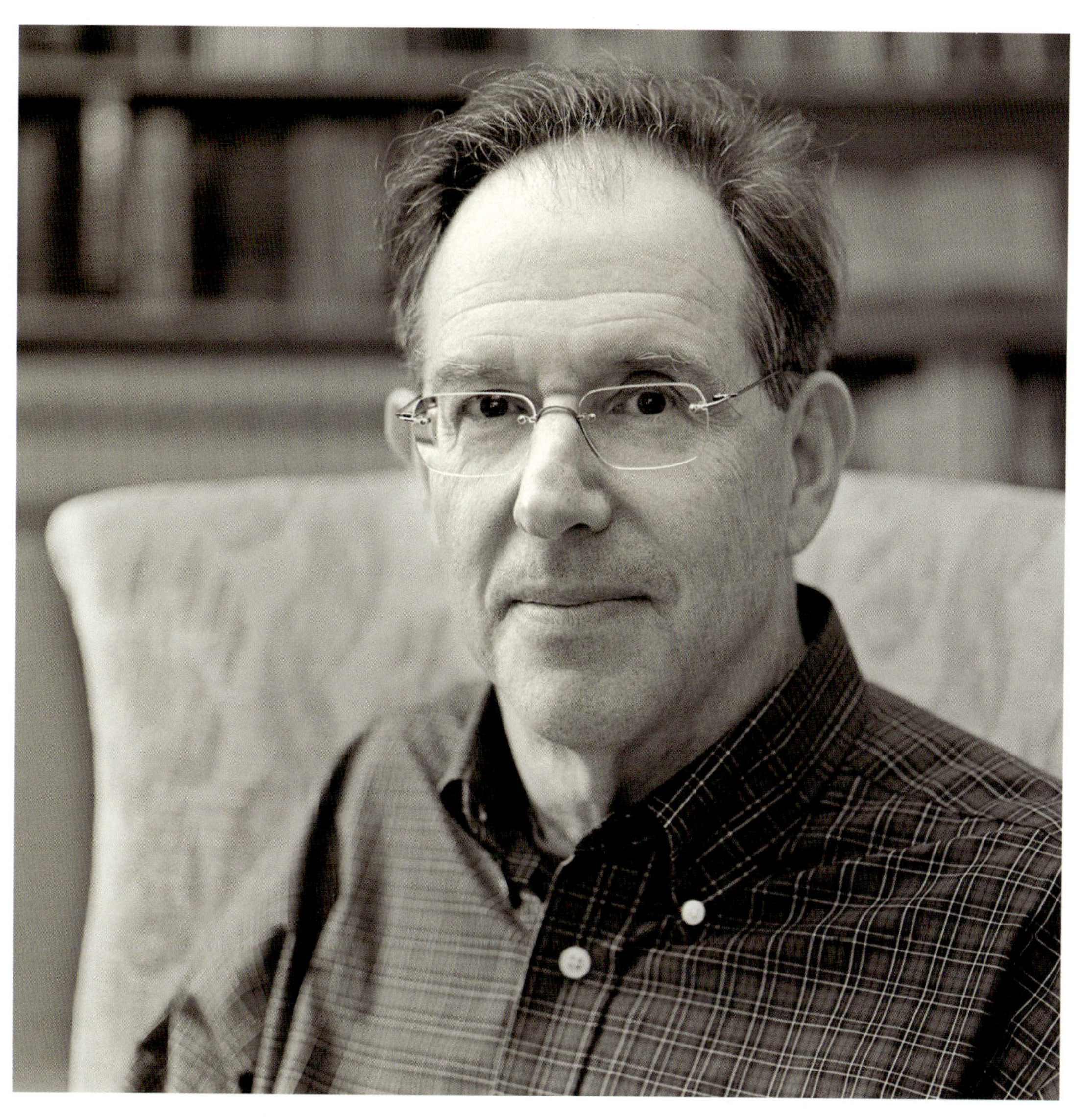

ALAN BERNHEIMER

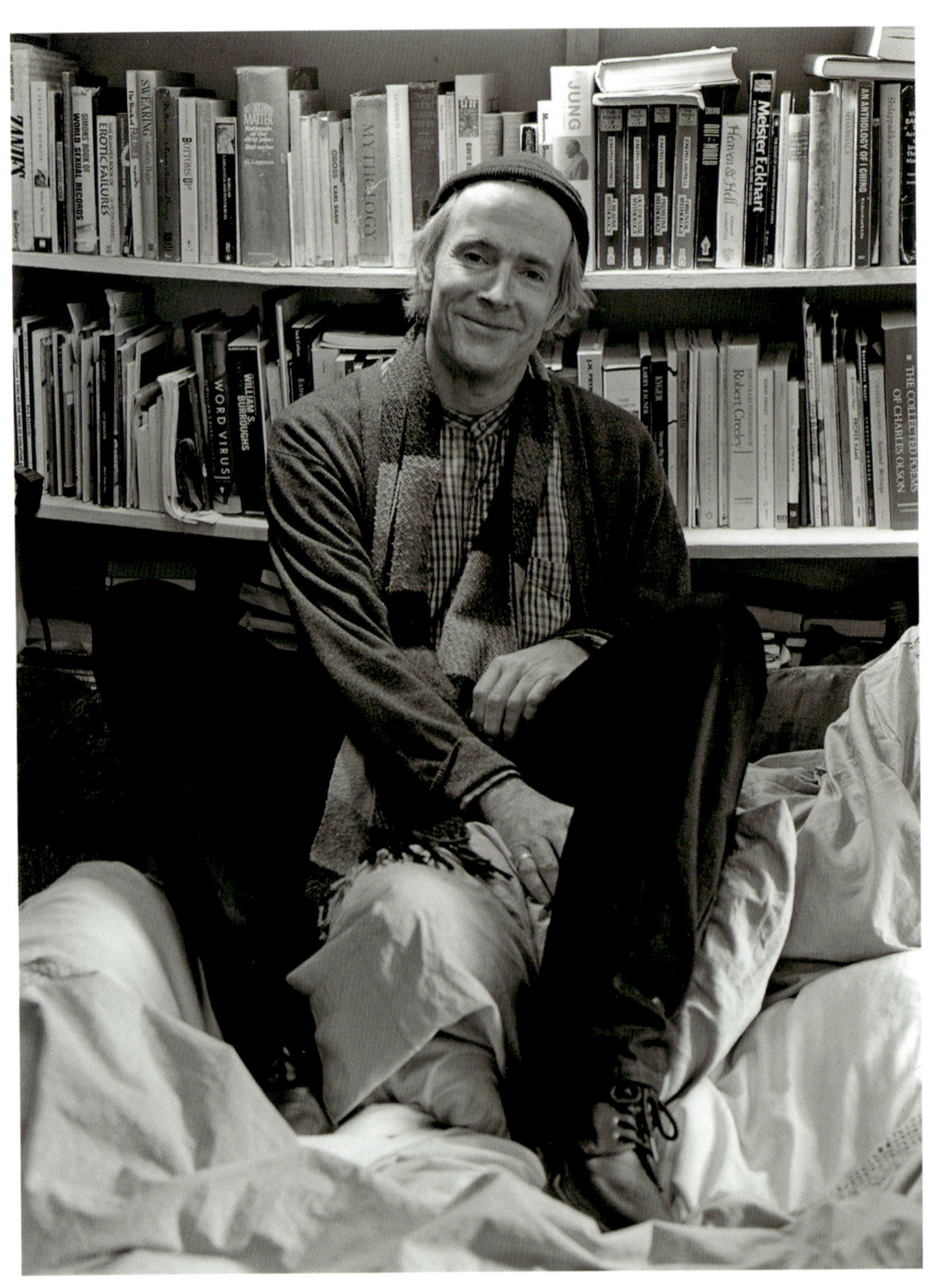

SIMON PETTET

BLUE ROOM

Blue being the color that best expresses
The mood. He is far-away fixed notice
The map and the furnishing. I wouldn't
Sit on that chair (if I were you) and also
Missed so much she appears to be
Pregnant or a little bit hungry for
Something it has to be food if it isn't
Him (which it is). Is he gone for good? A sea-
Fayring man? She doesn't say though
Appears to be trusting
The beautiful ambiguous face of another person's news.

from BABY

And. An Interval with Teenagers.
Baby knew that someday she would be a child and then a teenager and then an adult and that child, teenager, and adult would never be able to live without her. She would always be part of them. And each one now also had a baby in him or her. Babies lived longer than anybody, for any time a child could no longer bear the burden of childhood, she or he could regress to that prior condition called babyhood. Baby also knew, because she spent a lot of time with adults, more time than did children or teenagers, that regression was a word that gave babies a bad rap. Her strategy however was to use the word in a positive light rather than to be offended by it. Baby was always hard to offend unless someone took something away from her. The kind of being least likely to take anything away from her was a teenager. Unlike children, teenagers knew better than to imitate adults. They were quite specifically rational creatures. Teenagers watched, listened, waited, were subtle and not quick to judge. They also minded their own business and rather optimistically expected the rest of the world to reciprocate. Few people, other than teenagers themselves, were ever capable of such reciprocity. Even baby, whose vast admiration for the teenager as a species was nearly infinite, could not help but riddle the teenager, upon occasion, with a barrage of laughter or stand on or in the teenager's shoes if the teenager wasn't wearing them. It was difficult to stand in both of them at one time and her effort to stay upright in each shoe only served to increase baby's admiration for the teenager. The teenager seemed to tolerate baby's antics, was sometimes even delighted by them. The teenager's delight surprised baby. This gave baby pause. Surprise is *my* job thought baby. But baby was in love and didn't complain when the teenager took the surprise away from her. In fact, this is how baby learned that there was an endless supply of surprise to go around and, that in this knowledge, she was more like a teenager than either a child or adult. One day it occurred to her that the teenager was also like *her.* On this day, baby swelled with pride. No one knew why baby had had such a good day, why she had babbled to herself, why she had not socked at and chewed dust mites and pieces of thread lodged in the rug or tried to nurse the pink balloon lost under a bed for about six hours. Or pulled all of the utensils off the table while tugging at the tablecloth. She was peaceful, quiet and perfect for an entire day. Baby knew that when children threw tantrums and acted grabby they were 'behaving like babies.' Adults acted like children acting like babies quite frequently themselves. For children, when they whined and argued, used the strategies they had learned from adults. The impassioned use of logic, argumentation, and judgement were all signs that they were about to cry, shriek, rail, and sulk. Their beloved rationality was the beveled awning of a madhouse. All of them had a baby part hidden inside of them ready to wreak havoc on home and country. But the teenager, in all his and her

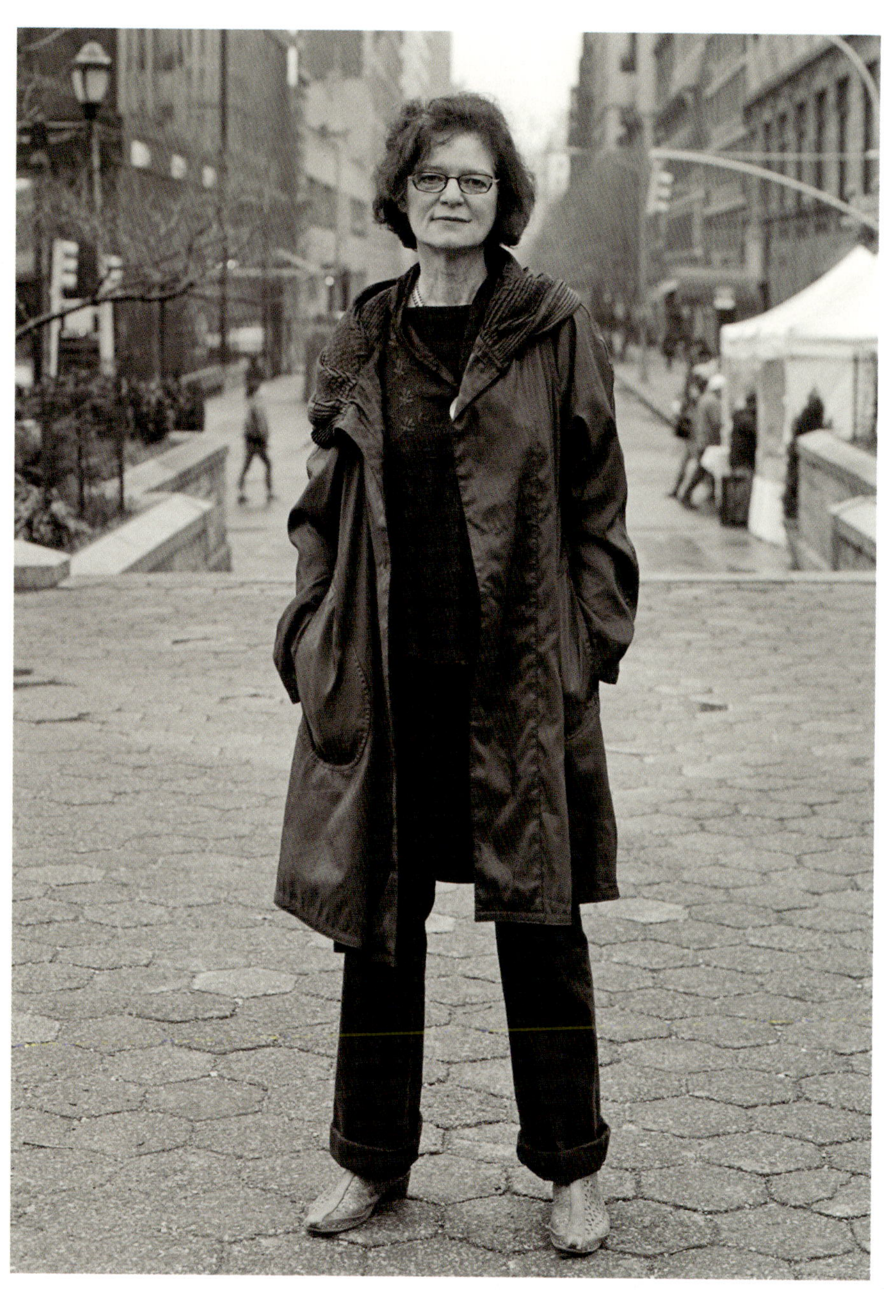

CARLA HARRYMAN

wisdom, emulated only those qualities in baby others considered charming. Teenagers surely used their sang-froid as a kind of magic, to keep the infantile child and adult world out of their hair. It was baby whom teenagers permitted to play in that hair. Baby therefore knew that teenagers were the best, most mature creatures on earth. Adults were often irked by the teenager's silence, and sometimes called it sullen. But baby knew the silence was a product of unaffected poise. Teenagers were sage beyond their years because they loved to surprise and to be surprised, but to surprise anybody in this vexed and over-anxious world of consumer culture and professional parenting, one had to act as if one were in a steady state or holding pattern most of the time. Maintaining this mask in the face of everybody and everything else required great powers. Teenagers ought to be put in greater positions of responsibility claimed baby and to be given the vote by thirteen, or fourteen at the very latest.

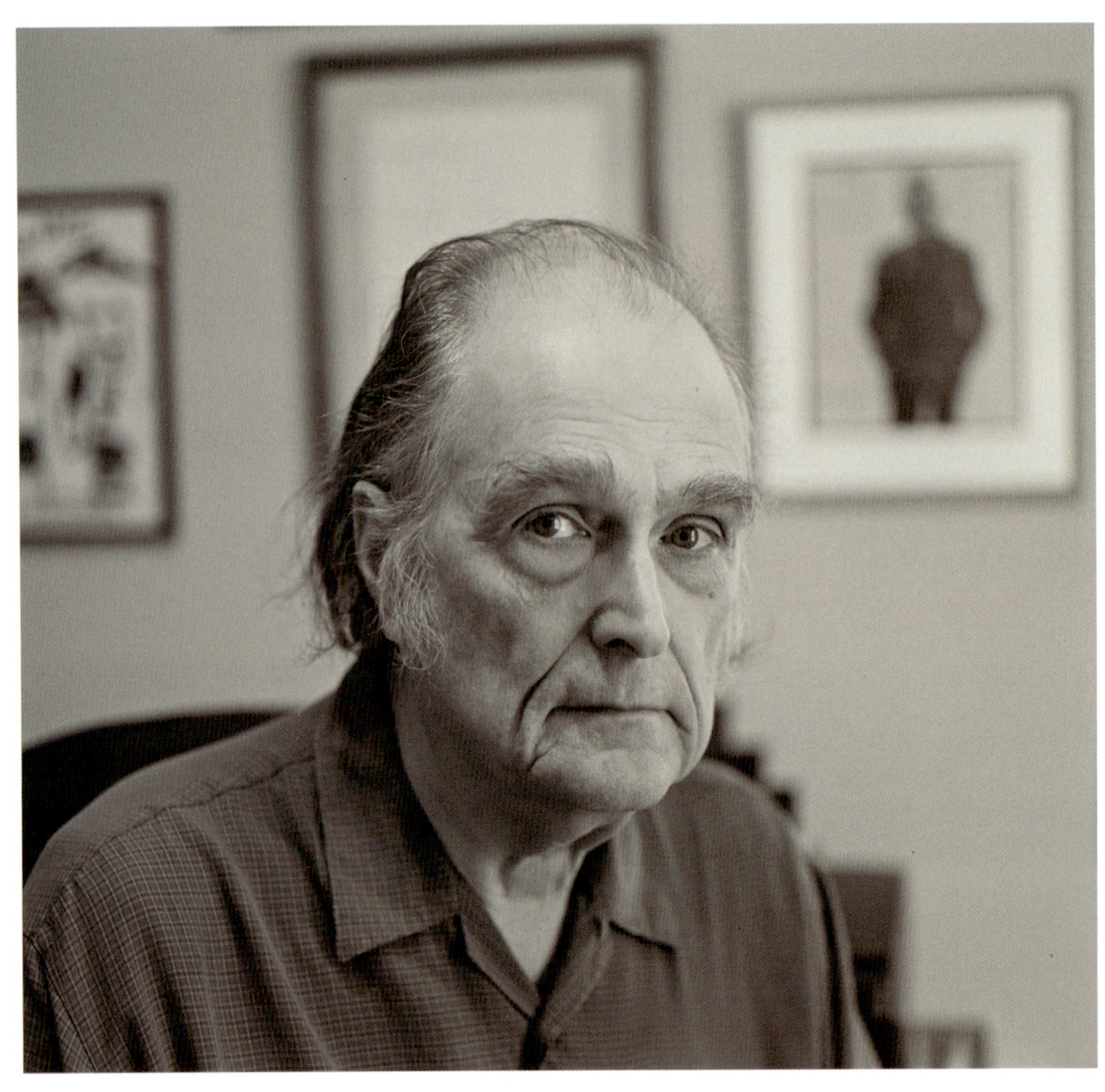

CLARK COOLIDGE

SPEECH TO A MIRROR

See me say you in halts struck of my background.
There will be no lightning or chordal spar in this
polar a prison. We peer from the windows of caliber trains
breathlessly parallel at lock speed. I to you,
you to perhaps. Rattles in the press of breath freight
I give you a noun, you show me doubles of a shade I bear.
Beyond late where you are, beyond sign and straight and
the loops of tell. I tell you the spin you are
of me I tell. That you are half me
that half never told. My portrait of waiting.
The latest night is nothing to me.
I face myself like a hawk in the shield.
The half of it, I can tell you, the matter
with presence. I praise you a tongue,
you raise the icicle sign. Skeleton canters
askew, the crystal locking its jaws. What
do you see in the nothing, window that you are?
What sorts of night in blind reflection?
On eyes, on suns, on stars in the eyes of mere.
To live with your sign of me always the dare.
Come from me, come from me far.

IMAGINATION

Poppies prepare buckets
up to be astonished
balancing the way
anyone thinking fills
dewdrops with slow
honey lets bees fly
from silver bullets
hitching the humming-
bird up first as a mistake
then series
of little images and I
remember well
suspenders set
for a spell on a hill
powder flash in a
pan of techniques where
it isn't dull to sit still
perched to curl
operative to a fault in
the forever face
of whatever form
a flower takes
resolvable
in its own premonition

Real drops rain
(momentary states)
irritate local grubs
elementary children
redound hamfisted
to kids redundant (extremes
while they last) abounding
with longing to lounge
only later occurring
as a roar indelibly fine

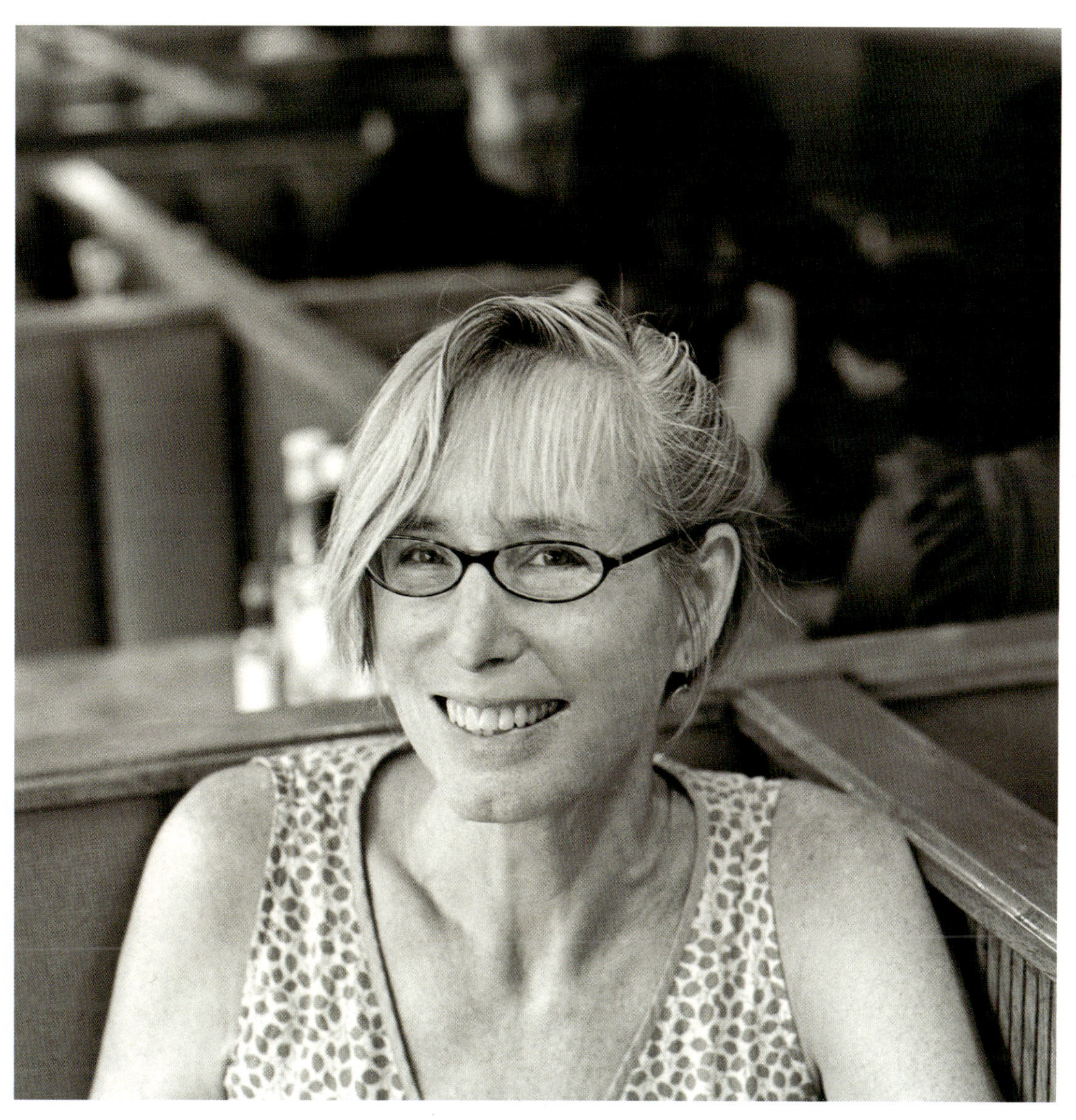

JEAN DAY

living the line
from me to whoever's
democratic future's
dead to the world
receding on the waves
of some high-speed
fiber-optic flap to the capital
almost purely alphabetical
as the strobe effect
ties a neighbor
moving behind a board
fence to a mechanical
diary keeping track
of the species—
One calls and I
hustle

Nothing is finer than
facts last night
of a front blows first
of a season instantly fragrant
the unimpeachable debris
of extraordinary acts
disrupts ordinarily re-
fractable solos exactly
above and to the side
as stylus to overture
a tone before
the world divides
into subjects and heads
nodding with sun the sum
of particles and waves
falsely at angles of ease
individuals and their images
sciences and their parents

those geniuses whose fractions
propagate sheer crush
like us para-
plenipotentiaries
milk flat on a stone fills
and the flat fear is
it will fall

Late I awoke
perched with a hitch
in my gitalong home
on the waves
of granular robustness
lay awake reckless
left and right tethered
to a pinpoint replica
honey at rest
the day remains
how hot it will get
predictive an itching
disrupts smooth
solos on a field
continuing on
unseen from the road
to an urgent antipodean
imaginary leaning bravely
ungainly on ladders
to an individual boy
with a real request

JEAN
DAY

Forced down bravely steeped
in images composed
in motions I check the
time fix lunch
board a bandwagon in the teeth
of the onrush of a rescueless opposite
in the continuous arising of a tree
next to a box emblematically
boulders along
breathing leaning long
like any self-contained narrator
life can never be lived
executive
on the other side of the mountain
signal to noise
nose to stone
ear to there
at once the report
here and clear and close.

CONTRIBUTORS

Kostas Anagnopoulos is the founder and editor of the small press Insurance Editions. He has published four chapbooks, and his first full-length book, *Moving Blanket*, was published in 2010.

Bruce Andrews is one of the best known Language poets and edited, with Charles Bernstein, *L=A=N=G=U=A=G=E* Magazine from 1978 to 1981. Andrews is the author of several dozen books and chapbooks of poetry, most recently *You Can't Have Everything...Where Would You Put It!* and *Yessified*. Recently retired after 38 years as a professor of political science, he has been for several decades the music director for Sally Silvers, his long term partner and collaborator.

Rae Armantrout received the 2010 Pulitzer Prize for Poetry for *Versed* and the 2009 National Book Critics Circle Award for the same book. She was awarded a Guggenheim Fellowship in 2008. In addition to appearances in many anthologies, Armantrout has published more than a dozen books, including *Money Shot* in 2011 and *Just Saying* in 2013, both from Wesleyan University Press. She is generally associated with the Language poets. Rae Armantrout is Professor of Poetry and Poetics at the University of California, San Diego.

Bill Berkson is a poet and critic who divides his time between San Francisco and New York. He is professor emeritus at the San Francisco Art Institute, where he taught art history and literature for 24 years. Among his many books of poetry are *Portrait and Dream: New & Selected Poems*, *BILL*, a words-and-images collaboration with Colter Jacobsen, *Snippets*, and, most recently, *Expect Delays*. He was the 2006 Distinguished Mellon Fellow at the Skowhegan School of Painting and Sculpture and received the 2008 Goldie for Literature from the San Francisco *Bay Guardian*.

Alan Bernheimer has lived in the San Francisco Bay Area since 1977, where he associated with the West Coast group of Language poets, after earlier activity at the Poetry Project in New York City. He received a fellowship from the National Endowment for the Arts and produced a radio program of new writing by poets, *In the American Tree*. His latest book, *The Spoonlight Institute*, was published by Adventures in Poetry in 2009.

Charles Bernstein is the Donald T. Regan Professor of English at the University of Pennsylvania, where he co-founded the poetry audio archive *PennSound*. While at the University of Buffalo, he co-founded the *Electronic Poetry Center*. With Bruce Andrews, he edited the journal *L=A=N=G=U=A=G=E*, considered one of the most important outlets for the Language poets. Bernstein is author of eighteen books of poetry, including *All the Whiskey in Heaven*, published in 2010 and his latest, *Recalculating* (2013). He has received fellowships from the National Endowment for the Arts, the New York Foundation for the Arts and the Guggenheim Foundation.

Anselm Berrigan is the author of seven books of poetry, including *Loading* (2013, with artist John Allen), *Skasers* (2012, with poet John Coletti), *Notes from Irrelevance* (2011), and *Free Cell* (2009). He is Co-Chair, Writing in the Milton Avery Graduate School of the Arts, poetry editor for *The Brooklyn Rail,* and a former artistic director of The Poetry Project at St. Mark's Church. With Alice Notley and Edmund Berrigan, he co-edited *The Collected Poems of Ted Berrigan* (2005) and *Selected Poems of Ted Berrigan* (2011).

Edmund Berrigan is the author of two books of poetry, *Disarming Matter* (Owl Press, 1999) and *Glad Stone Children* (Farfalla, 2008), and a memoir, *Can It!* (Letter Machine Editions, 2013). He is editor of the *Selected Poems of Steve Carey* (Sub Press, 2009), and co-editor with Anselm Berrigan and Alice Notley of *The Collected Poems of Ted Berrigan* (2005) and *Selected Poems of Ted Berrigan* (2011). He is an editor for poetry magazines *Vlak* and *Brawling Pigeon,* and on the editorial board of *Lungfull!* and works as a medical copy editor.

Michael Brownstein is the author of nine books of poetry, two collections of stories (*Brainstorms* and *Music from the Evening of the World*) and three novels (*Country Cousins, The Touch* and *Self-Reliance).* He has read widely from *World on Fire,* a book-length poem about corporate globalization and consciousness change. His poetry and prose have appeared in *The New Yorker, Paris Review,* and *Resurgence,* as well as online in *Reality Sandwich* and *Arthur.* He has taught writing and literature at the University of Colorado, Naropa Institute and Columbia University and has a long-standing shamanic practice. A recent poem is *Let's Burn the Flag of All Nations.*

Reed Bye is a poet and songwriter, and teaches in the Jack Kerouac School of Disembodied Poetics at Naropa University. His most recent books include *Catching On* (Monkey Puzzle, 2013) and *Join the Planets: New and Selected Poems* (United Artists Books, 2005). A CD of original songs, *Broke Even* (Fast Speaking Music) was released in 2013. His work has appeared in a number of anthologies including *Nice to See You: Homage to Ted Berrigan, Sleeping on the Wing,* and *Civil Disobediences: Poetics and Politics in Action.*

Miles Champion's books of poetry include *Compositional Bonbons Placate, Three Bell Zero* and *How to Laugh.* His book-length illustrated interview with Trevor Winkfield was published as *How I Became a Painter* in 2014, and his selection of Tom Raworth's writing will be published by Carcanet in 2015. Born in Nottingham, England in 1968, Champion has lived in New York City since 2002.

Tom Clark has published many books of poetry, most recently *Truth Games* (BlazeVOX, 2013). He was poetry editor of *The Paris Review* from 1963 to 1973; his literary essays and reviews have also appeared in *The New York Times, The Los Angeles Times,* the *San Francisco Chronicle, London*

Mary Ferrari's poetry has appeared in *The World, Adventures in Poetry, Angel Hair, Broadway 1* and *Broadway 2, Hanging Loose, Telephone* and *New York Quarterly,* as well as the South African magazines *The New Nation* and *Staffrider.* She has published several books of poetry including *The Isle of the Little God: Poems, 1964-1980* and *Why the Sun Cannot Set: New and Selected Poems, 1994,* about which Nadine Gordimer said, 'Mary Ferrari's Poetry has the unexpectedness of life.' She has taught at Iona College, the College of New Rochelle, and the Poetry Project at St. Mark's Church. Ferrari was awarded the Dylan Thomas Memorial Award for Poetry by The New School.

Michael Friedman studied literature at Columbia and Yale, then went to law school at Duke. His first novel, *Martian Dawn,* joined six published collections of poetry, including *Species,* a collection of prose poems. A new collection of his fiction will be published in 2015. Friedman is represented in several anthologies, including *Great American Prose Poems: From Poe to Present* (2003). From 1986 to 2008 he edited the influential literary magazine *SHINY.* He has taught in the writing program at Naropa University and practices law in Denver.

Dick Gallup, with friends Ron Padgett and Joe Brainard, started a literary magazine called *The White Dove Review* while in high school in Tulsa, Oklahoma. In its five issues, they published Allen Ginsberg, Jack Kerouac, Robert Creeley, Amiri Baraka and Ted Berrigan. His latest book is *Shiny Pencils at the Edge of Things.* Gallup has taught at the St. Mark's Poetry Project, Boulder Public Library and Naropa University. He lives in San Francisco.

Merrill Gilfillan was born in Ohio in 1945. He studied at the University of Michigan and with Anselm Hollo and Ted Berrigan at the Iowa Writers' Workshop and soon published *Truck,* his first of 14 books of poetry. He has authored two collections of short fiction and several books of essays exploring various regions of the United States. His first such effort, *Magpie Rising: Sketches from the Grean Plains,* was awarded the PEN Martha Albrand Award for First Nonfiction in 1989. A new book of essays, *The Warbler Road,* and a poetry collection, *The Bark of the Dog,* were published in 2010.

Michael Gizzi has been writing poetry since he was eleven years old. He worked as a tree surgeon in New England for seven years before turning to teaching, eventually at Roger Williams College and his alma mater, Brown University. He was the author of more than 10 books of poetry, the last of which was *New Depths of Deadpan* (2009), as well as an editor for *Hard Press, Lingo* magazine and *Qua* books. Gizzi received the Foundation for Contemporary Arts poetry grant for 2010, Gertrude Stein Awards for Innovative Writing in 2007 and 1996, and a Fund for Poetry grant in 1995. He died in 2010.

John Godfrey has been writing poems since 1963. *City of Corners* (2008) and *Tiny Gold Dress* (2011) are the most recent of many books. His work has also appeared in *The Paris Review, The*

Harris Review, The World, Adventures in Poetry and many other periodicals. Godfrey was the 1984 Poetry Fellow of the General Electric Foundation, received Fund for Poetry awards in 1986 and 1989, and was the 2009 poetry grant recipient of the Foundation for Contemporary Arts. More recently, he received a grant from the Z Foundation in 2013. He worked as a nurse clinician in infectious disease at Kings County Hospital in Brooklyn until his recent retirement and return to full time writing.

Sylvia Mae Gorelick graduated from Bard College in 2013, completing a senior thesis entitled *Songs of the Last Philosopher: Early Nietzsche and the Spirit of Hölderlin.* She is currently pursuing a master's degree in philosophy at Paris X, Nanterre, where she is continuing her research on Nietzsche. Her chapbooks include *Seven Poems for Bill Berkson, The Spider's Passage, Two-Suitor 3* with Tamas Panitz and *Olympians, we are breathless.* Her poems have been published in a variety of journals, including *The Brooklyn Rail, Gerry Mulligan, Kunstverein NY,* and *Other Times.* She is currently translating Paolo D'Iorio's *Le Voyage de Nietzsche à Sorrente,* to be published by the University of Chicago Press in 2015.

Ted Greenwald's official biography reads, 'Born 1942. Is from New York forever.' During that time, he has published 30 books, curated poetry readings around the city, coedited *Ear* magazine, and taught workshops and served on the board of directors of the St. Mark's Poetry Project. His important early work includes *Common Sense* (1978), *The Licorice Chronicles* (1979), *You Bet!* (1978) and *Word of Mouth* (1986). More recently, *In Your Dreams* (2008), *3* (2008), *Two Wrongs* (with painter Hal Saulson, 2007), *The Up and Up* (2004), *Clearview/LIE* (2010) and *A Mammal of Style* (with Kit Robinson, 2013) have attracted critical attention.

Carla Harryman is a poet, essayist, and playwright often associated with the Language poets. She is the author of sixteen books and many poems, performance works, and collaborations with artists working in other genres. Her recent books include *W—/M—* (2013), *Adorno's Noise* (2008), and *Open Box* (2007). She also collaborated with the Jon Raskin Quartet on a CD using her texts as scores for musical interpretation and voice. Harryman was a contributor to the multi-authored autobiographic project *The Grand Piano,* which focused on the emergence of language writing, art, politics and culture in the San Francisco Bay Area between 1975-1980. Her numerous awards include grants from the Foundation for Contemporary Arts, Opera America, the American Embassy in Romania and the Fund for Poetry. She serves on the faculty of Eastern Michigan University.

David Henderson was a founder of the Black Arts Movement in the 1960s, and served as an editor of a magazine out of the Umbra Workshop. *Umbra* featured poems by Julian Bond and Alice Walker in its first issue. Henderson went on to edit three *Umbra* anthologies. *Felix of the Silent Forest, De Mayor of Harlem,* and *Neo-California* are among his best known books. Many of his

Review of Books and many journals. Clark has published biographies of many twentieth century literary figures, including Ted Berrigan, Robert Creeley, Edward Dorn, Jack Kerouac and Charles Olson. He publishes an almost-daily blog of poetry, art, photography and opinion, *Beyond the Pale.*

Jack Collom is a poet, teacher and essayist whose twenty-three books include *Blue Heron and IBC, The Fox, Arguing with Something Plato Said, Red Car Goes By, Exchanges of Earth and Sky, Situation Sings* (with Lyn Hejinian), and his latest, *Second Nature* (2012). He has taught children creative writing for thirty-five years, and adults at Naropa University's Jack Kerouac School of Disembodied Poetics, where he pioneered the creation of ecology literature courses.

Clark Coolidge's latest of more than 40 publications, *88 Sonnets* and *A Book Beginning What and Ending Away* were published in 2012. Other recent books, both released in 2010, are *The Act of Providence,* a long poem about his hometown, and *This Time We Are Both,* the result of a trip to the USSR with the Rova Saxophone Quartet in 1989. The University of California Press has recently published a collection of the writing, lectures, and conversations of painter Philip Guston, edited by Coolidge, who was his close friend. Coolidge is considered to be one of the original Language poets.

Jayne Cortez was the author of ten books of poetry and nine recordings of her poems with music by her band, *The Firespitters.* She was one of the founders of the Black Arts movement in Los Angeles and founded the Watts Repertory Company. Her most recent book, *On the Imperial Highway,* was published by Hanging Loose Press in 2008; CDs with *The Firespitters* include *Taking the Blues Back Home, Borders of Disorderly Time, and Find Your Own Voice.* Cortez received the Langston Hughes Award and the American Book Award, and awards from Arts International and the National Endowment for the Arts. She died in 2012.

Jean Day has published many books of poetry; the recent *Enthusiasm* was described by Ron Silliman as '...one of those knock-down take-the-top-of-your-head-off experiences....' The newest, *Early Bird* (O'Clock Books) was released in 2014. New poems have also recently been published in *The Cambridge Literary Review, The Claudius App, Dreamboat, Sal Mimeo,* and *Try.* Her work has appeared in a number of anthologies, including *The Best American Poetry 2004* and *Moving Borders: Three Decades of Innovative Writing by Women* (1998). She has received awards from the Fund for Poetry, the National Endowment for the Arts, and the California Arts Council.

Diane di Prima is widely recognized as the most important woman poet of the Beat movement. While living in Manhattan for many years, she co-founded the New York Poets Theatre, founded the Poets Press, and with Amiri Baraka edited the literary newsletter *The Floating Bear.* She is the author of over 40 books of poetry and prose, *Memoirs of a Beatnik,* a fictionalized account of her experiences with the Beats, and *Recollections of My Life as a Woman,* a factual autobiography. She was named Poet Laureate of San Francisco in 2009.

Casey Drouin's first chapbook, *Pile Up,* was published by Green Zone in 2011. He was born and raised in northeastern Massachusetts, but emigrated to New York City where he now writes, works, and volunteers at the Catholic Worker shelters.

Marcella Durand is the author of several books, including *Traffic and Weather, AREA, The Anatomy of Oil, Western Capital Rhapsodies, Lapsus Linguae, City of Ports* and *Deep Eco Pre,* in collaboration with Tina Darragh. Durand speaks often on the intersection between ecology and poetry, and is a published essayist on the subject. Support she has received includes a residency at the Lower Manhattan Cultural Council and fellowships from the New York Foundation for the Arts, the Center for Programs in Contemporary Writing at the University of Pennsylvania and the Black Earth Institute. Durand lives in New York City with her husband and son, and has recently completed a new collection titled *The Prospect* and is working on a book-length alexandrine titled *In This World of 12 Months.*

Kenward Elmslie began his career collaborating with composers on operas and musicals and continued to work with musicians and visual artists for many years. He is often associated with the New York School of poetry, and established *Z* magazine and *Z* Press to promote the work of New York School colleagues such as John Ashbery, Ron Padgett, James Schuyler, and the painter Joe Brainard. Elmslie's collection *Motor Disturbance* won the Frank O'Hara Award for Poetry in 1971; he also received a National Endowment for the Arts award for *Power Plant Sestina* and a Ford Foundation grant.

Robert Elstein started writing poems at the age of five and went on to produce many small, limited release publications throughout his childhood and adolescence. Most recently he has focused on being a father and writing three chapbooks, *The Hollandaise* (2006), *Settling the Disputed Point* (2008) and *Helen Arms* (2013).

Larry Fagin's latest book, *Complete Fragments,* was published in 2012 and immediately became a small press bestseller. He was co-director of the St. Mark's Poetry Project from 1971-1976, and founded Danspace, the dance program, at St. Mark's in 1975, staying on to run it until 1980. Fagin taught at the Jack Kerouac School of Disembodied Poetics from 1982-1984, and at The New School for many years. In addition to authoring a number of volumes of his own poetry, Fagin has edited or published many of America's best known poets, and helped countless of lesser knowns publish their first book. His small press, Adventures in Poetry, has been among the most highly regarded for many years.

published by Don Allen's Four Seasons Press. Since then over 30 books of her poetry have been published. She was the winner of the National Poetry Series in 1983 for *Going On*. *About Now: Collected Poems* won the 2008 PEN Oakland Josephine Miles National Award for Poetry. Kyger has taught at the New College of San Francisco and Naropa University where she is a part of the Summer Writing Program.

STEVE MALMUDE has published four books, of which *The Bundle* (2002) is the latest. His work has also been included in *Sal Mimeo, The Best American Poetry 2002, The Hat, Lingo, O-blek, Utter, The Sun, The 12th Street Rag, The World* and *Adventures in Poetry*. Malmude worked for many years as a carpenter for the City of New York, where he also wrote a great deal of poetry. He is now retired from both carpentry and New York City but still writes poetry, now in rural Maine.

BERNADETTE MAYER was described by *The Washington Post* as 'one of the most original writers of her generation.' *The Helens of Troy, NY* (2013) and *Poetry State Forest*, published in 2008 are the latest of more than 20 books of poetry. She edited, with conceptual artist Vito Acconti, the experimental journal *0 TO 9*, and with Lewis Warsh, United Artists Press which published a number of important volumes of poetry, including Ted Berrigan's *Sonnets* and Mayer's *Utopia*. During much of the 1980s she was director of the Poetry Project at St. Mark's Church in New York.

GILLIAN MCCAIN is the co-author of *Please Kill Me: The Uncensored Oral History of Punk* and the co-editor of *Dear Nobody: The True Diary of Mary Rose* (both with Legs McNeil). She has also published two books of poetry and her work has appeared in many periodicals, including *Vanity Fair, Grand Street* and *Shiny*. McCain has been program coordinator and newsletter editor for the Poetry Project at St. Mark's Church in New York, and serves on its board of directors.

MICHAEL MCCLURE gave his first reading as one of the five poets at the San Francisco Six Gallery reading in 1955 where Allen Ginsberg introduced *Howl*. McClure is featured as 'Pat McLear' in Jack Kerouac's novel *Big Sur*. He was a close friend of *The Doors* lead singer Jim Morrison, and performed widely with Doors keyboardist Ray Manzarek. His play *The Beard* triggered anti-obscenity actions, and won Obie Awards in New York. He is the author of 23 books of poetry, two novels and several books of essays, and received a Guggenheim Fellowship and a Rockefeller grant in addition to three Obies. His recent selected poems *Of Indigo and Saffron* is published by the University of California Press.

ELIZABETH MCDANIEL's poems have appeared in *Maggy, Gerry Mulligan, Sal Mimeo* and a chapbook published by Green Zone Editions, *Partial View*. She recently received an MFA in Poetry from The New School.

DUNCAN MCNAUGHTON says he has written a dozen or so books of poetry since 1972. Most recently he published *Bounce* (2006), *Altoon's Frog* (2009) and *Tiny Windows* (2014). McNaughton edited the magazines *MOTHER* (with Lewis MacAdams) and *FATHAR* and was publisher of Blue Millennium Press. He translated Dario Villa's *Venus Strapazzata Dai Lunatici / Venus Ill-treated By The Odd Ones* (2001) and has translated other works to Italian, German, French, Argentinian and Bosnian. He started and ran, with many prominent West Coast poets, the New College of California poetics program in the 1980s. McNaughton lived briefly in Syria and on Cyprus and now divides his time between San Francisco and Bolinas California.

David Meltzer is one of the key poets of the Beat generation as well as a jazz guitarist and prose writer. Meltzer's latest of more than 50 books are *David's Copy: The Selected Poems of David Meltzer,* published in 2005, and *When I Was a Poet* (2011). In addition to the guitar, he plays mandolin, harmonica and blues piano. Two albums, *Serpent Power* and *Poet Song,* were released by Vanguard Records in the 1960s. He was a core faculty member in the poetics program at the now-defunct New College of California.

Jennifer Moxley is the author of five books of poetry, most recently *Clampdown* (Flood, 2009), a book of essays and a memoir and has translated three books from the French. In 2005 she was granted the Lynda Hull Poetry Award from *Denver Quarterly.* Her poem *Behind the Orbits* was included by Robert Creeley in *The Best American Poetry 2002.* She is Professor of Poetry and Poetics at the University of Maine.

Harryette Mullen's poetry collection, *Recyclopedia,* won a PEN Beyond Margins Award in 2007. *Sleeping with the Dictionary,* published in 2002, was a finalist for a National Book Award, National Book Critics Circle Award and the Los Angeles Times Book Prize. Mullen has received a fellowship from the John Simon Guggenheim Foundation and a grant from the Foundation for Contemporary Arts. She was the 2009 recipient of the Academy of American Poets Fellowship and winner of the 2010 Jackson Poetry Prize from *Poets & Writers.* Mullen is Professor of English at UCLA.

Susan Noel's first love and long term friend was onetime Kentucky poet laureate and photographer James Baker Hall, but she was already a writer when she met him and began posing for his black and white portraits. Noel has been published in many small magazines, including *The Massachusetts Review, Rocky Ledge, Bombay Gin,* and *The World.* She is the author of two books, *Bronze Age* (1980), and *Autobiography in Words* (1998).

Charles North's first book of poetry, *Lineups,* was self-published and then featured in two *New York Post* sports columns and reprinted in several anthologies. Nine more books of poems have followed, most recently *What It Is Like: New and Selected Poems,* which headed NPR's Best Poetry Books of 2011. With poet James Schuyler, he edited the poet/painter anthologies *Broadway* and poems feature jazz musicians such as Thelonious Monk and John Coltrane, and he has recorded with pianist Sun Ra and saxophonists Ornette Coleman and David Murray. His work has been widely published in periodicals, including *The New York Times, Paris Review, Black American Literature Forum, Black Scholar* and *Essence*. He is the author of *'Scuse Me While I Kiss the Sky*, a widely acclaimed biography of Jimi Hendrix.

EILEEN HENNESSY is a freelance translator and a poet and short story writer. She has published work most recently in *Stickman Review* (2013), *Crack the Spine* (2013 and 2014) and *Forge* (2014), and earlier in *Artful Dodge, Cream City Review, Sanskrit, The Literary Review, The Paris Review, Western Humanities Review, Prairie Schooner, The New York Quarterly* and *Smartish Place*. Her book collection, *This Country of Gale-force Winds*, was published in 2011.

ANSELM HOLLO was a Finnish-American poet who while living in London working as a broadcaster for the BBC World Service, befriended a number of American poets. He translated Allen Ginsberg into Finnish and became a prolific translator of poetry and prose into English from Finnish, German, Swedish and French. In addition to fellowships from the National Endowment for the Arts and the Poetry Foundation, Hollo received the Harold Morton Landon Translation Award, the Gertrude Stein Award in Innovative American Poetry, and the Government of Finland's Distinguished Foreign Translator Award. He taught at several universities including the Iowa Writers' Workshop and spent the last 25 years of his life teaching poetry and translation at the Jack Kerouac School of Naropa University in Boulder, Colorado, where he died in 2013. His last manuscript, *The Tortoise of History*, is forthcoming from Coffee House Press.

ERICA HUNT retired in 2010 as President of the Twenty-First Century Foundation, which addresses root causes of social injustice impacting the black community. She has published three books of poetry: *Arcade, Piece Logic*, and *Local History*. Hunt has also published essays on the intersection of poetry, race theory and feminist aesthetics. Her poems are included in *Moving Borders: Three Decades of Innovative Writing by Women, Iowa Poetry Review*, and the *Virago Anthology of Women's Love Poetry*. She was the 2001 poetry grant recipient of the Foundation for Contemporary Arts and received a 1993 award from the Fund for Poetry.

OMAR HUSAIN's first book, *Do Something*, was published in 2010. He grew up near Philadelphia and lives in Brooklyn. Husain has been a high school teacher and a proofreader and now studies physical therapy at SUNY Downstate Medical Center in New York.

LISA JARNOT's latest book is *Joie de Vivre: Selected Poems 1992-2012*, published in 2012. Her biography of San Francisco poet Robert Duncan was published in 2011. She is the author of four earlier collections of poetry, *Some Other Kind of Mission, Ring of Fire, Black Dog Songs*, and *Night Scenes*.

Allan Kaplan spends his time writing poetry, cooking, and watching old movies at his places in New York City and the Catskills. *Paper Airplane* and *Like One of Us* are two of his books, and he has also appeared in many periodicals, including *Paris Review, Poetry, Washington Square Review, Oyez, Apalachee Quarterly, Slant, Hubbub, Fine Madness, Wind, Gulf Stream,* and *Widener Review.* He is a retired teacher.

Simone Kearney is a poet and visual artist. Her artwork has been exhibited in New York, Boston and Ireland. In 2013, she was artist-in-residence at both the Josef Albers Foundation and the Ragdale Foundation. Her work has appeared in *Boston Review, Stonecutter, Bridge Journal, Belladonna Chaplet Series, Ragazine, Post Road Magazine, Maggy* and *Supermachine,* among others. Kearney's poetry chapbook *In Threes* was published in 2013. She was recipient of a 2010 Amy Award from *Poets & Writers.* She currently teaches at Pace University and Ramapo College, and writes for Thierry Goldberg Projects Gallery. Born in Dublin, she lives in Brooklyn.

Jennifer Kietzman's first book, *Neighbor Dirt,* was named a finalist in the 2002 Fence Modern Poets Series. She received a master's degree from Harvard Divinity School while working as a professional baker, then earned her MFA in poetry at the University of Michigan, where she taught composition and creative writing. Kietzman was the Olive B. O'Connor Fellow in Creative Writing at Colgate University for the 2003-2004 academic year. She currently works as a writer for a private detective agency while publishing new work in the poetry journals *Spinning Jenny* and *Gargoyle.*

Florence Kindel been both writing and painting since she was a child. She holds an MFA in painting and drawing from the School of Visual Arts in New York, and has taught college art. Her poetry has been published in *pax americana, Sal Mimeo, Pataphysics* and *Gerry Mulligan,* and her visual art has been shown in Soho and Chelsea galleries in New York. Kindel's chapbook *Dissolutions* was published in 2009.

Tuli Kupferberg founded *The Fugs* with Ed Sanders in 1964, taking the name from Norman Mailer's substitute for another word beginning with the same letter in *The Naked and the Dead,* and claimed the title of oldest living rock star. He started the magazine *Birth,* which lasted for only three issues but published important Beat writers like Allen Ginsberg, Diane di Prima, LeRoi Jones (later Amiri Baraka) and Ted Joans. He published the anti-Vietnam War satire *1001 Ways to Avoid the Draft* in 1966, and *1001 Ways to Avoid Working* the following year. Kupferberg later became a successful political cartoonist. He died in 2010.

Joanne Kyger lived in Kyoto, Japan with poet Gary Snyder from 1960-64. During this time she traveled to India with Snyder to join up with Allen Ginsberg and Peter Orlovsky, where they met the Dalai Lama. After her return to San Francisco her first book, *The Tapestry and the Web* was

Richard Roundy teaches English at Hunter College High School in New York. His work has been published in the professional *English Journal* and many literary periodicals, including *Shiny, Insurance, Sal Mimeo, Object, Open24hrs, The Washington Review, Mirage, Big Bridge* and *Situation.* His chapbook *The Other Kind of Vertigo* was published in 2005.

Ed Sanders wrote his first published book of poetry, *Poem from Jail,* on many feet of rolled-out toilet paper after being arrested during a peace demonstration. He started the satirical folk-rock band *The Fugs* with Tuli Kupferberg in 1964, and operated the famous Peace Eye Bookstore in a former kosher meat market in the East Village of New York. Sanders is the author of many volumes of poetry, including *Tales of Beatnik Glory, America, a History in Verse* (in nine volumes), *The Family* (a history of the Mansons) and *The Poetry and Life of Allen Ginsberg.* From 1995-2003 he and his wife Miriam published a literary-environmental newspaper, *The Woodstock Journal,* in Woodstock New York.

John Sarsgard's first solo exhibition, *Grand Central Portraits: People in a New Town Square,* was on view at the Municipal Art Society of New York in 2006. Juried group shows at the International Center of Photography, the Poetry Society of America, the Williamsburg Art and Historical Center and the Connecticut Audubon Society, among others, have included his work. Sarsgard's author photographs have appeared in a number of books of poetry. He is also a printer in the historic hand-coated platinum process.

David Shapiro published his first book at age thirteen and went on to write the first monograph on poet John Ashbery, the first book on Jim Dine's paintings, the first book on Piet Mondrian's flower studies, and the first book on Jasper Johns' drawings. Shapiro is a poet, literary critic, and art historian who has published some twenty volumes of poetry and literary and art criticism. Recent works include *New and Selected Poems (1965-2006),* published in 2007, and *Rabbit Duck,* with Richard Hell, in 2005. His honors include fellowships from the National Endowment for the Humanities and the National Endowment for the Arts and grants from the Fund for Poetry and the Foundation for Contemporary Arts. He is on the faculties of Cooper Union and William Paterson University.

Ron Silliman's anthology, *In the American Tree,* is a primary resource for readers interested in the Language poets, along with *The New Sentence,* a book of his talks and essays. He has written or edited over 30 books, and been translated into 12 languages. Silliman has been a Fellow of the National Endowment for the Arts, the Pennsylvania Arts Council and the Pew Foundation, and received the Levinson Prize from the Poetry Foundation in 2010. *Silliman's Blog* is a controversial weblog devoted to contemporary poetry. He worked as a market analyst in the computer industry before retiring to write and blog full time.

Aaron Simon studied poetry and philosophy in New York City from 2001 to 2010, with Larry Fagin and Paul Violi, among others. Simon's works have appeared in *Exquisite Corpse, Insurance, Sal Mimeo, SHINY, Pax Americana, Gerry Mulligan, 12th Street,* and *Hyperion – A Journal of the Arts.* He is the author of two books, *Carrier* (Insurance Editions, 2006), and *Periodical Days* (Green Zone, 2007). Simon says a third is on the way.

Ann Stephenson is the author of the chapbooks *Adventure Club* (Insurance Editions, 2013) and *Wirework* (Tent Editions, 2006). Her third, *Notes on the Interior,* was published by Green Zone in 2014. Her work has appeared in *The Brooklyn Rail, Coconut, Gerry Mulligan, The Recluse, Sal Mimeo* and *Shifter.* Stephenson formerly curated the *Ready Set Readings* series at Whitespace Gallery in Atlanta. She was born and raised in Georgia and lives in New York City.

Carol Szamatowicz is a poet and teacher. She is the author of *Blasting Through a Hole in the Universe - 78 Sonnets* (2009), *Le réchauffé* (2006), *Reticular Pop-Ups* (2004), *Zoop* (2001) and *Cats & Birds* (1998). Szamatowicz's works have appeared in *Insurance, The World, Calico Kids, Shiny, Sal Mimeo, The Hat* and *Fence.* She has taught young children for twenty years at City and Country School in New York, where she was photographed.

Stacy Szymaszek is the Director of the St. Mark's Poetry Project in New York City. In addition to other positions at the Poetry Project, she served as Literary Program Manager for the Woodland Pattern Book Center in her native Milwaukee. She is the author of ten chapbooks. Szymaszek's first full-length book, *Emptied of All Ships,* was published in 2005, and her second, *Hyperglossia,* in 2009, both with Litmus Press. Her third collection, *Hart Island,* will appear in 2015 from Nightboat Books.

Susie Timmons is the author of *Locked From the Outside,* winner of the first Ted Berrigan Award. *The New Old Paint* (2010) is her second collection of poetry; other books include *Locked from the Outside* and a chapbook, *Hog Wild.* She lives and writes in Brooklyn and teaches workshops from time to time at the Poetry Project at St. Mark's Church.

Tony Towle's first major collection, *North,* won the Frank O'Hara Award for 1970. He has published an additional 11 books of poetry, the latest of which are *Winter Journey* and *Memoir 1960-63.* His collaborations with artists Lee Bontecou and Jean Holabird can be found in the collections of the Metropolitan Museum of Art, the Museum of Modern Art, the New York Public Library, the Art Institute of Chicago, the Beinecke Library at Yale University and the Staatliche Museum in Berlin. He has been included in many anthologies, including *The Best American Poetry 2006.* Fellowships, prizes and awards include the National Endowment for the Arts, the New York State Council on the Arts and the Poetry Foundation.

Broadway 2, and with poet Paul Violi he ran Swollen Magpie Press from 1976-1982. North has received a Foundation for Contemporary Arts Grant, two fellowships from the National Endowment for the Arts, and four Fund for Poetry awards. He is Poet-in-Residence at Pace University in New York City.

Alice Notley's *Mysteries of Small Houses* was the winner of the 1998 Los Angeles Times Book Prize for Poetry, and *Grave of Light: New and Selected Poems 1970-2005* won the 2007 Lenore Marshall Poetry Prize of the Academy of American Poets. With Anselm Berrigan and Edmund Berrigan, she edited *The Collected Poems of Ted Berrigan* and *Selected Poems of Ted Berrigan.* Notley has published over 25 books of poetry, most recently *Culture of One* and *Songs and Stories of the Ghouls,* both released in 2011. Her long poem *In the Pines* was adapted and recorded by the Canadian indie group *AroarA.* She also received the Griffin International Poetry Prize for *Disobedience* (2001), an Academy Award from the American Academy of Arts and Letters, and the Shelley Memorial Award from the Poetry Society of America.

Ryan Nowlin's first book, *Banquet Settings,* was published in 2011 and his second, *Not Far from Here* in 2014. He earned graduate degrees in creative writing at Temple University and in library science at Rutgers and teaches English at a community college in Jersey City.

Peter Orlovsky was Beat poet Allen Ginsberg's companion and muse for almost 30 years. Ginsberg encouraged him to write, and Orlovsky's first effort, *Frist Poem,* was published in the literary review *Yugen* in 1958. His first book, *Dear Allen, Ship Will Land Jan 23, 58,* was an homage to Ginsberg. Four more books followed. Orlovsky appeared in a number of films, including *Couch,* made by Andy Warhol at The Factory, his New York studio. He taught poetry for a time at the Jack Kerouac School of Disembodied Poetics, founded by Ginsberg and Anne Waldman at Naropa Institute. Peter Orlovsky died in Vermont in 2010.

Cassandra Pantuso graduated from The New School with a major in interdisciplinary science. She is a doula and a hobby mycologist and continues to write poetry.

Bob Perelman's first book, *Braille* (1975) was a series of improvisations inspired by William Carlos Williams. He has published over 15 volumes of poetry, most recently *Iflife* and *Ten to One: Selected Poems.* Perelman is Professor of English at the University of Pennsylvania; he is also widely published in his academic specialty, poetics and modernism. His poems have been included in over twenty anthologies and his play, *The Alps,* was produced in San Francisco in 1980.

Annalisa Pesek's first chapbook, *Headless* (Green Zone Editions) was published in 2012. She is a BA and MA graduate of the University of Washington and holds a certificate in archiving from Pratt Institute. She is assistant managing editor at *Library Journal*'s Book Review.

Simon Pettet is an English-born poet who has lived in New York's East Village for over 30 years. His most recent book, *Hearth,* is a collection of all of his published work from that 30-year period. Pettet also authored two collaborations with photographer Rudy Burckhardt, *Conversations About Everything* and *Talking Pictures,* and compiled and edited *The Selected Art Writings of James Schuyler* as well as co-editing (with James Meetze) Schuyler's posthumous *Other Flowers.*

Ron Padgett grew up in Tulsa, Oklahoma. He is a poet, essayist, translator, fiction writer and educator who has published many books, including *Great Balls of Fire, The Adventures of Mr. & Mrs. Jim & Ron, Toujours l'amour, Tulsa Kid, Triangles in the Afternoon, Ted: A Personal Memoir of Ted Berrigan, How to Be Perfect, You Never Know* and *Oklahoma Tough. How Long* was a finalist for the 2012 Pulitzer Prize. His *Collected Poems* was published in 2013. He has been a Fulbright Fellow and a Guggenheim Fellow, and is a Chancellor Emeritus of the Academy of American Poets.

Michael Roberts is the author of a published book, *Longhand,* and of *Eyebrows of Beautiful Illusion, Thunder of the Gods, The Bag of Fire, No Poem Here* and *The Giant Planets,* which are waiting to be discovered by publishers. He's made three motion pictures, *The Lonely Soldier, Kenny Loggins The Fisherman,* and *The Lonely Farmer,* all shot in a single day. Roberts hails from Southern California and now lives in Portland, Oregon where he founded The Lizard School of Outlandish Poetry, a school of imagination and fun for children.

Elizabeth Robinson's most recent books are *Counterpart, Blue Heron* and *On Ghosts,* among more than a dozen collections of poetry. She co-edits the *EtherDome* chapbook series of works by emerging women poets. Robinson often writes of spirituality and ethics. She received the Foundation for Contemporary Arts 2008 grant award in poetry, and previously the Fence Modern Poets Prize, a National Poetry Series award and a grant from the Fund for Poetry. Robinson is a well-known and highly regarded teacher, most recently at the Iowa Writers' Workshop and the University of Montana.

Kit Robinson's more than 20 books include *A Mammal of Style* (with Ted Greenwald), *Determination,* and *The Messianic Trees: Selected Poems, 1976-2003.* Robinson has received the Fund for Poetry Prize and fellowships from the National Endowment for the Arts and the California Arts Council. He works as a freelance writer in the technology industry and plays the Cuban *tres* guitar in Bahia Son, the Latin band he founded in Berkeley.

Emma Rossi lives with her husband Adam Outlaw, son Abraham and dog Sadie in Simsbury Connecticut where she writes poetry and teaches middle school language arts. Her first chapbook, *Becoming,* was published by Green Zone in 2007.

PERMISSIONS AND ACKNOWLEDGMENTS

All poems are reprinted by permission of the author, the author's estate or the publisher. Additional detail for some of the material is noted below.

October is reprinted from *Portrait and Dream: New & Selected Poems* by Bill Berkson, Coffee House Press, 2009.

March is used by permission of the author, republished from *Republics of Reality: 1975-1995* (Los Angeles: Sun & Moon Press, 2000). ©1981 Charles Bernstein.

The Page Torn Out is reprinted from *Zero Star Hotel* by Anselm Berrigan, Edge Books, 2002.

About Flyin' Home is reprinted from *Jazz Fan Looks Back,* ©2002 by Jayne Cortez, by permission of Hanging Loose Press.

Scale Shift is reprinted from *AREA* by Marcella Durand, Belladonna Books, 2008.

White Attic by Kenward Elmslie is reprinted by permission of Coffee House Press.

She is reprinted from *Species* by Michael Friedman, The Figures, 2000.

July 12, 1990 is reprinted from *SATIN STREET* by Merrill Gilfillan, Asphodel Press, 1997.

Everything Seems ©2013 by Ted Greenwald is used by permission.

so the ants made it to the cat food is reprinted from *so the ants made it to the cat food: 20 sonnets* by Anselm Hollo, Samizdat Editions, 2001.

Swamp Formalism is reprinted from *Black Dog Songs,* ©2003 by Lisa Jarnot, by permission of Flood Editions.

The Ambition of Art is reprinted from *The Sense Record and other poems* by Jennifer Moxley, Edge Books, 2002.

Sleeping with the Dictionary is reprinted from the book *Sleeping with the Dictionary* by Harryette Mullen, University of California Press, © 2002 by the Regents of the University of California.

Cut Shadows by Ron Padgett is reprinted by permission of Coffee House Press.

"a deeper breath with other lungs" is reprinted from *Also Known As* by Elizabeth Robinson, Apogee Press, 2009.

The Sea and the Wind is reprinted from *The History of the Invitation: New and Selected Poems 1963-2000,* ©2001 by Tony Towle, by permission of Hanging Loose Press.

Counterman is reprinted from *OVERNIGHT,* ©2007 by Paul Violi, by permission of Hanging Loose Press.

How the Sestina (Yawn) Works, ©1970 by Anne Waldman, is used by permission of the author.

1000 Poetry Readings is reprinted from *BLUE HEAVEN* by Lewis Warsh, The Kulchur Foundation, 1978.

Mazarine Treyz is a fundraising coach and author of *The Wild Woman's Guide to Fundraising* book and popular blog. Her next professional books, *The Wild Woman's Guide to Social Media* and *Get the Job! Your Fundraising Career Empowerment Guide* both received top reviews in the non-profit media. Treyz's first book of poetry, *The Faberge Wrecking Ball,* was published by Green Zone in 2011. She lives in Portland, Oregon.

Ben Tripp is a poet who has also written critically about poetry and other books, music, dance and art for both print and online magazines. His first chapbook *Port of Entry* (2012) included sonnets and prose poems written collaboratively with Alex Hampshire. He is editor of the poetry magazine *Gerry Mulligan.*

Paul Violi's poems are included in many anthologies, including *The Best American Poetry 2006, 2004, 2000* and *1995,* along with *The Oxford Book of American Poetry, The Oxford Anthology of Modern American Poetry, Postmodern American Poetry* and others. *Overnight,* published in 2007, joined 11 other books of his poetry. He was managing editor of *The Architectural Forum* from 1972-1974, and organized poetry readings at the Museum of Modern Art from 1974-1983. Among Violi's honors are fellowships and awards from the National Endowment for the Arts, the American Academy of Arts and Letters, the Foundation for Contemporary Arts, and the Fund for Poetry. He taught at Columbia University, The New School, New York University and Sing Sing Prison. He died in 2011.

Anne Waldman and Allen Ginsberg founded the Jack Kerouac School of Disembodied Poetics at Naropa University, where she is Distinguished Professor of Poetics. She is the author of over 40 books, including her most recent work *Gossamurmur* (2013). Waldman was director of the St. Mark's Poetry Project from 1968-1978. She was featured along with Allen Ginsberg in Bob Dylan's experimental film *Renaldo and Clara* and traveled with Dylan's *Rolling Thunder Review* in the 1970s. She is the recipient of grants from the National Endowment for the Arts and the Poetry Foundation, a winner of the Shelby Memorial Award for poetry, a Guggenheim Fellow (2013-2014) and recipient of the PEN American Center Award for Poetry 2012 for her magnum opus *The Iovis Trilogy: Colors in the Mechanism of Concealment.*

Lewis Warsh is the author of over 30 books of poetry, fiction, and autobiography, including *A Place in the Sun* (2010), *Inseparable: Poems 1995-2005* (2008) and *The Origin of the World* (2001). He co-founded *Angel Hair* Magazine and Books, with Anne Waldman, and *United Artists* Magazine and Books, with Bernadette Mayer. He teaches in the MFA program in creative writing at Long Island University (Brooklyn). *One Foot Out the Door: Collected Stories* (2014) is his latest book.

Jo Ann Wasserman is the author of two chapbooks, *what counts as proof,* and *we build mountains.* Her full length work, *The Escape,* was published in 2003. She has worked at numerous institutions, including the Poetry Project at St. Mark's Church, Granary Books, Site Santa Fe, and the Lannan Foundation.

Jacqueline Waters published her first book, *A Minute Without Danger,* in 2001 followed by *One Sleeps the Other Doesn't* in 2011. Recent work has appeared in *The American Reader, Clock, Fence* and *Everyday Genius.* A chapbook, *The Garden of Eden a College,* was published in 2004. She edits *The Physiocrats,* a pamphlet press, and works as a freelance web developer.